PREMARITAL INTERCOURSE AND INTERPERSONAL RELATIONSHIPS

PREMARITAL INTERCOURSE AND INTERPERSONAL RELATIONSHIPS

A research study of interpersonal relationships based on case histories of 668 premarital intercourse experiences reported by 200 college level males.

LESTER A. KIRKENDALL
Professor of Family Life, Oregon State University, Corvallis, Oregon

FOREWORD BY BROCK CHISHOLM

GRAMERCY PUBLISHING COMPANY • NEW YORK

To Karl, Bob, and to Karen, Lew, Tamara and Glen

FOREWORD

The findings Dr. Kirkendall reports in this book remind us again that we face problems in our customary and traditional ways of looking at sex and our interpersonal relationships. It challenges us to re-examine our approach to these issues in terms of developing an important and needed maturity.

It has been clear for many years that sexual maturity never is, and can not be, attained by an automatic leap from non-existence to a full-fledged adult level at the moment of marriage. Many marriages, many families, and many lives have been ruined in the service of the belief that it could and should be.

In fact, there are necessary and continuous stages of sexual development from earliest infancy that are highly significant for the success of this long process, and there are many factors that will facilitate or hamper, distort or block, that progression. This book is a sympathetic and understanding record of the kinds of developmental problems that are met by young men, of a particular culture and at a particular time, and of their attempts to meet or avoid those problems, using the variety of behaviour patterns typical of their place and time. As such, it brings valuable information to serious students of the problems of human growth and development, both personal and cultural. It brings light into areas usually left obscure and misunderstood. It indicates areas of success and of failure of many community institutions, and points to much more research which needs to be done.

The study most certainly has an important meaning for those working with the family. The family with its internal and external relationships is a highly significant social unit, and is probably the most important factor in determining the nature of the interpersonal relationships which the children and adults it produces will experience throughout their lives. The family provides the training ground, the instructors and the models for the development of love, understanding, tenderness and co-operation, or of suspicion, hate, hostility and callousness on the part of the children. Such results are of great importance to the whole life of the children, to their capacities to create stable marriages and effective families themselves. In turn, the development of such capacities are highly important to the community in which they live, and even to their nation and that nation's world relationships.

Whether one likes it or not, the basis of the family and the cement which guards or disrupts its integrity is the sexual relationship between the parents. This will largely determine their ability to help their children to attain sexual maturity along with emotional maturity generally, both of which are essential to sound mental and social health.

In every field of human interpersonal relationships, from the family to the world, it is highly desirable that the specific responsibilities for satisfactory development be seen clearly and that these be accepted and carried forward effectively by the appropriate people at the appropriate times. This book is concerned with one of the most important areas for the development of interpersonal relationships and indicates far too high an incidence of blind fumbling and persistent unsuccessful experimentation. With unashamed knowledge and clear thinking it ought to be possible for families and communities to provide the kinds of help that Dr. Kirkendall's informants have demonstrated is needed, but to do so will require this generation to outgrow and cast off the prudery and shame which has so effectively and for so long shrouded this whole area of human development. This book constitutes a notable step in that direction and should be reassuring even to those among us who tend to characterize any such investigations as "stirring up filth." It is a sincere and, as far as it goes, a successful attempt to bring the light of reason into areas largely peopled by the hobgoblins and demons engendered by, and left over from, the ignorances and prejudices of our ancestors. Through this study Dr. Kirkendall helps to fulfill a major responsibility.

DR. BROCK CHISHOLM
Former Director-General
World Health Organization

Victoria, B.C.

CONTENTS

TABLES AND FIGURES

PREFACE

Although this study will probably be regarded as a "sex" study, I hope it will be read as a study in interpersonal relationships as well. Its purpose has been to find how premarital intercourse affects the relationships of the participants, utilizing a concern for the improvement of human associations as a value framework by which to guide the research procedures, and direct the analyses. Does premarital sexual experience create better or poorer interpersonal relationships, according to the standard for judging as set up in this study? Does it tend to strengthen or weaken relationships? These are some of the questions to be discussed in the following chapters.

The data in this study could never have been obtained without the understanding co-operation of the 200 young men who were my subjects. Fully aware of the use to which I intended to put the information they gave me, they nevertheless discussed their experiences with me objectively and in detail. In fact, many of them expressed the hope that their participation might smooth the way for those young people who will follow them, for many of the subjects, I am sure, felt that in some manner the fullness of life was escaping them.

The data presented in the succeeding pages may be construed by some readers as an indictment of one segment or another of our population, and it will be especially easy to use them to attach blame to youth for their sexual behavior. I am very hopeful that this will not be the outcome for my experience convinces me that young people, regardless of sex, are desirous of and are seeking satisfying interpersonal associations. They are confused, rather than exploitive; they have been unable to establish satisfying values, rather than being hopelessly self-centered; they have lacked guidance and help rather than being sex-obsessed. We are all, male and female, old and young, caught up in the failure of our society to deal positively, intelligently, and constructively with the powerful sexual impulse.

I return now to the comments in the opening paragraph of this preface in which I expressed the hope that this book may be regarded as a study in interpersonal relationships as well as a study in sex. I believe a monumental task faces us in the management of the sexual impulse. My study convinces me that what is needed is the development of a moral insight which will encompass in a consistent manner not only sex, but all facets of behavior. Only as we embrace a morality based upon a broad concern for the improvement of human relationships will sex become a constructive rather than a destructive force in our individual and social life. This book, it is hoped, will contribute a bit to this outcome.

Acknowledgments are owed to many people for their help and support; weaknesses and shortcomings are my own. I want first to thank my administrative officers, Mrs. Katherine H. Read and Dean Miriam Scholl, for permitting me to carry a lighter load of other duties while I was doing the research and writing involved in the study. I want particularly to express appreciation for support and helpful assistance to H. D. Schalock, James Mabry, Theodore B. Johannis, Jr., Jerry Li, Curtis E. Avery, Mrs. Margie Lee, Isadore Rubin, O. H. Mowrer, Mrs. Vida June Krantz, Miss Jean Hobart, Gerold Sliger, Douglas Johnson, Mrs. Carol Cramer, and still others who, because of numbers, must remain unnamed. My family deserves special thanks for the endurance they have shown while I have been absorbed in this work. Thanks also to the two hundred subjects among whom I count warm friends.

Thanks must also be extended for the financial support without which this study would have been impossible. The Committee for

Research in Problems of Sex, National Academy of Sciences, National Research Council, in particular, was generous, and the helpful efforts of its chairman, Dr. Frank Beach, are especially appreciated. In addition grants were received from the Graduate Council of Oregon State University, and the E. C. Brown Trust of Portland, Oregon.

LESTER A. KIRKENDALL

PREMARITAL INTERCOURSE AND INTERPERSONAL RELATIONSHIPS

1

THE PROBLEM AND THE

RESEARCH PLAN

"Is premarital intercourse right or wrong, and why?"—"Will having sexual relations strengthen a relationship?"—"If both persons in a dating relationship are agreeable, then is premarital intercourse all right?"—"What determines whether premarital intercourse is right or wrong—simply social custom?"—"If conventional opinions were changed, would sexual freedom be practical?" —"How far should a couple go?"

Such questions are familiar to anyone working with young people and adults on problems of dating, male-female associations, and sexual standards. Obviously they cannot be answered categorically. The complex circumstances surrounding premarital sexual associations make simple "yes" or "no" answers impossible. Attempts to specify exactly "how far to go" fail. Dogmatic definitions of right-wrong, which rule out all concern with circumstances and the motivations or feelings of the persons involved, break down very shortly.

Modern young people are unwilling to accept such rigid, irrational solutions to their problems. This is as it should be. As mature individuals, functioning freely and effectively in a democratic environment, they need to know and understand the problems involved in human behavior, and the rationale of possible solutions. They need help in coping with unique problems and rapidly shifting social circumstances, not only with reference to sex but to all aspects of behavior.

The rising concern over sexual conduct and standards results from many circumstances. Almost unlimited opportunities for the free association of unmarried men and women, the virtual disappearance of the chaperone, the decline of parental and religious authority, the freedom to acknowledge sex and sexual feelings, the near-collapse of a moral code based upon fears of pregnancy, disease, and social ostracism, the availability of automobiles, contraceptives, and general knowledge and information about sex— these conditions mean that young people encounter situations which pose problems their parents and grandparents never faced. Modern young people are aggressive in seeking answers to their questions and solutions to their problems. In their quest they are very much in need of better help than they are getting.

To meet this need, a value framework for orderly, logical, and meaningful thinking on questions of standards, right-wrong decisions, and acceptable behavior is essential. This need for some yardstick by which people may check decisions is stressed by many writers, and young people are urged to make their decisions accordingly. However, at this point their problem is twofold.

First, what value framework shall they accept? Shall it be the social mores ("When in Rome do as Romans do"), or rigid adherence to a certain pattern laid down by an authority ("Don't ask questions. Do as you are told"), or shall they be guided by an inner feeling of rightness ("If you think it's right, it's right for you. Let your conscience be your guide")? These represent the common value systems within which decisions about human relations are made.

Differing value frameworks produce conflicts because they are inconsistent, or lack inclusiveness. Thus, if we are relying on common social practices, or authority, what behavior is appropriate when customs or authorities differ? May not one be able to live with his own conscience yet engage in some behavior very harmful to himself and others? Can not the conscience be salved?

Second, once one has sincerely accepted a value framework, what behavior and attitudes are consistent with it? A person may feel satisfied with his own value framework but lack the knowledge or insight to move toward the goals he has set. Will one practice or one pattern of behavior be more appropriate than another? At these decision points research which assumes a specific value framework and provides tested insights can be most useful.

If this analysis is sound, the questions about sexual standards with which this chapter opened can be answered satisfactorily only if two conditions are met:

1. An understandable value framework is found. This framework must be applicable to the decisions necessary in our everyday associations.

2. Established facts and experience must be built about this value framework in such a way as to relate pertinent behavior and attitudes to it.

THE VALUE FRAMEWORK

The problem outlined above has long been a major concern of mine. It has generated a persistent pressure which has motivated my study and teaching. What is a satisfactory value framework within which one can reach ethical-moral decisions, not only about sex, but about other aspects of living? Once this value framework has been clarified what should be said about premarital sex standards?

The quest for a value framework has led me to lay an increasingly strong emphasis upon the importance of interpersonal relations[1] as an approach to understanding people and helping them

---

[1] Interest in interpersonal relationships as a school of psychological thought has grown rapidly in the past few decades. Much impetus has come from the work and writings of Harry Stack Sullivan (89, 90), Patrick Mullahy (78), Erich Fromm (35, 36, 37, 38), Karen Horney (52, 53), Alfred Adler (5), and others.

This interest is based on the experience of psychiatrists and other clinicians working with emotionally disturbed individuals. Such persons are commonly found to be involved in frustrating and unfulfilling interpersonal relationships. Their unhappy, disturbed associations have been accounted as responsible, at least to a large degree, for their emotional difficulties. O. H. Mowrer (76, 77) and Rollo May (73) are other authorities who have expressed similar points of view.

Interest in interpersonal relations is by no means confined to those involved in counseling, psychiatry, psychotherapy. Sullivan (90) and Mulwith their human-relations decisions. This concept has already been elaborated in several articles (Kirkendall, 59; Kirkendall, 61; Kirkendall and Avery, 63).* A statement of this point of view as contained in one of the articles (Kirkendall) follows:

> Whenever a decision or a choice is to be made concerning behavior, the moral decision will be the one which works toward the creation of trust, confidence, and integrity in relationships. It should increase the capacity of individuals to cooperate, and enhance the sense of self-respect in the individual. Acts which create distrust, suspicion, and misunderstanding, which build barriers and destroy integrity, are immoral. They decrease the individual's sense of self-respect, and rather than producing a capacity to work together they separate people and break down the capacity for communication.

This concept can be put in chart form. When it is, it reads this way:

---

lahy (78) regard an understanding of interpersonal relations as essential in the understanding of personality. Their interest in interpersonal relations is, in fact, elaborated into a theory of personality development. Sullivan defines personality as "the relatively enduring pattern of recurrent interpersonal situations which characterize a human life" (90, p. 111). Gardner Murphy (79) takes essentially the same point of view as he develops the "field" theory as an approach to the understanding of personality.

Brief discussions of the interpersonal, or "social psychological" approach as a theory of personality structure are found in Arieti (6, Ch. 70), and Hall and Lindzey (46, Ch. IV). Heider (49) and Leary (66) each has developed a psychology of interpersonal relations. The importance of satisfying interpersonal relations in early life is stressed by Bowlby (11), Erikson (33), Goldfarb (42) and Ribble (87). Peck and Havighurst (82) have extended this idea to a study of late childhood and adolescence.

Interest in interpersonal relationships is by no means focused on psychotherapy and personality development. Chisholm (17) has related this point of view to international affairs and the attainment of enduring peace. Allee (2) and Emerson (31), as biologists, emphasize the importance of cooperation in survival and the evolutionary process. Friend and Haggard (34) applied the concepts of interaction to occupational adjustment.

Montagu (74), an anthropologist, has assembled the scientific evidence which provides validity for this theory, and has argued its significance (75). Fromm (37), Montagu, and Allee (3), among others, suggest that the quality of interpersonal relationships may constitute a criterion for moral judgments.

* The numerals following the names of authors refer to numbered items in the bibliography.

BASIS FOR MORAL JUDGMENTS

Those actions, decisions, and attitudes are:

Right—Moral   *Wrong—Immoral*

which produce

1. increased capacity to trust people	1. increased distrust of people
2. greater integrity in relationships	2. deceit and duplicity in relationships
3. dissolution of barriers separating people	3. barriers between persons and groups
4. co-operative attitudes	4. resistant, unco-operative attitudes
5. enhanced self-respect	5. diminished self-respect
6. general attitudes of faith and confidence in people	6. exploitive behavior toward others
7. fulfillment of individual potentialities and a zest for living	7. thwarted and dwarfed individual capacities and disillusionment

Two closely-correlated conditions affect this concept in an important way.

First, the dissolution of barriers needs to extend beyond the two-person association,[2] or a tightly-knit small unit. This is to say that a good relationship leads its members toward an increasing acceptance of others, and others to an increasing acceptance of them. A good relationship between two or a few persons is like a

---

[2] Harry Stack Sullivan takes a position very similar to his own, though he is concerned mainly with primary dyadic relationships. Sullivan writes (78, p. 105):

> Whenever two people are collaborating toward the achievement of a common goal, they and their interpersonal relations make up, compose, and are integrated into a personal situation. Factors in this two-group which improve the collaboration, which increase the probability of achieving the goal, are constructive; factors that hinder the collaboration, diminish the probability, are destructive—with reference to the personal situation.

The assumption underlying the investigation being reported in this book is that if the "common goal" is living satisfactorily and happily with one's fellows, there should be the development of trusting, sincere, co-operative relationships between and among people. Sullivan referred in his statement only to the "two-group," but we have extended the idea to the larger social group as well.

stone cast in a pool of water. It creates an ever-widening circle of ripples which eventually reach the farthest bank. This capacity to extend to and receive acceptance from an ever-expanding world is basic both to the mental health of individuals and to the stability and preservation of a society.

Second, consideration needs to be extended to long-range consequences. Certain experiences may create a closer relationship between two or more persons at a particular time, but how will it work out eventually? This is an important consideration.

Clear-cut, unequivocal answers to the questions posed by these two conditions will be impossible in many situations. Yet it is important to establish integrity and develop interpersonal relationships based upon trust, co-operation and good-will, which, over the long run, will include more and more persons within their range.

Once the above formulation had been developed, my next concern was to relate it to sexual behavior. This led to the research project, the results of which will be reported in the following chapters. In this research the focus has been upon the meaning of the interpersonal relationship concept as it relates to premarital sexual intercourse. In a broad, inclusive manner the purpose of this study may be suggested by two questions: In our society, does premarital intercourse generally lead (a) to trusting, honest, outreaching, co-operative relationships, or (b) to self-doubt, withdrawal, mistrust, recriminations, and deceit?

This study represents an attempt to think about premarital sexual intercourse not as an act that is good or bad, or right or wrong in itself. Neither is it regarded as an experience isolated from a total life situation. The attempt is rather to understand how premarital intercourse relates to, affects, and is affected by the interpersonal relationships context in which it occurs. In other words, this research has been done and is being reported in a specific value framework, and value interpretations will be made within that framework.

WORKING RULES FOR THE STUDY

Research bearing upon the correlation between premarital intercourse and the quality of the preceding and succeeding interpersonal relationships presents many difficulties. The study of interpersonal relationships is almost entirely uncharted territory as far as non-clinical research is concerned; there are few guideposts. No clear consensus as to what elements constitute an interpersonal relationship exists. There is no easy way of probing the nature of interpersonal relationships. Procedures for this research were thus necessarily devised on an experimental and tentative basis.

Couple these uncertainties with widespread, restrictive cultural attitudes toward sex, and it adds up to a number of perplexing questions. How does one do research on premarital sexual intercourse in a conservative community-setting and avoid arousing criticism which might jeopardize the entire study? What data are necessary to answer the questions posed? How reliable are the data when they relate to such a highly personal experience as sexual intercourse? Should one attempt to obtain a random sample, and, if so, how does one obtain such a sample when selection is based upon the understanding that the subjects shall have had premarital intercourse?

These uncertainties and possible or actual difficulties led to certain decisions. These decisions may be stated in the form of working rules which I used as guides in developing the design:

1. *The research would emphasize descriptive, clinical-type data rather than statistical, taxonomic facts.* In designing the research I was seeking first and primarily to understand the nature and quality of the interpersonal relationships as they related to premarital intercourse. I was interested only secondarily in the extent or frequency of sexual conduct. I was not conducting a survey from which generalizations would be extended to the total population. This decision led to the next working rule:

2. *No attempt would be made to set up sampling procedures or to collect an array of personal background data.* Since the study was definitely exploratory in nature, it seemed premature to set up an elaborate sampling procedure, or to proceed with the collection of a vast amount of personal background data. If research in the area proved practicable, an extended study was envisioned. Sampling problems and the collection of background data could be attacked at that time.

Another justification for foregoing the collection of personal background data was that the population from which the subjects were selected was a relatively homogeneous one. The subjects were white, college students, primarily middle-class, Protestant, and in their late teens or early-to-middle twenties. About half of the subjects came from a rural or small-town background, and the other half from urban communities. A very few were already married. These were the known facts concerning the background characteristics of the population.

Since no particular sampling procedure was involved, the subjects who participated in the research were secured by personal, face-to-face invitations. No group appeals were made.

A number of subjects were obtained through personal acquaintance with students whom I met after visits to their college living groups. I occasionally accept invitations to conduct discussions in these college living organizations, i.e., dormitories, fraternities. Following such a discussion there were always personal conversations during which I might extend an individual an invitation to stop at my office, with the idea that he might participate in the research. Other persons were invited after an informal, casual conversation, and many of the interviewees were members of my Marriage classes. As I became acquainted with the prospective enrollees the research was described to them and they were asked if they could participate in the research. No subjects were included who came originally for personal counseling.

3. *Only male subjects would be used.* This decision was made for several reasons. First, the research project was undertaken entirely on a personal, individual basis. There was no commission by a foundation or educational agency to do research. Premarital sexual conduct is a subject about which people are sensitive. Inquiry into it offers possibilities for criticism and public disapproval. There seemed less chance of damaging repercussions and, conversely, better chances of success if the investigation was confined to males. I felt no hesitancy in mentioning the subject of the research to boys, or in asking them whether they had had premarital intercourse. Many women would undoubtedly have accepted this, but there was always the possibility that some girl would find the whole matter offensive. Thus criticism could result which would have prevented any further research with either men or women.

Second, my experience leads me to believe that when women are included in a research project, a mature woman interviewer is more likely to reach a wide range of female interviewees and have a better chance of securing valid and reliable data than a male interviewer. Of course, this would not be true for all women interviewers in contrast to all men interviewers, but true in general.

Finally, there was the simple fact that I was not yet ready for so ambitious a project.

4. *An interview-case history approach would be used.* Since little is known concerning the impact of premarital intercourse upon the course of the interpersonal relationships of those involved, it seemed important to go directly to persons with experience in those circumstances in order to learn. I felt a personal interview would provide an opportunity to develop rapport and a confidential relationship which would, in turn, permit explorations not possible through the use of a questionnaire. I felt also that more realistic hypotheses might be derived about the impact of premarital intercourse on interpersonal relations by face-to-face discussions than by impersonal checks or circles on a questionnaire.

This study will, of course, be subjected to the usual criticisms of the case history method, such as distortions due to the forgetfulness of subjects, fabrication at a conscious or unconscious level, unwarranted interpretations of the subjects' statements, and inaccuracies in recording on the part of the interviewer. Certain of these criticisms will be discussed later in this chapter.

5. *A systematic, organized interview procedure was needed.* In accordance with this decision an interview schedule was developed. This schedule was tested, retested, and revised, in the light of experience gained in preliminary interviews.

Questions relating to the quality of the interpersonal relationship in which the subject was involved and in which intercourse occurred were included. They were designed to bring out the feelings of the subject toward his experience and his partner, and to explore the character of the relationship itself. The questions bore upon five aspects of interpersonal relations that seemed significant in arriving at the desired understanding. These aspects, which will be discussed in detail in Chapters II-VII, were the (1) motivations, (2) nature and extent of communication, (3) protective measures, (4) attitudes toward responsibility, and (5) the subject's own feelings toward the experience (self-evaluations). Questions were also included to find what the subject felt his partner's attitudes were toward the intercourse experience. Other leads were followed, and questions were asked freely, even though they were not included in the interview schedule. Inflections in voice and nuances in tone and expression were observed and their meaning explored.

Each subject was interviewed about his relationship with each sexual partner. The various relationships were discussed in the chronological order in which they occurred, and descriptive details concerning each association (hereafter called "liaisons") were elicited by questions from the schedule.

In order to assure anonymity each subject was assigned a code number. This arrangement meant that his name was not used, yet it permitted accessibility to his case history.

PROCEDURAL QUESTIONS

Certain procedural questions are frequently asked. How many potential subjects may have had experience in premarital intercourse but rejected the invitation to the interview? What kind of persons refused to participate? How many may have fabricated experiences? Are men willing to talk honestly about their premarital sexual affairs? Are the data reliable?

First, let us note the possibility that potential subjects might reject the interview. The most obvious way to escape the interview would be for a man to say that he lacked experience in premarital intercourse. How many men did this can not be ascertained. Some probably did. The rate of rejection, however, would undoubtedly depend in part on the motivation provided for participation. An attempt was always made to create good rapport before a man was asked the question which determined his possible participation. Incentives to gain participation were offered, e.g., the gift of marriage-family pamphlets, emphasis upon the potential value of this research, the worth the interview might have for the interviewee himself, and my readiness, once the interview was concluded, to discuss features of the subject's experience, if he so desired.

Potential subjects who denied experience in premarital intercourse were usually so direct and straightforward as to be convincing. There was little or no hesitation or equivocation to indicate evasion or untruth. No exact count was kept of the number disclaiming premarital sexual experience, but approximately half of those approached said they lacked experience in intercourse. This coincides roughly with other data (Kinsey, 58) which indicate that by age twenty, 44 per cent of the college-level men have experienced intercourse.

Some fifteen to twenty men with experience rejected the invitation to be interviewed. These individuals usually excused themselves on grounds of lack of time, rather than a lack of interest. In fact, practically all of them expressed an interest in participation of time was available, and a few who declined did find time later. A lack of time is a very plausible excuse for getting out of the interview, and in a college setting it can certainly be an authentic one.

Several would have liked to participate but felt their discussion would unduly involve their partners. After one boy had agreed to participate in the research, his girl friend learned of it. She emphatically disapproved, and he hastily withdrew his consent.

Several individuals indicated a willingness, but skipped the appointment. Three or four others did not return to complete their case history once they had begun their discussion. No one ever withdrew co-operation during the interview itself.

Some of the subjects may have fabricated experience in intercourse, but this seems doubtful. The interview questions were detailed enough to make fabrication difficult. The interview was conducted in such a manner that a subject had little chance to launch into a long, detailed discussion of his experiences. If a man reported numerous prostitute or pick-up liaisons, data might not be taken on all of them, and he might have then reported more liaisons than he actually had. The interviews with the subjects were almost without exception convincing. They seemed sincerely concerned with reporting honestly.

On three or four occasions reports reached me that a certain subject had made known his participation and said that he had "beefed up his story." This was usually accepted by the person conveying the report as evidence that my subjects had been untruthful. Possibly so, but it seems at least as likely that such an individual was meeting some social-cultural expectations. A sophisticated and worldly-wise youth is expected to joke about sex, and to be nonchalant. So far as this research is concerned, if the fact of his participation was known it would be in keeping for him to indicate that he had outfoxed the investigator.

In one instance I received a report that a "subject" had built up his story. It turned out that this individual had never been interviewed, yet he told a friend that he had been interviewed and that he had "laid it on thick."

Let us examine the charge of fabrication from still another angle. Suppose a particular subject had been interviewed and an adult important to him, e.g., a teacher or a parent, knew of the study and knew this subject had talked with me. Unless there was much more permissiveness in that relationship than in most youth-adult relationships, the youth would be almost compelled to assert that his story was a fabrication.

Concealment is more likely than exaggeration. All one had to do to conceal was to avoid talking. This possibility was available to all subjects. If there were details which might reflect unfavorably omission was an easy way out, and this method, I know, was used by a few. A subject might wish to protect his partner. He might become bored with the whole procedure and wish to take no further time with the study.

Numerous individuals, on the other hand, went through the interview at obvious personal sacrifices in time and convenience.

Another problem was to decide how much time one could reasonably ask of each subject. The interview focused upon each liaison separately. It might take thirty minutes or more to work out the details of a single but complex liaison. More liaisons would have extended the time proportionately.

One subject reported 21 liaisons. He was highly verbal, remembered his experiences clearly, and was quite ready to answer questions. This particular interview took about ten hours. During the interview it became apparent that the subject would be lost to the study unless he could be compensated in some way for the time he was giving. He was working as a busboy, and he arranged for a substitute who was then paid from research funds.

Notes were taken during the interview with the subject's knowledge. At first the interviewees were told that they might examine these notes if they wished. There was never any interest in such an examination or any objection to note-taking, so this practice was soon dropped. A few individuals wished assurance that no name or identifying features would be used. Following the interview the case history was organized as a continuous narrative, written in longhand or dictated into a tape recorder, and typed.

The first fifty or sixty interviewees were asked to return and each read his typed case history. This was done to check the reliability of the data. They were asked to indicate needed changes. This practice was later abandoned for two reasons. First, no changes of any consequence were suggested. Corrections always concerned minor facts which had no significance for the relationship itself. My basic concern was that the case history accurately reflect the attitudes and feeling tones in the relationship as expressed by the individual. This aspect of the case histories always remained unchanged.

Second, an occasional individual found it a somewhat upsetting experience to read his own case history. Some of the accounts certainly reflected upon the personal conduct of the subjects; others reflected behavior patterns of which the subjects were unaware. For some men it was a shock to read the details of their behavior impersonally condensed. Even though a few subjects were bothered by what they read none made any changes. If a subject displayed concern, his reactions were discussed with him.

Each subject was provided an opportunity to discuss his own feelings and experiences at the close of the interview. At that time he was encouraged to raise any questions he wished as well as to discuss his reaction to the interview. This proved to be a very profitable phase of the interview. Laying aside the paraphernalia of research seemed to create an even more casual, relaxed atmosphere than existed during the interview. At this time new insights were often gained concerning the individual's feelings and experiences. This also proved to be a check on the realiability of the interview.

Most subjects seemed to find the interview worthwhile. Many commented that "this has been very helpful." Another common comment was, "I've never talked with anyone so freely before." When I thanked the subject for his time the reaction very often was, "I should be the one to thank you."

Personal biases on my part may have affected the quality of the interviewing and recording, though conscientious efforts were made to avoid this. The case histories were a condensation of the verbal material. When an individual answers questions for half an hour about a particular liaison and this information is then summarized in a single page or so, obviously some selection has been made. Did I always record the equivalent information and did I interpret this information in the same way at different times? Did I procure the most important information? These are important methodological questions which bear upon the issue of personal bias.

THE SUBJECTS

The data upon which this study was based were gathered from two hundred college-level men between the ages of seventeen and twenty-eight. Their average age at the time of the interview was 20.6 years. Their ages at the time of their first experience in intercourse ranged from nine years to twenty-six, with an average age of 17.1 years.[3] These data are given in more details in Tables I and II.

---

[3] Other studies have obtained similar data in regard to age of initial intercourse.

In reporting on a study of his, Gardner (39) says, ". . . in a group of 221 late adolescent males (17-20) 172, or 78 per cent of them, had had heterosexual experience by the age of 15.5 years . . ."

Hohman and Schaffner (51) asked 4,100 white and 500 Negro men entering the military service about experience in premarital intercourse. Of the experienced men 36 per cent had had intercourse by the time they were sixteen, 63 per cent by the time they were eighteen, and 92.8 per cent by the time they had reached twenty-one.

Kirkendall (60), in a study made during the mid-1940's, reported on the premarital sexual experiences of 530 men. He wrote that over 40 per cent of them "gave a history including premarital intercourse by the age of seventeen. By the time these boys were in their eighteenth year—about the time most of them were graduated from high school—over 54 per cent of the total group and 80 per cent of the experienced group had already had premarital sexual experience. Seventeen is the modal or peak year for the beginning of intercourse."

Kinsey (58) found in the total population of his male study that of the sixteen-year-old boys interviewed, 51.6 per cent gave a history of premarital intercourse. In the seventeen-year-old group, this percentage rose to 61.3 per cent.

In a study of premarital dating behavior among male and female college students, Ehrmann (27) found that 57 per cent of 274 nonveteran male subjects, age 18-21, had had premarital intercourse. In a sample of 302 veteran men, age 20-26, 73 per cent reported premarital experience. A sample of 265 college women, age 18-22, revealed 13 per cent with experience in intercourse. Ehrmann (pp. 33-34) also collates the findings of a number of investigators relative to the incidence of premarital intercourse for both males and females.

These two hundred men gave case histories covering experiences in premarital intercourse with six hundred sixty-eight partners. This is the number of recorded liaisons and they furnish the data upon which the study is based.

PLAN FOR THE ANALYSIS OF DATA

At the time the interviewing began the focal points around which the data from the case histories might be organized had not been clearly developed. After some forty or fifty histories had been collected, a careful examination resulted in an organizational plan which was used throughout in the analysis of the data.

Table 1

Age of Subjects at Time of Interview								
Age	:	Number	Age	:	Number	Age	:	Number
Not recorded	....	7	20		42	25		4
17		1	21		45	26		3
18		20	22		21	27		1
19		39	23		10	28		2
			24		5	Total		200
						Average Age		20.6

Table 2

Age of Subjects at Time of First Intercourse								
Age	:	Number	Age	:	Number	Age	:	Number
Not recorded	....	8	14		15	20		8
9		1	15		21	21		5
10		1	16		29	22		5
12		1	17		38	23		2
13		6	18		37	24		1
			19		21	26		1
						Total		200

Average Age: 17.1

As the case histories were studied it became apparent that the character of the sexual relationship, and its impact upon the participants, was conditioned by the quality of the overall, interpersonal relationship existing at the time intercourse occurred.

This overall, interpersonal relationship obviously influenced the nature and amount of communication that took place, whether guilt was felt, attitudes toward protection and responsibility, the motivations that led into intercourse, and the appraisals the subjects made of the experience.

Significant variables in the overall, interpersonal relationship which seemed to influence the nature of the sexual relationship appeared to be the character of the male's consort, or sexual partner, and the degree of affectional attachment that existed. A continuum taking these variables into account was, therefore, developed.

The continuum[4] was divided into six segments, hereafter called levels, which were then used for the purpose of distributing the six hundred sixty-eight sexual liaisons along its range. The six levels were defined as follows:

---

[4] Burgess and Wallin (15) recognized the value of using such a continuum in this kind of investigation. In the report of their study on engagement success, they pointed to areas of needed investigation. In speaking about studies on "the incidence of premarital intercourse," they wrote (p. 777):

It is hoped that Kinsey and other investigators will make the necessary significant distinctions in their future studies of premarital sex behavior. In the case of men it is important to define carefully the sexual partner as a prostitute, a pickup, an acquaintance of the same, higher, or lower educational level, a friend with whom steady company is being kept, and a fiancée. It is also desirable to ascertain whether the first and later sexual relations with women, falling in any one of these categories, took place when not engaged to anyone, when not engaged to future wife, or during the period of engagement preceding marriage. Similar distinctions should be made in the case of premarital sexual behavior of women.

Ehrmann (27) made use of a continuum in his research on premarital dating behavior. His continuum involved progression from mild levels of physical intimacy in male-female relationships (holding hands, kissing, hugging) to the deepest level of physical intimacy (intercourse). He also recognized that the meaning of these intimacy experiences varied with the depth of the couple's emotional involvement and so made use of the continuum used in this study.

Reiss (85) distinguishes two types of attitudes toward sexual intercourse. These are in reality a continuum, as he recognizes. He speaks of body-centered, and person-centered sexual relations. "The first one accents the physical aspects of the act, and the second one emphasizes the particular person with whom the act is being performed." The two types may merge imperceptibly into one another.

Level	Character of Partner	Degree of Attachment
I	Prostitute	Single or episodic experiences in houses of prostitution. No emotional attachment involved.
II	Pick-up	Relationship strictly for the purposes of sex. Single or episodic experiences. No emotional attachment involved.
III	Casual acquaintance who was perceived merely as a potential sexual associate.	Dating began definitely for purpose of obtaining intercourse. No affectional attachment on the part of the male.
IV	Dating partner who became a sexual associate before a strong relationship had developed.	The possibility of intercourse arose after dating began and before male became affectionally attached.
V	Partner with whom a relationship of some strength existed.	Considerable emotional attachment.
VI	Fiancée	Strong emotional attachment.

Each of the sexual liaisons was classified according to the level at which it fell at the time intercourse first occurred.[*] The decision was made according to the circumstances of the experience, and the feelings of attachment the male ascribed to himself. Many of the subjects had sexual experience at more than one level.

After the liaisons were classified by levels, each one was analyzed for the purpose of isolating circumstances that would illustrate how the five characteristics accepted as important in determining the quality of an interpersonal relationship, influenced and were influenced by premarital intercourse. These characteristics were:

1. *Motivations.* The significant motivations that would clarify the meaning of the sexual part of the association were examined.
2. *Communication,* both verbal and non-verbal. Communication in this study is defined as the exchange of ideas and an awareness of feelings and attitudes between and among persons. Special attention was given to the extent and the nature of

---

[*] For the statistical data on liaison classifications and a discussion of them see pp. 253-57 and Table 10 in Appendix A.

the communication that occurred concerning the sexual relationships.

3. *Protective measures.* These included the efforts made by either or both persons to protect the other from unfavorable consequences of the sexual relationship. Usually these included such consequences as possible pregnancy, discovery, and emotional reactions of a negative nature.

4. *Attitudes toward responsibility.* Attitudes displayed by subjects toward the assumption of responsibility for both the sexual aspect of the relationship and for the overall responsibilities of the total relationship were examined.

5. *Self-evaluation.* The feelings of satisfaction or dissatisfaction resulting from subjects' experiences in the sexual relationship were probed.

The results of the analyses are found in the form of descriptive data in Chapters II-VII. The purpose of these chapters is to indicate the numerous ways in which these relationship characteristics may be manifested at the various levels when premarital intercourse occurs, and how they may interact with one another. The nature of the discussion, it is hoped, will give flesh-and-blood meaning to the generalizations that will be made and provide a keener awareness of the kind of circumstances and experiences which may surround associations involving premarital intercourse.

Chapter VIII deals with the possible strengthening or weakening effects of intercourse upon overall relationship, while Chapter IX deals with its possible effect upon marital adjustment. Chapter X suggests some of the factors facilitating or impeding the integration of premarital intercourse into the structure of a society concerned with the improvement of interpersonal relationships.

STATISTICAL ANALYSIS

In addition to the analyses from which descriptive data were derived, a category analysis system[5] was set up around the same five relationship characteristics for the purpose of securing statistical

---

[5] In perfecting the system, the writer acknowledges the indispensable help of Dr. H. D. Schalock and Miss Jean Hobart. Mr. Gearold Sliger and Miss Hobart did the content analysis.

data. The desire was to ascertain the extent to which certain of the relationship characteristics were found at the various levels. The data also permit inter-level comparisons and serve to indicate trends as they relate to these relationship characteristics. These data apply only to this sample. They can not be considered as being applicable to a general population.

In order to preserve reading continuity, the statistical data have been placed in Appendix I, "Statistical Findings." This appendix can be read independently of Chapter II-X if the reader wishes to do so.

2

ANALYSIS OF LEVEL I

LIAISONS

This chapter will analyze sexual liaisons involving prostitutes.

Level I liaisons are restricted to those sexual relationships that occurred in a "house" and/or with a woman who made it a business to provide men with sexual intercourse for money. If a subject merely described his partner as a pick-up, or even as a "whore," this did not result in a Level I classification. Nor were sexual liaisons resulting from chance meetings on the street, or in taverns, classified as Level I associations. The sexual relationship had to occur in a setting in which men were provided sexual access to women in exchange for money.

EMPHASIS ON THE PROSTITUTE

Much has been written about prostitution, and most of the attention by far has been given the prostitute herself. There is little concern or interest expressed in the male who patronizes the prostitute.[1] His motivations, attitudes, and personal adjustment

---

[1] In the book, *The Call Girl*, (Greenwald, 45) the author comments:

> In order to understand the call girl better it is necessary to understand her clients and her relationships with them. The word usually used by

are ordinarily given no consideration.[2] The research on American males conducted by Kinsey (58) was unusual in the extent to which it dealt with males who patronized prostitutes.

Three examples, out of many, of this almost exclusive concern with the prostitute will be offered. A recent book by Dr. Eustace Chesser (16) of London devotes three chapters to the attempt to understand prostitution. After pointing out that an adequate understanding can not be reached through historical analysis, Dr. Chesser comments: "What we have to look for is the defect in the personality which causes a woman—and sometimes a man—to divert the sex instinct from its proper aim . . . We must now turn our attention to the psychology of the prostitute."

Dr. Chesser's reference to men in the above quotation is not clear. He may be referring to males who patronize prostitutes, to male prostitutes, or to male sexual deviates. Regardless of what he meant this is the only reference made to males in the entire discussion. Why did Dr. Chesser not give equal attention to masculine psychology? If, for the female, prostitution represents a diversion of sex from its proper aim, is it not equally as much a diversion for men?

The second example is the widely publicized Wolfenden Report (96), prepared by an official British commission, on homosexual offenses and prostitution. This report almost completely ignores the fact that males are involved in prostitute relationships. In the opening paragraphs of the report the Committee remarks, "It would have taken us beyond our terms of reference to investigate in detail the prevalence of prostitution or the reasons which lead women to adopt this manner of life."

Since the Committee did not intend to investigate these details it would seem that this would have been an effortless way and a natural time at which to acknowledge the involvement of men.

---

call girls in speaking among themselves to describe a client is "John." Who are these Johns? What kind of men are willing to pay large sums for the impersonal sexual release that a call girl provides? (p. 161)

[2] Greenwald (45) does discuss, rather incidentally, the characteristics of those men who patronize call girls. These males, of course, are older, more sophisticated persons than those who participated in this study. Murtagh and Harris (80, Ch. 10) also comment briefly on the characteristics of both older and teen-age patrons. This book is an interesting non-technical study of prostitution in New York City.

But it did not, and nowhere in the report is there more than a fleeting indication that men patronize prostitutes.

A third book, *Social Problems In Our Time* (93) devotes three chapters to sexual deviations. One deals with deviations found in men. The male use of prostitution is not mentioned.[3] The other two chapters deal with female deviations; one is devoted to prostitution.

If masculine participation in prostitution is very largely ignored it is even more the case that the nature of the interpersonal relationship between patron and prostitute is overlooked. This is understandable since a relationship is an intangible thing at best. The relationship between a patron and a prostitute is certainly a casual and transitory one, and not easily subjected to scrutiny.

In this chapter the concern will be, so far as the data permit, with examining the significance of the patron-prostitute relationship for interpersonal relationships. The masculine viewpoint will therefore be under scrutiny, and will dominate the discussion.

The nature of the prostitute-patron relationship is such that strong barriers to communication between the participants are present from the beginning. In practically every liaison both the prostitute and her patron have every intention of making the relation brief and transitory. The possibility of any attachment or any later social relationships is actively rejected, certainly by the patron.

STATISTICAL DATA

The data analyzed in this chapter were obtained from thirty-eight men who provided information on ninety-two liaisons. The number of liaisons reported by each Level I individual is given in the following table.

These data, it should be remembered, were obtained from college men. Data collected from some other social-education group might present quite a different picture both with respect to the number who had patronized prostitutes and the attitudes toward

---

[3] The author does say, however, "The prevalence of prostitution itself and the very indication of female promiscuity, has the inevitable counterpart of male promiscuity as well." (p. 206)

prostitute liaisons. Kinsey (58) found that of his subjects who had reached twenty-five years of age "only 28 per cent of the males of the college level" had patronized prostitutes. Most of the men in this study have confined their experiences with prostitutes to a single, or two or three liaisons. Actually, six men accounted for forty-nine, or more than half, of the ninety-two prostitute liaisons.

Table 3

PARTICIPANTS AND LIAISONS—LEVEL I

Number of Subjects	Number of Liaisons Reported	Total Number of Liaisons
23	1	23
7	2	14
2	3	6
1	4	4
2	5	10
1	7	7
1	8	8
1	20	20
38		92

Kinsey (58 p. 601) found that college-level men had the lowest frequency rate for participation with prostitutes of men at any of the educational levels. "Between 16 and 20 males of the grade school level have intercourse with prostitutes 9 times as often, and males of the high school level have it more than 4 times as often as males of the college level."

Kinsey's data (p. 352) also indicate that the majority of college-level men with prostitute experience will have had this experience between their sixteenth and twenty-first birthdays. Most of the men participating in this study had had their prostitute experience while still in their teens. Average age of these men was 20.6 years and about half had already gone through the age period in which prostitute liaisons were most likely to occur.

What may happen in the future so far as the participants in this study are concerned? With increasing age and experience in the military service some of the subjects will probably multiply the number of their prostitute liaisons. Others, to judge from their comments, do not intend to patronize prostitutes again.

DESCRIPTIVE DATA—LEVEL I

The descriptive data for Level I liaisons will be analyzed under the relationship headings listed in Chapter I, namely; *motivation, communication, protective measures and assumption of responsibility,* and the *subjects' evaluation of their own experiences.* In addition, some general observations which have implications for understanding prostitute-patron relationships will be made at the end of the chapter.

Motivations

An obvious lead to understanding one of the masculine motivations which led to patronizing prostitutes was offered by one circumstance. This was the frequency with which "going to a prostitute" involved two, three, or four males at a time, rather than one. What happened took on the appearance of an adventure. It seemed to be primarily a male-group experience, rather than the efforts of an individual to secure sexual satisfaction.

Thirty-four of the thirty-eight men reporting prostitute liaisons went to the house with a friend, or friends, and never alone. These thirty-four included every one of the twenty-three boys who reported only a single liaison with a prostitute, plus six of the seven subjects with two liaisons. The subject who reported twenty prostitute liaisons was accompanied in every instance by other men. For four other men, who reported two, three, five and eight prostitute liaisons respectively, information as to whether each of these liaisons was a part of a group experience was not obtained. In the case of the one subject who reported eight prostitute liaisons there was probably no group participation. He described himself as a "lone wolf" and said that he went to prostitutes at times when he was moody, downcast, and lonely.

Several ways in which prostitute visitation was used as a male group experience emerged from an analysis of the case histories.[4]

---

[4] Murtagh and Harris (80) write:

> Prostitutes all say that the teen-agers, in striking contrast to their elderly customers, are coarse and offensive. They are exhibitionists, inclined to come in groups and perform for each other's benefit. Many of

The experience was used to test and dare, as an occasion for excitement and adventure, as a method of gaining status, or as a way of putting pressure on an individual. Seemingly there was much less desire for sex than for something which would prove that one was sophisticated and wordly-wise. The prostitute often seemed an incidental aspect of the total situation. She was the medium through which the boys were demonstrating something to themselves and to each other.

The first case history illustrates several motivations. It is quoted at length to provide a clearer overall picture of what "going to a prostitute" may mean to a group of boys. Here one can see the process of daring, nudging and jockeying, and of gradual commitment, which continues until no one can retreat without loss of face. This process seems to occur often when boys of the age and level of sophistication of the subjects in this study are anticipating intercourse with a prostitute.

> **59**[*]   M's[†] first experience in intercourse occurred the day he was inducted into the army. M met five or six other young fellows at the induction center who were also being taken into the service. In the evening, after their physical examinations, they got together and, because it was daring, went to one of the worst sections of town. They went to a night spot where they stopped outside, for they were somewhat afraid to go in. The proprietor observed them and invited them in. They accepted and in a short time they were drinking and feeling somewhat more at ease. After a while another man asked them if they would like to have "women for the night." The fellows talked this over at length, and all agreed that it would be a good experience. They stepped outside to make financial arrangements, and first one and then another of the fellows began to make excuses as to why he didn't think he would go in this evening. One was feeling somewhat ill

them request aberrant acts, not because they like them, but because they enjoy regarding themselves as sophisticates. Naturally the women resent the motivations almost as much as the requests. (p. 176)

[*] The case histories have been numbered consecutively from 1 to 200. Excerpts from a particular case history may appear at more than one level (or in more than one chapter). In such an event, the case history number remains the same.

[†] "M" is used throughout to designate the male of that particular case history, "F" to designate the female. "F1" means M's first sexual partner, "F3" the third, etc.

from the shots he had taken, another didn't know that he quite liked the looks of the place, and others had other reasons.

"Finally one of the other fellows said to me, 'Well, by God, I'm not going to chicken out, are you?'

"I said, 'No, I'm not! These other guys can chicken out, but I'm going through with it.'" After this exchange of dares M and his companion completed arrangements and went to the house. . . .

"As soon as I was done I got out of the bedroom and went down to the living room where I found my friend waiting for me. The rest of the fellows had gone to the hotel so we had a chance to talk alone. We found that neither had had a satisfactory experience and that the relationship had not amounted to much for either of us. However, he had not had the trouble in reaching a climax that I had had, and he had been waiting outside for me for some little time. . . ."

Nevertheless, the boys did not tell the rest of the fellows what their actual reactions were. "Oh, gosh, no! We told them what a wonderful bunch of girls we had found, how much fun we had had and how much they had missed. We really built it up."

M thinks after this experience there was some looking up to him and the other fellow as leaders in the group. He doesn't know whether it was the result of their having gone ahead with the prostitutes, but from that time on if there were questions to be asked or decisions to be made, M and his friend were accepted as the leaders. That continued for as long as the group remained together.

The following three excerpts are further illustrations of the use of prostitutes to test and dare, or to serve as an occasion for excitement and adventure with friends.

57 M's first experience took place after a fraternity initiation. In order to relax, three pledgees, close friends, went for a drive. One of them, who had been to a prostitute before, suggested they go some place and have intercourse. As he put it, he was "horny." The other fellows were receptive. As M reviews the situation he realized they nudged and dared each other until all of them were in a position from which they were unable to withdraw without being considered "chicken." M thinks that secretly they wanted it to be that way. He feels that they were curious, yet no one could have gone by himself. "We had to sort of dare each other."

197 F2 was "a whore with whom I had relations when I was in Tiajuana, Mexico." At this time M was nineteen years old, and visiting Tiajuana with two friends. They started drinking about noon and continued drinking and "walking around the place." That evening they started to drop in on floor shows. "The dancing girls were downright lewd. They would come over as they danced, and you could play with them right while they were dancing. Some of the girls would grab for your penis. We did whatever we wanted to with them." The boys did not quite dare in the earlier part of the evening to accept intercourse. Later M and his friends went to a Lesbian show. About 1:00 A.M. they started back to their hotel. On the way they were accosted by a fellow who "asked us if we wanted a girl." So they said they did, and the pimp took them into a house where they could take their pick from among the various ones.

125 One evening a bunch of fellows about M's age, around fourteen and older, were "fooling" around town. They got to talking about sex, and as a result of the discussion all chipped in enough to raise $5.00 so one of the group might go to one of the local houses and have intercourse with a prostitute. M drew the lot so the fellows took him to the house and waited in the living room for him while he went in for intercourse.

Sometimes prostitute experiences may be preceded by a long period of planning and much anticipation, as is indicated in the two excerpts which follow.

99 M has just recently had one experience in intercourse with a prostitute. He had heard so much talk from boy friends about intercourse that he felt a strong desire to experience it. His boy friend had the same feelings. They were aware of each other's desires and decided that on a forthcoming vacation to San Francisco "we would go to a house."

They made considerable preparation for their experience. M stopped masturbation for four or five days before they expected to visit the prostitute. He and his friend talked quite a lot about what the experience would be like. The day they arrived at San Francisco they attended several "peep shows" and in general built toward the anticipated experience. "We spent the day getting 'sexed up' in a big way." The actual experience was a "big letdown."

124 M had his first experience in intercourse when he was fifteen. He was on the football team which each fall went to S. to play. It was generally known that the year before members of the team had gone to a "whore house." Knowing that he would be going to S., M and a couple of his friends looked forward to this time as the occasion on which they would have their first intercourse. They went to a show after the game, then about 2:00 A.M. M and his two friends went to the house and had intercourse.

"Going to a prostitute" makes an exciting conversational topic. Obviously they become shared experiences which create at least a temporary sense of group solidarity.

2 "Intercourse with a prostitute gives you something to brag about to the other boys." Usually after intercourse was over and the fellows were leaving, there would be an exchange of conversation, somewhat like this: "Well, what did you get tonight?" The reply might be, "Oh, I got half and half," or "an old-fashioned." Sometimes some of the girls would use their mouths on the boys and "this was almost as good as intercourse. This also gave us something to talk about."

57 After they decided to go to a house the boys went back to the fraternity and let their plans be known. As a result another carload of fellows followed them to see if they actually went. Their experience later was the subject of a good many conversations.

The use of sexual experience to make oneself feel "one of the boys" is illustrated in the following excerpt. Once M got his experience, though, he found his friends too occupied in recounting their own experience to listen to his. Evidently they needed, just as much as M, to make others aware of their accomplishment and sophistication.

148 M, then seventeen, felt a little reluctance about going to a prostitute, but he didn't let the other boys who were planning to go know how he felt. Still, he wanted to go. So many of his friends had had intercourse, and many of them were younger than himself. "I thought it was high time I did something about it. It was a case of putting pressure on myself, you might say." After he was through, M tried to tell the rest of the boys about his experience, but they were too busy talking about their own to listen to him.

Sometimes an individual may feel definite pressure from members of his group to participate in the experience that other members of the group are planning or having.

> **149** M's first sexual experience came at age nineteen after two friends suggested that he go with them to a house of prostitution in a neighboring town. They knew that M was a virgin and when he showed reluctance, they began to urge him. Their argument was "you've got to do it sometime, so you just as well get started now." M went with mixed feelings. He was curious about the intercourse and really wanted the experience. On the other hand he was scared. When he reached the house, "I didn't particularly want to go in."

A combination of boredom and liquor sometimes provides the incentive for seeking a prostitute association. M, in the following excerpt reported twenty prostitute liaisons.

> **2** "As I think of my experiences, going to a prostitute follows a regular pattern." The moves which ended in going would begin when a group of fellows, usually about five, and usually the same five, drove to a tavern to get some liquor. After drinking a bit and driving around a while, someone would say, "Let's go down to one of the houses." This suggestion would be accepted and they would go as a group. "In all my experiences of going to prostitutes, I have never gone alone."

The need which some boys feel to accept group standards and to meet group expectancies seemingly resulted in certain of the subjects' concealing dissatisfaction with their prostitute experience. Few have the hardihood to express feelings of disapproval, disillusionment, or disgust openly even though they may have felt them.

Participation in sexual intercourse is accepted by many young men as a test of masculinity. The normal male is expected to strive for and to appreciate intercourse. The boy who feels dissatisfied either keeps his "mouth shut," or tells his friends what he thinks they expect to hear. An illustration of this is found in case history #59, previously used in this chapter.

An additional excerpt from another history has been selected to illustrate this reaction.

> **54** After they had left the house the fellows did a lot of laughing and talking about their experiences. They commented on the

various girls, how long it took to have a climax, and "which girls they were going to get the next time they went.

"I just sat back and listened and said nothing. I had made up my mind. They could go back all they wanted to, but I wasn't going. So far as I was concerned, it wasn't at all satisfactory and was a waste of money."

Even when a boy has convictions about sexual conduct based on principle, he may remain silent about them in face of possible adverse reactions from friends.

148   M has come to regard prostitution as socially and morally undesirable and definitely not worth the money. He would not consider going to prostitutes again. He has never voiced his true reactions to his friends, however. In talking with them he· has treated his and their experiences as fun and as though they had his full approval and acceptance. "When a bunch of fellows get to talking about sex, you're not going to be the one to throw a wet towel on the fun."

Some boys who have patronized prostitutes have experienced failures in sexual functioning which they wish to conceal. The reaction expressed in the following excerpt is typical of a number of others who experienced the same problem.

125   M's first experience with a prostitute (his second sexual experience) was during the fall of his freshman year in high school. He was then fourteen years of age.

"I was so damned scared that I didn't know what to do." M was also embarrassed and had difficulty in getting an erection. In intercourse he couldn't reach a climax. His partner did not help him any. She indulged in no foreplay and "was too business-like." M put on as bold a front before his friends as possible. He told them nothing of his embarrassment, or his sexual inadequacy.

Sometimes two or three very close friends will have developed a strong rapport. Under such circumstances they may be able to acknowledge to each other that their experience has been an unsatisfactory one, or that they have experienced failure. This acknowledgment will not be made to fellows outside the close circle. When talking to those outside their group, the boys are likely to indicate that their experiences were very satisfying. An additional illustration follows:

123 On the way home the boys talked very frankly at length about their relationships. All three acknowledged that when they were at the point where they had to go ahead with intercourse, they wanted to back out. None of them had found it very satisfactory. When they got home, though, they put on quite a different front before the rest of the boys. They said little for a day or two, but within three or four days practically all the boys in town knew what had happened. The three were heroes for a time. They were asked many questions, and were the object of excited and curious comments. They used the experience as an ego-building experience, and to emphasize the point that they were now men. None of the other boys had yet had that experience. "We didn't tell the real truth about how we felt."

The concern among boys for being a part of a male group, and for attaining group status will come as no surprise to those familiar with adolescent psychology. This is the age at which the average boy is trying to emancipate himself from home, and to establish himself as a person. He is attempting to earn a role identity for himself in his own right. This is done with behavior which excites the admiration of his peer group,[5] though it is often disapproved by adult society. The boy also gains a sense of achievement through having defied social convention,[6] and through having experiences about which his parents will never know. This aids him in achieving the desired sense of being mature and independent.[7]

---

[5] For an excellent discussion of the importance of group identification with its sense of masculine achievement to the adolescent boy, see Bloch and Niederhoffer (9). Many aspects of adolescent behavior, not the sexual alone, are discussed.

[6] Ellis (30) suggests that sexual orgies arise from the need of people to defy the extremes of rigid sexual abstinence prescribed by traditional morality and conventional codes. Occasional outbursts of license give a sense of freedom and recklessness. He regards prostitution as a refined form of sexual orgy.

[7] The prostitutes evidently sometimes see the same efforts to portray sophistication. Murtagh and Harris (80) quotes a prostitute as saying,

I hate those punk kids like poison because I know most of them need us girls like holes in the head. But if you listened to them talk, you'd think they were big men burning up for a woman. Funny, but they all seem to like my type. I'm sorry to say I can't return the compliment. Would you believe it, a funny-looking fourteen-year-old punk once told me . . . he liked his women fat . . . Fourteen years old, he likes his women fat! (p. 176)

Another datum which may have some significance at this point relates to the number of subjects who said that drinking had preceded their visit to a prostitute. Thirty-five men said either that each of their Level I liaisons, or some of them, had been accompanied by drinking. Three men failed to give information on this point, yet a study of their case histories would indicate that drinking might easily have been a part of their pattern of behavior. Of these three, two had had prostitute liaisons overseas and the third spoke of moodiness and despondency having preceded his visits to prostitutes. Among the thirty-eight subjects there are none about whom one could feel unequivocally that "this person does not drink."

The reason for this coincidence of drinking and patronizing of prostitutes needs further study. Both are probably symptoms of some underlying condition which calls for understanding. More research on this point would be of value.

Although the motivation resulting from the need to participate in a male group experience has been strongly emphasized, it would be incorrect to assume that this was the sole motivation. Evidence indicates that other motivations also exist.

Curiosity as a motivation appeared frequently in the case histories. Existing social attitudes toward sex stimulate it, and it is expressed in such comments as these: "I'd heard so much about intercourse, I wanted to find out what it was like."—"I was just plain curious."—"I'd been wanting to find out about sex for some time."—"I couldn't find what I wanted to know from reading, so I decided to find out for myself."

These subjects were curious not only about intercourse, but also about prostitution. Several mentioned their interest in asking the prostitute questions about herself, and how she came to get into prostitution. Some were too abashed to do this. In the following excerpt, M had the nerve needed to go through intercourse, but he was too embarrased to ask the girl questions about how she came to be a prostitute.

> 57 M would have liked to ask the woman some questions about what led her into prostitution. He felt a little embarrassed about asking such questions, however, so he said nothing. On the way home M found that one of the other fellows had asked his girl these same questions.

The desire for sexual experimentation is sometimes a motive for going to a prostitute. Some boys are interested in experimenting with sex, just as they are interested in experimentation with anything else. In the next history M was quite widely experienced sexually before he had intercourse with a prostitute. He was already an acknowledged leader and authority in his group on sexual matters. The prostitute involved in this excerpt was M's thirteenth sexual partner.

> 136 M and three friends had been drinking. After some talk they decided to go to "a whore house for some experience." M wanted this kind of experience also, so he was quite ready to go along. He had heard that women prostitutes knew how to bring fellows to a climax a great deal more quickly than inexperienced women could, so M told his friends that he was going to masturbate before he went so that "I would come more slowly, and get my money's worth." He did this, and as a result his climax with the prostitute was much delayed.
>
> In the bedroom M undressed completely, and the prostitute washed his sex organs with soap. At the same time she manipulated them quite vigorously. Since M had masturbated such a short time before, this did not produce an erection. This "fouled her all up." The result was that in order to help M secure an erection she used her mouth. That way "I got a 'half and half' job for only $5.00." They also experimented with four or five different intercourse positions.

The discussion thus far has been of obvious and conscious motivations. Unconscious motivations, without doubt, exist also. One wonders, for example, what unconscious needs motivated the subject who reported twenty prostitute liaisons, and gave no evidence of a desire for either social or sexual experiences at any other relationship level. This boy's history revealed no evidence that he had ever experienced or felt much tenderness in any of his relationships. His attitudes seemed to express marked impersonality toward all the girls with whom he had been associated. Does this represent a general incapacity to develop relationships with depth and permanence? Are some strong forces operating at the unconscious level? At this point these questions can only be raised, not answered.

Some deep-seated motivations are evidently operating in the

following case history, whether M's analysis of what they are is correct or not:

> 44 M, who has had intercourse with two prostitutes, describes himself as a person who "had never been around much," and who has been reared in a "secluded atmosphere." He has always been shy and ill at ease, even fearful, with girls. He was regarded as "naïve and uninformed" by his acquaintances.
>
> He discussed his second prostitute liaison, which was so sordid and revolting that "the next morning when I got sobered up and began to recollect what had happened, I was almost sick with disgust. It seemed like only a person who was mentally deficient or depraved could have done this." Time has not lessened the feeling, and even now M finds it quite painful to talk about it.
>
> M himself commented on his thoughts about his motives. He thinks the reason he entered these experiences was that he wanted to convince himself that he could break through the barrier of shyness and ineffectiveness that had troubled him. Also, he wanted group acceptance. He did not anticipate getting group acceptance by telling the group about these sexual relationships, for he knew he was regarded as naïve and even prudish. But as the result of these experiences, he at least hoped to prove to himself that such was not the case.

Nothing in these histories indicates that these boys have gone to prostitutes because of an overpowering physical sex drive separate from psychic factors. Several boys spoke about feeling strong physical desires at the time they went to prostitutes, but at the same time they recited circumstances, e.g., drinking, sexually stimulating. discussions, that clearly indicated conditions which might cause or contribute to sexual arousal. The sex drive which impels adolescent boys to seek sexual satisfaction through prostitutes is almost surely more psychologically induced than physically produced.[8]

---

[8] For discussions on this point see Kirkendall (62), Lion (69), Beach (7, p. 1-32), Olive (81), Safier (88). Significant portions of Lion and Safier are quoted in Kirkendall (60). Still shorter quotations are given in Chapter X of this book.

Communication

The discussion of communication[9] presents certain difficulties so far as Level I liaisons are concerned. The best approach to understanding the problems of communication in the patron-prostitute relationship seems to be, first, an examination of the relationship of the boy to the prostitute he is patronizing.[*] This relationship was by-passed earlier in this chapter in order to explore the more meaningful (to the boy) relationship which exists between him and his boy friends. The character of this relationship will explain some of the problems of communication.

In the first place the roles of the two participants—the prostitute and her patron—are quite clearly and sharply defined. This being so, there is little or no necessity for extended communication. The participants are unacquainted and, in their own eyes, of unequal social status, so casual conversation is not indicated. The circumstances define the event which is to occur. When a man goes to a prostitute the sequence of events is taken for granted. He made his decision when he decided to enter the house, and the business of the prostitute is to accommodate those who come, regardless of her feelings.

Thus, interchange is ordinarily reduced to a simple business transaction. There is no more need for the prostitute and her patron to discuss whether a sexual relationship should occur, than for a motorist to discuss with the attendant at a filling station whether he can or should purchase gasoline. Decision-making communication is conspicuously absent in Level I liaisons.

Nor did these subjects engage in communication which centered about the participants' emotional concern, or revealed their feelings about their personal successes and failures,[10] just as one does not discuss such matters in a business transaction.

---

[9] By communication is meant the exchange of ideas and awareness of feelings and attitudes between and among persons. In this study special attention is given to the capacity of individuals to express themselves fully and honestly about their feelings and attitudes toward their relationship.

[*] The word "patronize" itself has a semantic significance, carrying as it does the implication of condescension, or unequal status.

[10] This may be much less true in other circumstances. See for example some of the prostitute liaisons set up by men in the overseas military service. Some of these exist for a considerable length of time and may display certain of the characteristics of a husband-wife relationship. Also Murtagh and Harris (80)

Communication in a relationship is markedly conditioned by the concepts which people hold of each other, and of themselves. Communication between those who recognize that they are experiencing similar emotional reactions and who regard themselves as equals, or who would like to continue their association, will surely differ from the communication which exists between those who feel that a vast social chasm exists between them, who regard themselves as involved in an impersonal, business transaction, or whose relationship is based on contempt for each other. The relationship between the prostitute and her patron is certain to exhibit these latter characteristics predominantly.

One gets the impression as the boys speak that they definitely regard the prostitute as a person apart from themselves socially. She is often viewed as an individual who has willingly and willfully strayed and who must accept full responsibility for the condition in which she finds herself. She is "reaping the consequences" of her conduct. There was little evidence of any feelings that a general social responsibility might be involved in the status of the prostitute.

From time to time some male may be touched by what he sees, but he simply accepts it as "one of those things." [11] This detached attitude is illustrated in the following excerpts. Even when, in spite of themselves, both M's felt somewhat sorry for their partners, there was no evidence that they communicated their feelings, or that they had any desire to do so. One possible ameliorating action was readily available to each of them; both could have refrained from copulation. The boys still took advantage of the girl's presence for fulfilling their own personal desires.

> 33 The boys found two prostitutes at the house. One was about thirty-five, and the other about twenty-two. The younger one was unmarried and, according to M, "already had a kid, and no way to support it, so she was in this business as a way of making

---

describe how some prostitutes minister to certain of their emotional needs of their older patrons.

[11] This, as an individual attitude, is very similar to a common social attitude that "prostitution has always existed and always will." Chesser (16) seems to embrace this view, though Havelock Ellis (30) felt that prostitution was a product of certain influences which become operative as civilization develops.

some easy money. She was off on the wrong track, and I couldn't help feeling sorry for her."

M first had intercourse with the thirty-five-year-old woman who charged him $5.00. As M left the room, he met his friend who had just had intercourse with the younger girl. M asked him how much he had paid and he said $3.00.

The rate differential disgusted M, so he said to his friend, "Well, I'm going to go in and try it for $3.00." So he went in and had intercourse with the younger girl.

185 M, age nineteen, found a "whore, about fifteen," with whom he had intercourse. He felt "sort of sorry" for her, because "she was so young, and kinda cute, yet already at that age she was in a cat house."

Another attitude sometimes expressed is that prostitutes are incapable of any feeling, that nothing will injure or disturb them. For example, M, who reported twenty prostitute liaisons, commented in response to a question about what sex standards he would want for his children, as follows:

2 "The one thing I would want of a son would be that he not take advantage of girls. I wouldn't mind for him to have intercourse with prostitutes, though, because you couldn't hurt those girls anyway. Whatever you do wouldn't make any difference to them."

Two boys, on the other hand, expressed surprise and satisfaction at the humanness of their female partners when they found it possible to talk with some frankness. Their stereotyped concepts evidently had caused them to believe that prostitutes were devoid of feeling or sentiment.

In the first statement, M does not indicate what he thought a prostitute would be like, but evidently her human, friendly approach was not what he had expected.

148 M paid his money and went with the girl with whom he was to have intercourse. He told her frankly that he had never had intercourse, and was uncertain and a little fearful. She was very nice, and objectively, with no embarrassment, explained how to go about intercourse, the different positions, and similar matters. She was so relaxed herself that M was unembarrassed and was put quite at ease. She was a woman about thirty and married, so she told M. M was nineteen.

M's experience with her "kinda shook me up. She was so different from what I had expected." After they were done they talked a while longer. "She was a good conversationalist," and explained to M something of why she thought older married men patronized prostitutes.

In the next excerpt one wonders how much the satisfaction the boys expressed with their sexual experience was conditioned by the cordiality of their reception at the house.

156 "We were all kind of scared when we first went in." However, one of the girls met the three boys and put them very much at ease. She talked very cordially, asking them where they were from and what they did. Then she wanted to know "who was to go first."

On the way home the boys compared experiences and told in detail what had happened to each of them. They were all pretty well satisfied and felt that the experience was about as satisfactory as they had hoped. For M it was "actually a pretty pleasant experience."

From the standpoint of the prostitute or the establishment in which she works, taking time to engage in pleasantries is sometimes, evidently, an unwarranted trespassing on "company time."

40 "After intercourse was over, she softened up some and we started to talk a little bit, but about this time the Madam and the taxi driver came in and hustled me out. They said I was taking too much of her time."

The fact that the prostitutes are sexually experienced and are in their own quarters puts a young, inexperienced boy at quite a disadvantage. He is in a subordinate position in these associations and so is subject to the direction of the woman. He is in a poor position to open discussion, or to express himself freely. He finds himself being moved along in a process over which he has no control, and the procedures used make him quite aware that he is simply in tow.

The case histories are replete with phrases which make it clear that with this group of boys it was usually the women who called the turn.

"The first thing she did was to take my money—$5.00 of it."

———

"She asked me how I wanted it (intercourse)."

"She took me over to the wash basin and washed my genitals."

"She told me to get my clothes off."

"She said this must be my first time."

Whether in view of his inexperience the boy's subordinate position is a relief to him, whether his situation contradicts the role which he thinks he should assume in a sexual relationship, whether he feels demeaned, is not fully clear from the case histories. Undoubtedly, these feelings and opinions will vary from boy to boy. Several excerpts are quoted, however, which make it clear that some boys do have feelings about the subordinate circumstances in which they find themselves.

> 149 M ejaculated before he could make an entrance. When this occurred, the girl's comment was, "You must be a beginner." This was quite embarrassing to M, and he felt "very little-boy like. I had been trying to act so grown up and to make it appear that I knew everything, and that I had been around. Then she said that."

> 115 "When she came out she started talking with me and asked me what 'I would like.' I was so green at the whole business that I hardly knew what she meant. I knew though that she was using a lot of slang terms to describe what she had to offer." Since M didn't want to expose his ignorance he said, "I'll take it straight."

> 156 When M and his girl got into the bedroom she asked, "How do you want to do it?" M was shocked "that she would ask such a question." When he said, "Oh, it doesn't make any difference," she asked, "Do you want to do it the old-fashioned way?" "I said, 'Yes, that will be all right with me.' I was just bluffing my way through."

Hostility and contempt on the part of the prostitute seem to be communicated in the following excerpt:

> 139 After they were done they got up and F washed M's genitals. She then gave herself a douche. The sight of her doing this "made me feel sort of sick." They both dressed without talking. Before M completed his dressing, F had finished and "simply

walked out. As she did so, I said to myself, 'All in the course of a lifetime.' "

An older, more sophisticated boy will sometimes pit himself against the prostitute or set up the situation to suit himself. An example of this was given in the excerpt from history #136 in which M described how he masturbated before he went to the prostitute and "fouled her all up" when he did not attain an erection.

When several boys are able to retain their identity as a group they may also take command of the situation. This circumstance was illustrated in the excerpt from history #137 in which M described how he and his friends went from one house to another engaging in sex play with the girls they found there.

Further insights emerge when communication between members of the male group is analyzed. Discussion between the boy who patronizes the prostitute and his boy friends is relatively free as long as he actually finds or pretends to find pleasure in his visit to the prostitute. As has already been noted, when a boy is dissatisfied with his experiences he is unlikely to express his feelings freely in a group, though he may eventually do so to one or two of his most intimate boy friends. Among adolescent males the common assumption is that a normal boy will seek sexual experience and will, of course, enjoy it. A boy who is dissatisfied, or who rejects the opportunity for intercourse, is likely to expose himself to such reactions as the one expressed in the following excerpt.

137 Of the group of four boys who went to the house, three had intercourse. Of the fourth one, M commented, "He just stood in the hall and waited until we were done. I don't know why. I can't figure him out."

A feeling of need to communicate and communication problems may arise between the boy who has patronized a prostitute and his girl friend, or fiancée. Several references to this particular circumstance are found in the case histories. Three excerpts relating to it follow.

2 M told the girl he was "dating steady" that he had been to houses of prostitution. Her attitude was that she saw no use of making any point of it. This was "just something which had

happened. She was quite gracious about it." She thought that it was probably a good thing for M to have had the experience.

139 Concerning M's telling his fiancée, "this has bothered me. I have debated quite a while about it." His decision was made, however, by a chance occurrence. M's fiancée asked him if he was a virgin and he said he was. This untruth has bothered him ever since. He is fearful that if he tells the truth now she will lose respect for him.

57 When he becomes engaged M "thinks" he will tell his fiancée of this experience. He feels that "she will want to know." He knows that he would want to know "all about her," and if he is going to ask her about her past experiences he will have to tell about his. M feels such an inquiry is desirable. "It will help me know what kind of a girl she really is."

The above excerpts certainly imply an acceptance of the double standard of sexual conduct which permits freedom to the male, but denies it to the woman. Does the "graciousness" of women in accepting the previous experience of men reflect their implicit acceptance of the double standard? Or do they reason that acceptance is the only possible course open to them? What kind of reasoning enables M (#57) in the history just quoted to think that knowledge of his fiancée's inexperience or previous experience will help him to know "what kind of a girl she really is," without feeling that similar knowledge about him is a revelation of "what kind of a boy he really is"? What concepts about the nature of masculine and feminine sexuality are implied in the attitudes displayed in the above excerpts? How widespread are these attitudes? These questions need further investigation. An insight into common and current attitudes and concepts is important in developing effective educational and guidance programs.

Protective Measures and Assumption of Responsibility

The use of protective measures and attitudes toward the assumption of responsibility are closely related in Level I liaisons and will be treated under the same heading. The assumption has been made that persons associated in an emotionally-satisfying interpersonal relationship will be interested in protecting their associates.

Accordingly, Level I liaisons have been examined for evidences of protectiveness and responsible conduct toward others.

The prostitute-patron association is a relationship that brings together two persons, usually without previous acquaintance, for a very brief period of time, an hour or so at the most. There is no expectation that the relationship will be continued or renewed. It is devoid of emotional attachment. In fact, the idea of emotional attachment is practically always rejected. As a result, the relationship is a transitory association, and the participants are primarily concerned with attaining their own personal objectives. They concentrate on the physical and the commercial aspects of the relationship.

The most obvious protective measures reported in these liaisons are those concerned with the prevention of venereal diseases. These measures were almost always applied to the men by the women, and usually involved only the physical inspection, and/or sometimes the washing of the genital organs.

In one or two instances subjects reported the use of injections intended to prevent infection. There was no reference to the use of condoms, withdrawal, or any other male device which would prevent either venereal disease or pregnancy. One subject mentioned going to a military prophylactic station after completing intercourse and receiving treatment there. Another mentioned the use of a "pro" kit after he had left the prostitute.

The responsibility for protective measures seemed always to fall on the woman, and to be applied mainly for the benefit of the male. This arrangement seems a natural consequence of the circumstances associated with prostitution. The men are there for personal pleasure, and are not concerned with their consort.

Probably few men, especially those who are experienced, would accept or use the condom because of its anticipated interferences with their physical pleasure. Furthermore, the attitude which men generally bear toward a prostitute does not require them to be concerned with her welfare. The woman thus becomes the one who has to apply protective measures as a personal safeguard. The prostitute may also look upon the protective measures she applies as necessary in the successful conduct of her business. By preventing the transmission of venereal diseases the prostitute protects her customers and helps keep conditions favorable for her business. Though she may be seeking in what she does to protect herself against pregnancy, the male probably gives this eventuality little consideration. His general attitude is one of unconcern. He sees no need for being responsible for the woman. He may assume that she knows exactly what needs to be done, anyway. One subject said, "I figured she knew enough to take care of herself."

The impersonality of the relationship probably makes protective measures seem needless and even out of place.

> **183** In none of his prostitute liaisons did M use any kind of contraceptive, nor did he withdraw. "Naturally" he had no real feeling for any of the girls.

Still another subject made this comment about possible pregnancy: "I didn't worry about that. I was going to be gone the next day anyway." Another M said, "That was her worry, not mine."

The prostitute sometimes attempts to protect her customers from community talk and criticism. One way this is done is to make a clear distinction between the prostitute role and the role of social acquaintances. This distinction was noted by one subject.

> **2** The boys went often enough so that they got to know "some of the girls real well." Sometimes when business was not too pressing, they would "shoot the breeze" with the boys. Even though the boys got well acquainted with the girls at the house they never spoke to them if they met on the street. They simply passed with no sign of recognition.

In the next excerpt, the girl quite clearly indicated the separation which existed in her mind between the role of the prostitute and a role in which there might be emotional involvement. She evidently believed in maintaining impersonality, and in expressing her determination to do so gained the grudging admiration of her consort.

> **139** After he was through intercourse M started to talk. For a long time he had wanted to find out from a prostitute how she felt about prostitution and how she had gotten into it. M began by asking her, "Does anyone ever kiss you while he is having intercourse?"
>
> Her reply was, "I am a whore, Sonny, not a lover."
>
> "I kinda liked her for that statement. In fact, I liked her general attitude. This was her job and she was going about it. She

wasn't going to go any further than was necessary. She was going to keep it a matter-of-fact relationship."

The impersonal aspects of prostitution are in themselves a sort of protective shield or cloak. The impersonality of the situation prevents emotional involvement and, for some boys, it may aid their sexual functioning. In the excerpt below, the concept of the prostitute as being without personality probably enabled the boy to have intercourse with prostitutes of any age without being disturbed by it.

> 2   It has never bothered M to have intercourse with girls who were older than himself. "I have had relations with women who were old enough to be my mother." As M looks at prostitutes he thinks they are always "sort of ageless personalities.
>
> "In fact, you might say they don't have personalities. They are sort of like slot machines. You put in $5.00 and pull the handle."

Other boys find such impersonality upsetting. It may protect some, and enable them to participate casually and freely in Level I liaisons, but it may prove the downfall of others. Their feelings about the impersonal aspects of their experience are obvious in the following excerpts.

> 124   The experience was a very casual one. There was very little conversation and very little foreplay. She was "very impersonal" and "nonchalant" about it all. "I was disappointed in it; it was a complete failure as far as I was concerned. It was not as satisfactory as when I masturbate." M commented to his friends as he was leaving that he "was never going to spend $5.00 like that again."

> 57   M found the experience less satisfying than he had expected. He had always thought intercourse should be something one wanted to do because they liked it and enjoyed their partner. In this situation "it all seemed to be so mechanical. It was simply a business proposition."

> 40   "It was one of those 'pay-your-money, get on, get off' deals."

Some subjects gave clear evidence that their visit to a prostitute —particularly the first one—presented hazards for which they had not bargained. This shows up most clearly in the numerous references to failures and inadequacies in sexual functioning. These are found in about half of the reports. The usual statement is that the individual had difficulty in attaining or keeping an erection, and often in reaching a climax. Only one individual spoke of a premature ejaculation.

In several instances these inadequacies were associated with feelings aroused by the prostitute when she washed the boy's genitals. Boys described themselves as "surprised," "shocked," "embarrassed," or "bothered" by this experience. These boys were then likely to experience an incapacity in sexual functioning.

Not all boys have such difficulties, of course. One boy described the genital-washing experience as "rather pleasant." Another boy found that mouth-genital contacts were "almost as good as intercourse," and that they also "give us something to talk about."

Many of the case histories contain references to other experiences which the boys found upsetting and disturbing. These include such things as the nudeness which involved both sexes, the use of mouth-genital contacts, the fondling of the male genitals by the woman, the embarrassment at being in a situation in which one doesn't know what to do or what is expected, the chagrin and even fright over a failure in sexual functioning, becoming sick while in the house as a result of drinking, being in surroundings which in general are filthy or unaesthetic, and the fear that one's family may learn about this experience.

The following excerpt gives quite a clear description of the reactions which M had to his visit to a house of prostitution, and illustrates several of the points just made.

> **59** "When we got there we sat down in the living room and they began to bring women out for us to look over. I felt like I was a judge in a cattle show, and was looking over the prize stock. After a little while they brought out a girl named Mary, and I thought to myself, 'This is as near as I'll ever get to anything that looks good.' So I said, 'I'll take Mary.' When I said this she came over and sat on my lap, put her arms around my neck, and snuggled down next to me. It was so put on, and so artificial, that it almost turned my stomach."
>
> M went with Mary to the bedroom where they were to have intercourse. "When we got there Mary maneuvered me over to the wash basin, reached down and unzipped my trousers, took out my genital organs, and began washing them carefully. After

she had washed them she examined them minutely and I couldn't help asking, 'What are you looking for?'

"Her response was, she was looking to see if I had venereal disease.

"This close inspection just about ruined things for me, for I had never before experienced that kind of familiarity from a woman. However, still more was to come. Mary matter-of-factly pulled off her clothes, went over and got into bed, and indicated that I was to undress and come over myself. This came near ruining things completely. I had never before stripped down before a woman, and I could hardly bring myself to do it now. However, I went ahead, undressed, and got into bed with her."

M then found that he had a great deal of difficulty in achieving an erection, and once he got an erection, he had even more difficulty reaching an orgasm. "As I was working at it, and I mean working, every now and then she would say in a perplexed tone of voice, 'Come on, boy, come on,' and that would set me back even further than I was before. She finally decided that my way of doing it was not the best and that she would try something different. So she got me over on my back and got astraddle me. After a while this did the trick."

Another impediment to adequate sexual functioning experienced by some boys arises when they find themselves teamed with prostitutes considerably older than themselves. Under such circumstances some may identify the prostitute with their mother. Three subjects spoke of such an identification.

123 So far as M was concerned, "I was scared to death." He had a very unsatisfactory relationship. The prostitute was considerably older than M. He estimated that she was at least thirty-five. This made her about the age of M's mother, and M could not keep the idea of his mother out of his mind when he looked at her. This made it hard for him to go ahead. Another thing which added to this feeling was that before intercourse the prostitute had washed his genitals. "This repelled me because it reminded me again of the fact that she was about the age of my mother."

In intercourse M had trouble maintaining an erection and in reaching a climax. He stopped once, withdrew, and she helped him to get a stronger erection by fondling and manipulating his genitals.

57 When they got to the house, the boys had to wait. After a time the women with whom they were to have intercourse came

in. M drew the oldest one. This was a little upsetting, for she was very much older than he was. "I thought to myself, 'She is actually old enough to be my mother.'"

The third subject who was with a thirty-five-year-old woman had difficulty in getting an erection, but "after she turned out the light I was all right."

The prostitutes themselves must occasionally make similar identifications. In the instance related below (not one of the case histories collected for this study) the prostitute was probably identifying herself as a mother aiding a disturbed son. The incident is given as it was related by M.

M, when he was sixteen, went with a couple of older boys to visit a prostitute. The woman with whom M was paired was "quite an old woman; she must have been thirty or thirty-five." When it came time for intercourse, M found himself unable to get an erection. His impotence maintained itself even though she fondled and manipulated his genitals. "All the time this was going on I was getting more and more upset and embarrassed." After a time they gave up the attempt as unsuccessful.

Then F, taking notice of M's chagrin and disturbed reaction, said, "Now, son, don't be bothered by this. There is nothing to be worried about. The trouble is that you ought not be here. This is no place for a young boy like you. This place is for these old lumberjacks who have no women of their own, and more money than they know what to do with. You go on home, forget this, and find a nice girl to fall in love with. Then when you want to have intercourse, you can have it all right. There won't be any trouble."

Certain psychological reactions which cannot be guarded against are apparently associated with many of the Level I liaisons. One wonders about the long-term consequences of such experiences. If an individual protects himself by creating a shell of impersonality, does this blunt his sensitivity in later relationships? Do the feelings of shock, embarrassment, and chagrin, which many of these boys related interfere in any way with their sexual functioning in later years? Will it interfere with the father-role, especially when the father has to be concerned with the sexual behavior of his children? With repeated experiences will these negative reactions diminish or disappear? How permanent are the various dichotomies which seem to be part of the prostitute-patron situation, e.g., the classification of women as good and bad; the splitting of sex into a physical experience as against sex as an expression of love; the complete shedding of responsibility by the males in one situation and the assumption of it in another; the ruling out of tenderness at one time and the inclusion of it as an essential at another?

EVALUATION OF SUBJECTS

As each subject was interviewed he was asked if he was satisfied or dissatisfied with his sexual experiences. A tabulation of the replies from the thirty-eight subjects follows:

Number of Subjects	Reaction to Experience
6	Satisfied
9	Mixed Feelings
19	Unsatisfactory
2	No Feelings
2	No Information

Each of the six who expressed satisfaction with their experience did so because they had derived physical pleasure. Instances in which a high degree of satisfaction was registered were those in which the girl was physically active. For example,

> 197 "It was the best I ever had. It was a good one. She did most of the work. She worked right along with you."

Another subject expressed his satisfaction at having the opportunity to have intercourse in a bed when "we were both undressed." In addition to the physical pleasure several boys who were having their first experience mentioned that the experience gave them "a sense of accomplishment."—"I now felt on par with the rest of the boys."—"I suddenly felt much older. I felt that I had grown up."

Those who had mixed feelings also indicated that the positive aspects of their feelings centered about the physical pleasure. "The orgasm was the best part of it."—"I enjoyed the feeling I got out of it, but that was all."

Five of the nine subjects with mixed feelings had negative reactions because they felt that they had spent their money foolishly. One boy commented, "The next morning when I got up I felt like pounding my head against a wall for shooting $5.00 that way. I couldn't see myself spending money for it when it could be had free." One boy who had an ejaculation before he could make an entrance said, "That was the fastest five bucks I ever spent."

The strength of feeling the dissatisfied boys put into their expressions much surpassed the strength of feeling expressed by those who were satisfied. Several statements made by dissatisfied subjects expressing strong feelings follow:

8 "It° cost us only $3.00 each, but I wouldn't be caught dead there (in the house). Conditions were terrible."

71 "It was utterly disgusting. I told the other boys that I didn't enjoy it and that I might as well have masturbated."

124 "It was very disappointing. It was a complete failure as far as I was concerned."

42 "It is repulsive even to think about. It was such a one-sided affair."

Others expressed dissatisfaction on the basis of unsatisfactory physical expression.

139 "I could hardly tell I had had a climax."

99 "There was no feeling about it at all."

Two boys expressed a fear that their families might find out about their experiences. The statement made by one of the subjects is given below:

57 On the way home they stopped for a cup of coffee. While in the café, M saw two fellows from his home town. He thought they recognized that he and the other fellows had been to a house. He was somewhat worried for fear that they would spread the information, and that it would come to the attention of his family.

° The repeated use of the neuter pronoun "it" to designate the situation or to refer to intercourse undoubtedly reflects the impersonality of the situation, and the inability of the boys to feel or accept the prostitutes as persons. Sometimes one gets the feeling that the boys consciously avoid the personal pronoun "she" or "her."

Another boy enjoyed the experience but was "so worried for the next week for fear I would catch something that it wasn't worth it."

Without doubt the self-esteem of a number of boys was altered by their prostitute experience—and not always in the same direction.

A few boys, as has been noted, said they felt a sense of accomplishment. Others felt demeaned. Five boys made statements which definitely indicated that result. "I felt dirty after I was through."—"I felt cheap."—"I was a little ashamed."

The most pronounced feeling of all came from #44 who expressed himself as being "almost sick with disgust." He felt "only a deficient or mentally depraved person" could have done what he had.

Some individuals develop rationalizations which relieve them of their feelings or self-depreciation or guilt. For example, one boy commented that he was glad he had not enjoyed his experience. Since he had not, he felt less guilt than he would have otherwise.

More knowledge about how boys who have strongly negative reactions handle their feelings would be of considerable value.

GENERAL OBSERVATIONS

The concluding section will contain a few general observations which should help in getting a better perspective on what has been said.

1. The boys from whom these data were obtained represented a select group. They were college men. For the most part they were relatively unsophisticated, and not broadly experienced. A good many of them had their first intercourse experience while they were in high school. Only two of them had overseas military service experience. This is by way of saying that if similar data had been secured from older men who were in, or had been in, the military service, or who had had a long experience of being on their own in a wide range of circumstances, the picture of their Level I liaisons would likely be quite different. The same might also be said about data from boys in a lower socio-economic class. These data are most likely to be

typical for boys who are the products of middle-class homes, who are college-bound, still under the influence of and controlled by their parents to a considerable extent, and who are in their late teens or early twenties, and are insecure in their masculine status.[12]

2. The prostitute experiences of these boys have for the most part been ones in which they were seemingly trying to demonstrate their grown-upness to other boys. Some of them may have regarded their experience as an act expressing social rebellion and defiance.

3. Their sexual experiences were ones for which they could hardly be considered ready. Their sheltered existence, and their paucity of knowledge about the nature of the experience, means that many have been shocked, or experienced traumatic episodes in their blundering experimentation.

4. The circumstances point to much needed but generally nonexistent types of communication. Boys in general would profit from opportunities to talk about their own insecurities and perplexities while growing up. As a result of their sexual experiences, some of the subjects of this study felt a need to discuss their reactions and explore their feelings. Several of them undoubtedly utilized the research interview as an opportunity to expose their feelings and to revise their concepts of themselves and the experience.

5. In terms of the central concern of this study—an interest in the improvement of interpersonal relationships—Level I liaisons have raised many questions.

  a. Have the prostitute experiences related by these boys been good preparation for later relations which must be based on trust, nourished by communication, and sustained by mutual feelings of trust and respect?

  b. Are the boys who are the least sensitive to relationships in

---

[12] Kingsley Davis (23) in his interesting article would appear to have older, more sophisticated individuals in his mind as he discusses motivation. Davis sees male motivation almost exclusively as a matter of satisfying, in some form or another, the biological sex urge. He writes, ". . . in addition to the sheer desire for sexual satisfaction, there is the desire for satisfaction in a particular (often an unsanctioned) way . . . the craving for variety, for perverse gratification, for mysterious and provocative surroundings, for intercourse free from entangling cares and civilized pretense, all play their part."

general the ones who are able to participate in Level I liaisons without traumatic effects?

c. If, as has been suggested, the motivation for many of these
relationships is a need for male group experience, are there
other experiences which can be substituted for the satisfaction of this need? What experiences can give an adolescent
boy a sense of male achievement which will make such experiences as prostitute liaisons unnecessary?

d. Are "patronizing prostitutes" and drinking symptoms of
some underlying condition which needs to be understood
and dealt with in some manner? Or should they be regarded
as normal experiences?

e. What are the long-range consequences of these experiences
on the boy's concept of sex, his adjustment in marriage, and
his ability to give sex education and guidance to his children?

f. How deep and persistent are the relationship values experienced when there is occasionally a real attempt on the part
of the prostitute or her patron to be considerate of, or concerned for, the welfare of the other?

6. These data raise a question as to how much emphasis should
be placed in sex education programs on the significance and
meaning of prostitution, and masculine participation in it. If in
this group of relatively unsophisticated boys almost 20% have
had intercourse with prostitutes this cannot be regarded as a
minor phenomenon.[13] Sexual liaisons at this level are quite
easily and quickly developed. All that is required is the boy's
decision to go to a prostitute, and the availability of the prostitute.

7. We need more factual data to understand what we are dealing
with. Some suggestions have already been made. Other studies
might give us an idea as to whether a boy who experiences intercourse at Level I usually moves on to other levels. Do boys
who begin intercourse at Levels V or VI fall back to Level I
and under what conditions? How many boys are fixated at this
level and why? How do the effects of prostitute experiences occurring in the military service differ from those experienced in

---

[13] Kinsey (58) found that 28% of all college men had sexual experience with
prostitutes.

civilian life? What effect has age, and broad social experiences, on the kind of sexual associations a boy seeks and their influence on him?

8. All these data have been gathered from men, and the masculine point of view is emphasized. Prostitutes are persons, too, and it would be helpful to know much more than we do about their feelings, the effects of their experiences on them, and what sort of relationships they are capable of building.

3

ANALYSIS OF LEVEL II

LIAISONS

Level II liaisons were defined as those in which intercourse was obtained from a partner who had been picked up in some kind of casual circumstance, and in which the purpose of the male was definitely to obtain intercourse. No liaison that grew out of dating association was included. Most Level II liaisons involved a single sexual contact, and generally might be more accurately defined as episodes rather than relationships. The distinction between prostitutes and pick-up liaisons (Level I and Level II) held up well and the distinction between a prostitute and a pick-up liaison was easily made.

STATISTICAL DATA

The data used in developing this chapter were taken from the case histories of sixty men who gave detailed reports of one hundred eighteen Level II liaisons. Thirty-four of the sixty subjects reported a single Level II liaison. Case histories were not developed for all Level II liaisons experienced by the subjects. Omissions occurred with subjects who had many liaisons to report.

Table 4

PARTICIPANTS AND LIAISONS—LEVEL II

Number of Subjects	Number of Liaisons Reported	Total Number of Liaisons
34	1	34
10	2	20
7	3	21
4	4	16
3	5	15
2	6	12
60		118

DESCRIPTIVE DATA

In this chapter, as in the preceding one, direct quotations from the subjects and a recital of specific incidents will be incorporated in the discussion. This policy is being followed in order to give as accurate and realistic a picture of Level II liaisons as possible.

As in the preceding chapter the liaisons histories will be examined to provide insight into *motivations, communication, protective measures and attitudes toward the assumption of responsibility,* and *self-evaluations.* The chapter will conclude with a summary and general observations.

Motivations

One of the major motivations at Level II is clearly an interest in physical sexual satisfaction. This purpose appears very clearly in a good proportion of the case histories. Although boys many times did not find much satisfaction, they nevertheless held this objective. Evidence leading to this conclusion appeared in several forms. The subjects themselves stated that they were seeking physical satisfaction. A number of them mentioned the fact that they had not one but several copulations with the girl in the span of a few hours and found them satisfactory. Some referred to their interest in further sexual associations with the girl. Others mentioned specific features of the relationship which made it enjoyable to them, e.g., long periods of foreplay, active participation in the sexual act by their partner, the physical sensations experienced, a feeling that they were secure from discovery, adequate time for intercourse, the opportunity to have intercourse without clothing.

Discussion of or participation in the sexual relationship are sometimes used by boys to prove their sophistication. This can be observed in Level II liaisons. These activities sometimes assume the nature of a game or contest among boys. Our cultural attitudes have tended to make sex a mystery, an enticing and forbidden fruit, and a source of fascination and merriment. As a result, play at sex seems daring to many adolescent boys. It serves as an avenue for demonstrating their sexual prowess, and it provides group adventure. Two excerpts showing this attitude are given below.

> **20** "When I got back, I told the boys that I had had intercourse. They wanted to know every detail—every parry and thrust. They got a big kick out of it. There was a lot of laughter, back-slapping, suggestions about how my technique could have been improved, and similar points."

> **97** M and four boy friends picked F up one evening after they had been engaging in a little beer-drinking. They knew that F was "an easy make." They "took her out in the tulees" where each boy had intercourse with her. While one boy was in the car the rest would stand outside and kid and joke about the sounds and movements, and speculate on what was happening.

The discussion of motivations which led into prostitute liaisons emphasized male group influences, and the need of the individual to feel himself a part of the group. Participation in prostitute relationships seemed to provide a way through which boys hoped to prove their masculinity to each other and to themselves, as well as to build group feeling.

The need to prove masculinity is also a motivation in Level II liaisons, though not to the same extent as in Level I. Whereas almost every boy who reported a prostitute liaison said that initially he had gone to the house with a friend or friends, only half of the boys experiencing Level II liaisons experienced them with a boy friend or friends. In the cases when boys did make pick-ups in pairs or in groups, there was little of the challenging, daring, nudging behavior so common in Level I liaisons. In Level II liaisons subjects reported that pick-up experiences were sought and agreements were reached through group participation, but there was less evidence that boys were pressured into the experience by their friends or made to feel "chicken" if they did not participate, than was the case at Level I. Once the suggestion was offered that a pick-up be made, the members of the group ordinarily readily assented. Several reasons may account for this difference:

1. The boys may feel more familiar with and aware of what will happen in a pick-up liaison than in a prostitute liaison. Therefore, going to a prostitute seems more unusual, more daring, and more unconventional, than securing a pick-up association.
2. Boys feel more in control and more at ease in entering a pick-up association than they do in a prostitute association. Usually the boy makes the approach and so far as observers are concerned he maintains control. He has some chance to arrange the circumstances under which the sexual association will occur. If a car is used it belongs to him or a friend. As a consequence a boy may not feel as much pressed to go through intercourse with the pick-up as with a prostitute, if he is not in accord with the idea. He and the girl can go away together, and his friends can see him leave. He can even tell his friends that the girl refused intercourse and be believed. Thus he need go no further than he wishes, and he is still able to "save face." This much freedom can not be had in a prostitute situation.
3. The girl is sometimes known personally to the boy or boys making the pick-up. The boys already have some idea of what approaches to make, and what reactions to expect from the girl.
4. An opportunity for a pick-up sometimes comes quickly, i.e., a group of boys drive past a girl on the street. There is no time to engage in a period of debate and interchange if the pick-up is to be made.

Some individuals become quite ingenious, and even adept, in developing seductive approaches. Thus, one boy possessed an unusual sweater with a striking emblem. He used the sweater as a means of striking up conversations with girls in places where he thought he might effect a pick-up. He wore or handled the sweater ostentatiously enough that it provoked comment from girls, and from this he was able to develop a conversation.

The satisfaction of some kind of fixated or emotional need through pick-up associations seemed to be still another motivation. Excerpts illustrating this follow. M (#134) reported numerous liaisons equally divided between prostitutes and pick-ups.

> **134** "I've wondered why I spent as much time with prostitutes and pick-ups as I have. I think it may be that my first love relationship broke up and left me so upset. I really thought a great deal of this girl and when she quit me I was both hurt and angry. I still feel that way somewhat. I remember thinking at all times that I would never give another girl a chance to hurt me that way."

> **84** M thinks he started making pick-ups because "a romance of mine had just blown up." In these various experiences "I kinda got my fill. I haven't had much interest in pick-ups since. I don't think that I would have done it then, except that I was sort of down on the world. These girls would show me a little affection at the time we were having relations, and I think that is what I was wanting."

If the self-analyses made by these two subjects are correct, one wonders why they should take a break in a dating relationship so hard. Other boys have met such experiences without so much disturbance. Does this reflect some kind of insecurity, or instability?

The subjects were asked to supply as much information as possible about the motivations they imputed to their liaison associates. These data provide some interesting insights into the images the boys develop of their sexual partners. Their reports also provide the basis for speculation as to possible feminine motivation for engaging in Level II liaisons.

An examination of the case histories indicates that in reporting the subjects divided their female partners into two equal-sized groups:

In the first group are those girls who, according to the boys, found definite physical enjoyment in intercourse and who, they felt, were participating in it largely for that reason.[1] Comments like the following indicate this motivation:

---

[1] Some of the boys who provided autobiographical statements for the Kronhausens (65, pp. 198-219) note the strong sexual desires of the girls with whom they had intercourse.

6 "She might have been nothing but a slut; she might have been a very nice girl. I don't know. One thing I am sure about is that she liked it as much as I did, and was as eager for it as I was."

18 M's first experience in intercourse was "with a girl with a reputation." He had heard stories that "she was hotter than a fire-cracker" from a number of fellows she had had intercourse with. When M had relations with her she was quite aggressive and inviting. She "got into position," played with M's genitals, and when he went to make an entrance helped him place the condum on his penis. "She was all fired up." M thinks she had an orgasm. After they were through she seemed "relaxed and contented."

Other evidence to substantiate this point of view is the frequency with which boys mention having been with girls who were very aggressive and seductive in their conduct. Such girls might attempt to excite the boys through discussing previous sexual experiences in a manner which seemed to invite approach, or by participating with active movements in the act of intercourse, or by unzipping their trousers and stimulating their genital organs.

9 "She took my hand and put it at the right place on her genitals."

47 "We had hardly got out of town before she reached over and unzipped my pants."

Some females apparently arrange pick-up associations just as overtly as do males. This is very obvious, as in cases when a woman goes to a tavern in which pick-ups commonly occur and goes from table to table talking with the men, or when she flirts openly with men as she meets them on the street.

Other pick-up arrangements initiated by women are less often common knowledge, yet they are just as clearly pick-ups. The following illustration showing how women make pick-ups has been selected from among a dozen possible ones. In this instance M was a popular professional athlete who, because of his physical appearance and public renown, was a very attractive figure to women. He was twenty-one years of age at the time of the interview.

16 F11 was a twenty-one-year-old married woman with whom M had a relationship when he was twenty. M first noticed her at the ball park where his football team was playing. She was frequently on the sidelines taking a great interest in the game and in the players. "She was good-looking, well-built, and a really fine appearing person." M first found who she was when he received a letter from her saying that when he was next in her city she would like to see him. "She wanted me to call her the next time I was in town." M wasn't too excited because he knew from his experience in professional football that "many women really go for professional athletes."

The next time M's team was in her city she was on the sidelines, and made herself known to M. After the game was over and M had returned to the hotel, she sent word to M through a couple of his teammates that she would be waiting outside the hotel for him. The fellows who brought M the word indicated they thought she was "a knockout." After M had finished dressing he went down to the street, and found F11 in her car waiting for him.

An intercourse relationship developed in this situation immediately, and continued as M returned to the city from time to time.

M, who was quite articulate and insightful, made some useful observations about the situation faced by professional athletes, and their relationship with women.

M's observations led him to believe that most of the girls who picked up professional athletes were from seventeen to twenty years old. He thought that they were usually "girls of low intelligence who were trying to break away from their home, and prove that they were grown up." They would ordinarily work, then get an apartment of their own and begin inviting men to come to their apartment. "They seem to think it is a big deal, but in terms of what they want it is actually getting them nowhere." M feels they are wanting an experience with a man which will lead him into marriage. They are using "sex as a bribe." However, men who meet women under these circumstances are interested in sex—not marriage. "Even sex every night gets old. You sort of get tired of that kind of thing." M thinks that "practically every woman has marriage in the back of her mind. You can't meet a woman like that who isn't trying to get married."

In one of the communities in which M's team played there was a large apartment house for girls, with two or three girls to each apartment. The existence of an apartment like this was well-known, and fellows exchanged information readily about their experiences there. As many fellows as girls would get together in one apartment. The girls would get dinner, they would spend the evening, and later have intercourse. Nobody ever paid any attention to the use of contraceptives. "There were so many guys going in and out of the apartments that they couldn't prove anything on you."

M has sometimes come out of the field house and found a girl with whom he was not at all well-acquainted waiting for him in his car. She might have seen him drive up in the car, or had been told by others that it was his automobile. Some of the girls followed the team from one place to another. M mentioned in particular two girls who moved into a certain town near the headquarters of the ball club. As the club played one town or another, these girls would frequently be in the ball parks and after the games M and his friends would go out with them. M had intercourse with these girls often. They were college girls who seemed to be enamored with the boys and followed them.

In some cities there are well-to-do women who have nice apartments. The athletes can practically move in and live with them at no cost. Most of them can give the fellows more satisfaction in the sexual relationships than they can get from ordinary girls. They also know "how to take care of themselves and one doesn't have to be so careful."

M himself has no real respect for girls whom he meets in this manner, and it is his opinion that other men who have similar experiences have the same reaction. M does feel, though, that the kind of sexual experiences he has been having while in professional football have been good. He has enjoyed them, but he has come to know he will get out and forget them. He plans to marry in a year or two (as he has since done) and raise a family. He doesn't want to continue this kind of life.

The next excerpt illustrates a much more common pick-up situation. In fact, similar experiences were related by several Level II subjects.

171 M and his boy friend had spent the evening in the apartment of two girls whom they had picked up at a dance. After several hours of talking and drinking "we were just getting ready to leave. The two girls disappeared into the bedroom for a short time. They must have gone in to talk for they came back out in a few minutes, and invited us to stay overnight."

The second group of girls as seen from the subjects' point of view were apparently attempting to satisfy some important psychological need.[2] Basically, the central problem with these girls seemed to be that they were seeking acceptance, affection, and the satisfaction of a continuing relationship. Sex was being used as a vehicle for accomplishing this, even if the duration of the relationship was no longer than overnight, or even a few hours. Several boys provided evidence that pointed very directly toward this need. Four excerpts which support this statement follow.

> **148** "Fll was a girl who was starved for affection if I ever saw one." M thinks this was what she was seeking in the relationship. She indicated as much while M was trying to talk her into intercourse. She wanted him to promise, if she agreed to go ahead, to return to see her, and M had to do this before he was able to secure her consent to intercourse.

In the next excerpt, M's boy friend whose intercession made it possible for M to have intercourse with F, was using F strictly as a medium for attaining sexual satisfaction. In order to do this he worked at keeping her in an accepting attitude toward him personally.

> **33** One thing that made M realize that F1's interest was centered on his friend was that she would not permit M to have intercourse unless his friend was along to intercede for him. M thinks that F1 was trying to work up a marriage between herself and M's boy friend, and he was "playing along" with her as much as necessary to keep her as a sexual partner.

This kind of effort to maintain a relationship, made by the girls in the following two excerpts, is not uncommon. Similar experiences were reported by several other boys.

> **52** M and a boy friend picked up two girls who were "just pigs" at a football game. "Both of them had put out before and every-

---

[2] The suggestion that some of the Level II partners were reflecting some important unconscious need is in harmony with the conclusions reached by a number of other investigators. See particularly Abraham (1), Deutsch (24), Glover (41), Greenwald (45), Lion (69), Loeb (71) and Safier (88). For a brief generalized discussion of the importance and the difficulties inherent in recognizing unconscious mechanisms and motivations in the study of sexual behavior see the remarks of Dr. Norman Reider (American Psychiatric Association, 4) in a symposium appraisal of the research by Dr. Kinsey.

one knew it. Both of them were doers." F2 "was the kind of a girl I'd be ashamed to be seen with in public."

The sexual experience was so poor that "it wasn't worth trying to take her out again." F2, however, did try to be friendly with M by speaking to him on different occasions at school. One time she asked him if he would be her date at a girl-ask-boy dance. M refused. During her senior year she got to the point where "she would hardly speak to me, which was okay with me."

40 M had only one sexual relation with F2. After this she wrote him several letters, and for a couple of months thereafter called his home on week ends to see if he was there. M asked his parents to tell her when she called that he would not be home that week end. M heard later that she was sent to the State School for delinquent girls, and that she also had had an illegitimate child.

Such motivating needs are almost certainly deeply rooted in personal and personality inadequacies. Several excerpts from case histories support this point of view.

16 F1 was "a kind of sloppy girl, the kind who didn't appeal at all." M told the fellow who had fixed him up that he, too, had been able to have intercourse with her. M never tried to see her again.

33 "She had no family whatsoever. She was 'a pig' and her mother was just like her. Her mother ran around with men and had men at the house all the time. So did the girl. There was just a pile of guys around her house all the time to see her."

40 Though F1 was a girl who lived in the neighborhood, M never attempted to see her again. This was probably because he felt a little ashamed of his relationship with her. Also, because "she was no raving beauty. She just didn't appeal to me at all." As soon as M had finished intercourse with her, "I wanted to get out of the room as fast as possible. I didn't want to have anything more to do with her." However, as he has seen her afterward, "I have kind of nodded to her."

If this interpretation is correct, the efforts made by the girls to satisfy their psychological needs take different forms. Some may be very aggressive in using sex to set up a relationship; others may attempt to gain their objective by being utterly pliant. Many, perhaps all of them, appear to lack sensitivity and insight, and exercise poor judgment about human relationships. Perhaps their need for support and attention is so great that it overwhelms all else.

Several illustrations follow which illustrate an aggressive approach on the part of the female.

> **62** "She (F2) asked me if I wasn't going to ask for what all the other boys were always wanting. I said, 'Well, will it do any good?' She indicated it would so I accepted the invitation."
>
> M continued seeing F2 for several weeks and had intercourse with her several times in that interval. Then one evening she was quite cool toward his advances. M asked her what the difficulty was, and F2 asked him what his intentions were with reference to marriage. M told her he might be interested after he was through school. This seemed to satisfy F2 and she went ahead readily.
>
> M had several more dates with F2 at which times they had intercourse. He decided, however, that F2 was wanting to be "too serious," and anyway he "was tired of her," so he quit seeing her.

The following information provided by a nineteen-year-old subject shows how a woman's unsuccessful marriage may have influenced her aggressive approach to M.

> **47** F7 was a twenty-eight-year-old married woman whom M met just after he had graduated from high school. Her husband owned a filling station and M was working for him. He drank a lot, "shacked up with other women," and left the station pretty much in M's charge.
>
> One night when the husband was gone F7 came over to the station. She asked M if he would take her into town for a bite to eat after he closed the station. This M agreed to do. Both ate, and afterward got into the car to go home. F7 then asked M if he would take her to "the place where the kids parked." M hesitated, but agreed to do this also. He was wary since she was married, but she took the lead, initiated petting, and he went along. They had intercourse, then went to F7's home where it occurred again. M had intercourse with F7 about sixty times in a period of six to eight months.
>
> M feels her motivation was probably sexual pleasure. "She just about goes nuts in intercourse. I came out of it all scratched up." F7, however, tried once to get M to run off with her. She suggested she would divorce her husband. M was not interested in this proposition.

The next excerpt illustrates an aggressive pick-up effort on the part of the female followed by continued efforts on her part to arrange a sexual liaison.

> **44** M met F4 on a blind date while he was visiting a friend in another community. They went to a party together, but nothing of any significance occurred. M returned home the next day without seeing her.
>
> In the next two weeks, however, F4 called M by long distance five times, and expressed a very real interest in him. Finally she made arrangements to come to M's home town the following week end. She came on a Saturday and stayed until Sunday afternoon.
>
> M met her and they went to his home for dinner. Later they went out for the evening. M mentioned his fraternity, and F4 expressed an interest in seeing it. This gave M the idea that intercourse might be possible. It was vacation time and M knew the house was empty. He took F4 to it and they started a tour. They went upstairs and looked around. Then F4 asked where the fellows slept, so he took her onto the sleeping porch. Here they sat down on a bed and began to neck. It was clear immediately that F4 was ready for intercourse.
>
> After F4 returned to her home, there were more long distance calls and an effort on her part to get the two of them together again. At first M was favorable, but at the same time he had begun dating another girl. As he became more interested in her he lost interest in F4. All F4 "had to offer was sex."

Girls who are very aggressive almost invariably overplay their hand, if what they are seeking is a continuing relationship with a boy. Boys may have different reactions to such aggressiveness but are seldom or never interested in establishing a permanent relationship with a girl when intercourse occurs at this level of emotional involvement.

While some girls are aggressive, others are reported as being very passive and submissive.[3] One of the latter kind will permit a boy to do as he wishes without protesting any mistreatment she

---

[3] Greenwald (45) who made a study of the backgrounds and personality characteristics of call girls notes their marked incapacity to establish satisfactory interpersonal relationships. His subjects "felt the need of relationships so deeply that they frequently put up with a great deal of mistreatment and brutality rather than break them" (p. 122).

may experience. Such girls seem dependent and lack any assertiveness of their own. One way in which this characteristic is manifested is in the girls' inertness and immobility in the sexual relationship itself. As many as a third of the subjects made such comments about their partners as the following: "She was just like a log."—"She wouldn't move a bit. She just laid there and you could do anything you wanted."—"It was just like she was dead. She never made a movement."

This extreme passivity also shows itself in the girls' readiness to submit to any experience in which the boys wish to engage, even to gross indignities. One gets the picture of individuals who are completely and utterly submissive, and who will agree to anything.

Three illustrations were chosen from among several that could have been used.

> 172   M, now twenty-one, has had three partners in intercourse. The first was a girl involved in a "gang bang" (a common term for group intercourse experience) situation. M went one evening to visit two friends of his who kept a bachelor apartment. When he got there and after he was admitted, he found the two fellows who rented the apartment, plus three friends whom they had invited, were having intercourse with a thirteen-year-old-girl, known about town as a prostitute. This was the first time M had seen F1 though he had heard about her. All five of the fellows had had intercourse with F1 twice before M came in. M had intercourse with her, then she came out of the room and sat around with the fellows for a time. Then one of the older ones, age twenty-five, took her back into the bedroom for intercourse again. F1 "was so beat up by that time that she couldn't react."

Nine subjects gave histories in which they had participated in group intercourse experiences. One of the subjects described a situation in which he and twelve other boys in succession had intercourse with a girl in the back seat of a car. The details bore the marks of truthful reporting, and his statements remained consistent as questions were asked. The story is one of rank exploitation, and one so stark and crude, that it seems pointless to relate the details.

Two final excerpts illustrate the abject acceptance by some girls of whatever advances are made.

87 M's second partner was a girl, sixteen, who had been out with two other boys, acquaintances of M. M and two friends were driving around aimlessly one evening when the first two boys stopped them, and asked them if they would like to have intercourse with a girl whom they had in the back seat of their car. M and his friends accepted the invitation, and each of them had intercourse with her. They had never seen the girl before, nor have they ever seen her since.

M received no pleasure from the experience, "nor did the girl." She simply lay there and let them go ahead. They used no contraceptive methods, for the girl was "four months along." At least that is what she had told the other boys.

78 F5 was a nineteen-year-old girl with whom M had intercourse when he was still seventeen. M and one of his high school buddies stopped while on a trip to visit a mutual friend who was attending college. The friend told the two he had been having intercourse with a girl, and that he knew the two of them could have it with her if they wanted. They were both ready for the experience, so the friend took them to her apartment.

"It was a funny deal. Our friend had a key to her apartment, but when we got there, it wasn't locked. Instead, the door was propped shut with a little table. We pushed the door open and walked in, and found a high school boy in bed with F5. Both of them were naked. We kicked him out, and then all of us had intercourse with F5."

One boy in talking about the tendency of some girls to submit to any proposal or advance, and to continue to accept the boy despite mistreatment, said, "We boys have an expression to describe this. We say, 'No matter how much you gore 'em, they still come back for more.'"

Some girls seemed to display a marked degree of gullibility. Several subjects gave case histories in which this appears. One of the clearest illustrations is given below.

33 M fell into a sexual relationship with F1 in this manner. A close friend of his had picked her up and had been having intercourse with her and told M and three other fellows about it. He agreed with them that he would arrange with F1 to take her to the beach. If they would come down to the beach, he would try to talk her into having intercourse with them. The boys followed this plan, and pretended to run across M and F1 on the beach as they "were playing around." They then accused M's friend of monopolizing F1's sexual favors, and threatened to "beat him up" if they didn't get a chance to have intercourse with F1.

M's friend said to F1, "You see, if you don't give the boys some, they are going to beat me up."

"It was easy to talk F1 into anything." She accepted the situation, and permitted the boys to have intercourse with her. She was aware that everyone knew she had a reputation for that kind of behavior.

In another instance a girl apparently accepted sexual advances for the sake of revenge. One subject reported picking up a girl who had just broken with her boy friend. She was furious, and was hoping to make her ex-friend jealous. M anticipated that these circumstances might make her ripe for seduction. When he picked her up and made advances, he found he was correct in his assumption.

Communication

Communication in Level II liaisons has several interesting features. In the prostitute relationships the intent of the prostitute and her patron, and the outcome of their association are clearly defined and understood. Participants in Level I liaisons functioned in a highly-structured situation. This makes anything more than simple arrangement-making communication unnecessary.

Level II liaisons as a group are usually not so highly structured, though some may be quite cut-and-dried. Suppose a girl who has gone through a number of pick-up sexual experiences is accosted by a boy who knows her reputation, and she knows he knows. No more extensive communication is needed in this situation than in a prostitute relationship.

As a matter of fact, certain circumstances will define a pick-up relationship almost as sharply as they define a Level I liaison. If a boy meets a girl in a tavern and she makes overtures by smiling, or by bringing herself into close bodily contact with him, and if she dresses the part, the situation is pretty clearly structured. She hardly needs to ask him if he would like to come to her room.

As a matter of fact non-verbal cues and exchanges are a common part of Level II liaisons. Some of them are about as delicate as the use of a sledge hammer.

20 As soon as I got her back of the tavern and out of sight, I put one hand inside her blouse and reached between her legs with the other. I gave her a little push and she went over backwards and just laid there. That's all there was to it.

Other non-verbal expressions are more subtle and difficult to catch. At the time the overtures are made they may be tentative. What will finally culminate will depend on how the first cue is accepted.

47 "I passed her on the street, and just by the way she smiled I said to myself, I'll bet she is just the type." (She was.)

146 "She walked in a real slinky way."

134 "There was just something about her that tipped me off—I don't know just what it was."

98 "The first time I saw her I said to myself, That thing gives out."

6 "The way she laid up against you in the car was enough to tell you what she was willing to do."

34 "She just hung all over you."

Non-verbal cues growing out of the total situation may be so vivid or so well-established that they are automatically accepted by both partners.

98 M was driving around town one evening and saw a girl standing at a bus stop. He stopped and asked her if she would like a ride. She said she would, and got in. They drove about a bit chatting aimlessly, and M started to "head for the country." As he did F3 said, "I want to eat first." Nothing more than this was said, but M knew that she knew what he wanted, and he knew she was willing after she had something to eat.

16 "She knew what I wanted, and I knew she knew, and nothing needed to be said."

One of the non-verbal cues which is evidently weighed heavily by boys in deciding "how far to go" is the kind of resistance a girl makes to their advances. The lack of resistance, or ineffective resistance, encourages many boys to move ahead. Such remarks as the following were made by a number of boys reporting Level II liaisons.

> "She didn't put up any resistance."

> "She was aggressive in a submissive sort of way."

> "She put up a little resistance, but you could tell she didn't mean it. I think it was only because she felt she should."

> "She kept saying she didn't want to have intercourse, but she didn't put up any physical resistance at all. So I didn't pay any attention."

> "A girl doesn't have to resist very much to stop a boy. I have always felt if a girl really meant it, she could at least cross her legs."

The case history material indicates that the traditional idea that the male should be the aggressive, controlling person in a sexual relationship is much more observed in Level II liaisons than in Level I liaisons. In several instances the woman apparently wanted the male to establish the lead by making the first move. Once he had done this the female herself became aggressive. The following is an example:

> 8   When M was seventeen he met a twenty-year-old girl in a tavern. During the evening he drank and danced with her. After a time M sensed that intercourse was possible, and suggested that they "go for a ride." F2 replied that "rather than going for a ride, why not go to my motel?"

This need to communicate sexual desires, yet to do it unobtrusively, or with some regard for conventional attitudes, also shows up in two other illustrations, both given by the same subject. Here we see good illustrations of double talk in which much is implied but nothing is said overtly.

> 100   M saw a girl of about fifteen walking down the street. He stopped and picked her up. After a bit of talk M said, "Where are you going?" F1 replied, "Anywhere you are." "I knew enough to know what to think. I didn't hesitate any. I simply said to myself, O.K., sister."

> M and a girl whom he had picked up had stopped to park. They were having a casual conversation and M asked F what her father did. She replied, "Oh, he's a carpenter. He *makes* things." M replied, "Oh, he does? Well, I *make* things, too." F then commented, "Oh, do you? I like people who *make* things."

When it comes to overt discussion of the sexual relationship, the capacity to communicate may vary greatly. Communication ranges from saying nothing to frank and free discussion.

8 "After we were through we talked about our relationship. I found that she hadn't reached an orgasm, so we tried again, and this time she did."

9 "There wasn't a word spoken about sex. I simply started petting. She put up no resistance, and we went right into intercourse."

186 "There wasn't a word spoken after we were through. I took her right home."

Communication barriers may be erected to prevent the establishment of any long-time or continuing relationship. Several boys spoke of giving only their first names. The omission of identification, e.g., of names and addresses, is a device very easily used for concealment. In another instance, M would have liked to keep contact with a pick-up associate whom he met on a summer trip, but feared the consequences of revealing himself.

4 M has thought a number of times of writing F3 "I didn't use any contraceptive, however, and I wondered whether she might have got pregnant. I'd like to know, but the possibility that she might have is what kept me from writing."

Protective Measures and Assumption of Responsibility

The reader will recall that certain assumptions relative to protection have been made in this study. The assumption has been that in a relationship built upon trust, integrity, and mutual respect, attention will be given to protecting the partner from possible detrimental consequences of the relationship. Certainly a relationship involving premarital intercourse ordinarily calls for some attention to protection. The possibility of upsetting emotional reactions to sexual experiences; the marked likelihood of criticism in case of discovery, especially for the female; the chances of pregnancy; the possibility that the impact of sex on a relationship may alter values and goals—all of these suggest that concern for such consequences needs to be considered in a good quality relationship.

What is the attitude toward protective measures and how great is the acceptance of responsibility in Level II liaisons?

In the first place, concern for protection at Level II would seem to be low, particularly anything which would go beyond the use of contraceptive, or prophylactic measures in intercourse. The protection of a sexual partner against such psychological hazards as criticism, feelings of guilt, a decrease in self-respect, or resentments over misplaced trust or confidence, probably is given little weight by the subjects engaged in Level II associations.

Twenty-eight of the sixty males with Level II liaisons reported using some kind of prophylactic-contraceptive measure. These measures were about equally divided between the use of the condum and withdrawal before ejaculation.

Certain circumstances make for ineffective use of contraceptives, especially withdrawal and condoms, both of which are dependent on the conscientious attitude of the male. Drinking, though less common than in Level I liaisons, was reported by twenty-seven of the subjects who had experienced Level II liaisons. The participation of more than one male in a sexual relationship with a girl may render ineffective any use of contraceptives in that relationship.

> **97** "The five of us had intercourse with F on three different occasions. The first time I used a rubber, but I didn't after that. The other fellows didn't use one, so what was the use of me doing it?"

There is no record among these liaisons of a woman either using, supplying, or asking the male to use any kind of contraceptive. This is in contrast to Level I liaisons. Here the woman usually assumed the responsibility for such contraceptive-prophylactic measures as were taken.

The comments made by the subjects, however, would indicate that their concern, if they had any, was for themselves. The following two comments are typical.

> **16** "I used a condom, for I couldn't see myself getting tangled up in a situation like that."

> **40** "My dad told me when I was a sophomore in high school that if I was going to have intercourse I should use a rubber so I would be as safe as possible. He didn't want me taking unnecessary chances."

Even if a boy engaging in a Level II liaison wished to protect his partner, or to assume the responsibility for his conduct, the extreme casualness of many of the relationships would make this most difficult. Dealing responsibly with a possible pregnancy is a case in point.

Several boys cited instances in which they had had intercourse with girls who were complete strangers to them, and with whom they used no contraceptive methods. In addition, identities were sometimes false or concealed, possibly by both partners. It would, therefore, be quite easy for a boy to impregnate the girl, yet never be aware of it.

Realistic analysis of the personal and social attitudes centering about such sexual associations as occur in Level II liaisons makes it obvious that at this level much exploitation and irresponsible behavior is to be expected, particularly on the part of males. The typical social, double-standard attitude safeguards the male from the consequences of his acts, and at the same time leaves the females vulnerable. It also means that the male approaches his potential sexual partner with an attitude of disdain and disrespect. The responsibility for the relationship and for what happens is on her shoulders. He is simply behaving in a socially understood and acceptable way for a male. To complicate the girls' situation, some of them are apparently physically unattractive, or have such unacceptable personalities that the extension of sexual favors is perhaps their only method of attracting a boy. Once a reputation for being easy, sexually, has been established, such girls find their only opportunity for male associations is to live up to this reputation.

All of the above points are illustrated in the following excerpts.

9 M had no feeling for F1 before intercourse. He knew that she had a reputation for being an "easy make." After intercourse "I thought nothing of her. I had no respect for her—no nothing." Feeling that way M had no interest in ever looking her up again. In fact, he has never seen her since.

18 "I saw why she had the reputation of being hotter than a firecracker and why each boy was telling all the others about her. That's the only reason boys went to see her."

31 "F2 was known about town as a girl who would accept sexual relations from anyone. She was the kind to whom you could say,

'Will you do it now or later?' This was the only way she could get anybody."

42 "From what I had been hearing about her, F1 sounded like a hot number. However, she was anything but good-looking, or interesting as a person."

The next two excerpts indicate how many boys are able to— and do—shift the responsibility for consequences to their partners.

20 "I figured she had been over the road before and could take care of herself."

105 "She made no effort to stop me so I went right ahead. If she wasn't going to stop me, I wasn't going to make the effort. It was her life, not mine."

The subjects with experience in Level II liaisons then made comments about their sexual partners which indicated that, so far as ability to set up dating relationships was concerned, many of these girls were already disadvantaged persons. Instead of providing them safeguards, or offering protection, many times the boys contributed to the already disadvantaged position of the girl. It seems fair to say that these girls are being "used." As a matter of fact, this word was selected by at least three young men who were reporting Level II liaisons. One commented that he knew that the girl he had picked up would have intercourse because "I knew several fellows who had used her." Another boy referred to a girl who had been penetrated by five or six different boys, one after another, in a group sexual experience as "all used up." Still another boy mentioned buying liquor for a pick-up whom he hoped "to make," because "I'd heard of guys using liquor on girls" to impair judgments and release inhibitions.

The subjects may, and often do, subject their partner to the risk of an unwanted pregnancy through failure to take adequate contraceptive measures. A boy will often make the girl's position even more untenable by telling other boys that he had had intercourse with her, and that "she can be had." This is even more likely if the girl had been aggressive, or had aroused the hostility of the boys. The boys may use deceit and duplicity on the girl. Naturally, such experiences must surely undermine a girl's spirit and morale.

Several illustrations of subjects reporting the use of deception and duplicity have been given. Deception is easy when girls want to believe desperately that the relationship has some strength in it, as many of these girls seem to. They are apparently ready to grasp at straws, and to believe whatever is told them, hoping that this will turn out to be an enduring relationship. When girls show such a predisposition, it is easy for boys to take advantage. It might be put this way: whenever one wants something so badly that he is willing to pay any price for it, someone is likely to charge him that much.

The element of differential social maturity also enters to complicate the situation. Girls in the middle teens have a much greater capacity for heterosexual loyalty than have boys of the same age. Many a girl finds herself disillusioned because she thought the boy to whom she was attached was ready to associate himself with her exclusively, and to regard whatever happened in their relationship as confidential. Instead of confidential behavior and loyalty to her she finds his principal loyalty still attached to his male group. His companionship interests and his emotional attachments are there. Thus, instead of holding their experience in confidence, she finds he has reported everything to his male friends.

This situation is especially likely to redound to the disadvantage of the girl in case of suspected or actual pregnancy. In such a circumstance a girl is likely to find herself in a vulnerable and unprotected position with a whole group of boys arrayed against her. The subjects at Level II liaisons usually seemed ready to protect each other against a girl in difficulty, e.g., one premaritally pregnant. The girl in such a circumstance may find herself defenseless against their unbroken front.

The following excerpts will illustrate this particular point.

87 F4 told M that she was pregnant and that she intended to name him as responsible. "While I didn't think she was actually pregnant, I was pretty badly scared and I didn't want to take any chances. So I talked with some other fellows who knew F4 and we got a list of eighteen fellows who said that if she came back on me they would say that they had had intercourse with her also. After F4 found this out, I heard nothing more from her."

146 F2 was not a virgin, and M used no contraceptive method whatsoever. "All of us were very careless and brash at this time.

We were under the impression that if three or more fellows made a girl, and she got pregnant, she would be called a whore and no one held legally responsible. For this reason we were quite careless about what we did in our sexual relations."

This mutual protection association between some of the male subjects in this study was displayed in another way.

114 "I wanted a car to go pick up this girl. A friend of mine loaned me one. It had an out-of-state license, and I figured if anything happened he would be long gone before any attempt to trace the car could be made."

179 M had a sexual experience with F4 during his sophomore year in college. He was driving a cab and received a call from the dispatcher. He was told that a certain address had called for a cab. It was generally known that this call came in once or twice a year, and was from a married woman. It usually meant that she had been drinking, and was seeking intercourse. M, therefore, went with an understanding of what might occur. The dispatcher said he would note his cab as not on duty while he was gone. M found, when he arrived, that the statement he had received about the situation was correct.

146 M began to make sexual advances to F11, and she seemed receptive. At this point M's friend "took off, saying that he would go down to a restaurant a couple of blocks away and get a cup of coffee." It was two hours before M had secured intercourse and went to get his friend. M regarded his friend's conduct in this situation as very thoughtful, and M told him that he really appreciated what he had done. He also told him that if ever a situation came up where he could do the same for him, he would be sure to do so.

Scheming, deception, and duplicity are not strictly masculine characteristics—to imply this would be a distortion of fact. Deception is not a one-way street, and girls also scheme and deceive boys. The male may be exploited through an actual or pretended pregnancy. Some girls may use pregnancy as a way of getting into a marriage. In the following excerpt both M and his boy friend had had intercourse with the same pick-up, and an actual pregnancy resulted.

52 "As a matter of fact, my friend had to get married to her later because he got her pregnant. They got married near the end of her sophomore year in high school, and she was already six months along."

Sometimes boys suspect that girls are seeking a pregnancy in order to ensnare them. In the excerpt next quoted the girl pretended pregnancy, in the boy's opinion, to effect a marriage.

33 M thinks that F1 was scheming for marriage between herself and M's boy friend. She told M's friend on one occasion that she was pregnant, but M's friend wouldn't "let her pull that kind of a gag." He told her he "knew better than that" and for her to "get wise to herself on that kind of stuff."

188 "I always used a rubber. F had had intercourse with my boy friend, too. Once he caught her lying about when she was to menstruate and she admitted it. He thought she was just trying to get pregnant, so I wasn't taking any chances."

The analysis of Level I liaisons included a discussion of certain psychological hazards which seemed inherent in the relationship. Such hazards for the boy are less evident in Level II liaisons than in Level I. For example, whereas many boys complained of inadequacy in sexual functioning with a prostitute, only one boy in a Level II relationship referred to an inability to attain an erection, and two others spoke of difficulty in reaching a climax.

One of the most obvious psychological hazards is the highly unaesthetic, even revolting setting in which some of these boys obtain their sexual experiences. This is true especially in some of the experiences involving several boys and one girl. The smearing of semen, perhaps blood, the odor of urine and perspiration, have been described by several boys who participated in such experiences as "nauseating," "revolting," "sickening." One subject commented, "It was so gross you wouldn't believe it."

Other boys, however, speaking of the same kind of circumstance have regarded it as a joke, as in the following excerpt.

52 "It (the group sexual experience) occurred in the back seat of my buddy's new car. You should have seen the mess! It took us hours to clean it up, and get the smell out. It was a good joke on us, though."

Certainly, there is evidence at this level to indicate that many of the boys see their associates only as sexual objects[4] and that their awareness of or consideration for them as persons is at a very low level. Some excerpts indicating that this is the case have already been given. These are added for the sake of emphasis:

> **34** "I haven't the faintest idea as to whether she got any satisfaction. As soon as we were done we got her in the car and took her home. There wasn't a word said on the way back."

> **40** "As soon as I was through I wanted to get her out of there. I didn't want anything further to do with her, and I didn't want to see her again."

> **169** M and his boy friend picked F1 up as she was walking along the street. On the way to the secluded spot where they were to have intercourse, F1 tried to make out that she was acquainted with M as well as his friend, but M told her he was sure she must be mistaken. "I didn't want to be connected with her in any way. I had a marked feeling of distaste for her."

EVALUATION OF SUBJECTS

A tabulation of the replies to the question relating to the subjects' satisfaction or dissatisfaction with the Level II relationship shows the following results.

Number of Subjects	Reactions to Experience
8	Satisfactory
9	Mixed Feelings
22	Unsatisfactory
15	"Just an experience—no feeling in particular."
6	No Information

The satisfactory appraisals came very largely from individuals who found the experience physically satisfactory. Some found a certain psychological satisfaction also.

---

[4] The frequent use of "it" to describe the sexual association was noted in Level II liaisons as it was in Level I. "It didn't amount to much." "I didn't enjoy it."

74 M had intercourse with F4 three times during the evening. It was a very satisfying experience. She "knew the ropes," having been married, was quite vigorous in her movements during intercourse, and had orgasms.

145 So far as M is concerned the experience was "just plain sex." He enjoyed the relationship, however, because F3 was so co-operative in her movements and actions.

47 M's sexual experience made him "feel more grown up and like one of the boys."

Those who reported mixed feelings usually found the act physically satisfactory but felt some sense of guilt or depreciation, or they reported that although the physical experience was unsatisfactory they felt a sense of achievement or accomplishment.

Those who reported dissatisfaction found a number of reasons for their unsatisfying experience.

88 M definitely had the feeling as a result of these experiences that sex was not "what it was cracked up to be."

97 The five boys picked up F and all had intercourse with her. M had the impression that F "was a little bit—maybe quite a bit —off." The whole experience was "sort of nauseating."

Sometimes one learns positively from a negative experience. Such seems to be the case with M in the following excerpt.

84 "I learned from these experiences (pick-ups) that they were not the kind of relationships I wanted."

GENERAL OBSERVATIONS

After a study of the case histories involving Level II liaisons these observations seem pertinent.

1. The kinds of associations which are involved in Level II liaisons seem to be associations which from the standpoint of interpersonal relations are shallow and limited in their concept of the total personality. From the point of view of human relationships there are certain points to be made:

a. Level II relationships seem clearly to be based on the idea that participation in sex is a paramount value. From the standpoint of the male in particular, participation in intercourse is a value that seems to override any concern the individual might have for the general welfare of his consort. Members of both sexes, however, seem to see members of the other sex as sex objects. This concept is even embodied in the slang in which, from the male point of view, a woman may be referred to as "a good piece" or a "piece of tail," or a man referred to by a woman as "a prick." Sex seems to have been pretty thoroughly divorced from the total personality. Some of these men snapped at the opportunity for intercourse with a woman who might be very repulsive to them personally. The divorce of sex from personality values was not always complete, however, as was attested by the fact that some of the boys who participated in intercourse under unaesthetic, exploitive conditions were disturbed over the experience.

b. Another concept which produces a relationship problem is the double standard. This discussion might be approached from many points of view, but only one will be noted. This is the concept that seems to regard the woman as the sole repository of moral values and releases the man from any responsibility for his actions, if the woman will permit him to go ahead. The most striking illustration of this was found in one of the case histories which reported a group intercourse situation. Five boys had intercourse with a girl who was described by the subject reporting as "a little bit— maybe quite a bit—off." As one of the boys finished his experience in copulation with the girl and was leaving her, he turned to her and asked, "Don't you have any morals?"

This particular attitude seems to be one which leaves the male free to practice irresponsible conduct, and at the same time make the woman an object for exploitation. It also requires her to control and direct very strictly the same emotion which the man declines to discipline or direct at all.

c. One wonders what gives rise to patterns of conduct in which such marked insensitivities to human values are displayed as in several of these Level II liaisons. Or, what kind of an adjustment causes some girls to submit limply and lifelessly to such glaring indignities as some of these girls did? What enables other girls through their aggressive sexual approach to violate so crassly common social conventions in male-female relationships? Is some kind of profound individual or personal need pressing for satisfaction? If it is, what produced it? What can be done to help such persons?

    d. What in the personal adjustment of either a boy or a girl makes sex a factor of such paramount value? For some persons the individual's addiction to sex seems equivalent to the addiction of other persons to alcohol or drugs. What causes this? Is it something in the biology, or the psychology of the individual, or are both involved? What can be done to help an individual in a reappraisal and readjustment of his values?

2. Experiences in Level II liaisons—especially some which violate common concepts of human dignity and humane associations so grossly—must have some effect on the later feelings and conduct of people. How do they influence the individual's concept of sex, male-female relationship, one's self-image, and the parent-child relationship, both now and later? How do these effects vary from person to person, and according to what factors do they vary?

3. What in our culture contributes to a condition in which such crass experiences as some of the Level II liaisons can occur? What in our sexual attitudes needs to be corrected? What can be done to produce more awareness of the needs of others and of the need for promoting relationships which have more integrity in them? A culture which makes participation in sex a game, but which at the same time demeans and debases those who participate in it, has opened the way for exploitation and confusion. Girls are pressed to set up a relationship with boys, yet are subjected to experiences which impair their capacity for relationships. Do we not need to scrutinize our cultural values and practices?

4

ANALYSIS OF LEVEL III

LIAISONS

This chapter provides descriptive data on Level III liaisons—defined as associations which the male enters specifically for the purpose of obtaining intercourse—and is successful. The male regards the female, as judged by his avowed purpose for entering the relationship, as an object for sexual gratification. He is willing to invest time in the relationship only because he hopes that she will eventually accept intercourse.

In contrast to Level I (prostitute associations) and Level II (pick-up associations), the relationships at Level III typically begin as the usual "dating" relationships. The boy ordinarily asks the girl for a date, or has a date which has been arranged by a friend, and the two go out together. Frequently the couple have a car or are in a car with others, and are ordinarily setting out for some kind of social or recreational activity. As a rule they are unencumbered by adult supervision, though probably not free from parental admonitions. These are the external appearances people around the couple may observe. What can not be perceived are the purposes of the two as they enter upon their association.

STATISTICAL DATA

Data on the two hundred twenty-two Level III liaisons were supplied by ninety-eight men. The data on the number of subjects and liaisons reported at this level are given in the following table.

Table 5

PARTICIPANTS AND LIAISONS—LEVEL III

Number of Subjects	Number of Liaisons Reported	Total Number of Liaisons
48	1	48
24	2	48
11	3	33
6	4	24
4	5	20
1	7	7
2	9	18
1	11	11
1	13	13
98		222

Almost precisely one-third of all the sexual liaisons gathered in this study were Level III liaisons. No other level has such a large recorded proportion of the total. Likewise, just a shade under half of the subjects (ninety-eight, or forty-nine per cent) had engaged in Level III liaisons. One might hypothesize from these data that a good proportion of all premarital sexual liaisons, and as many as half of all men with experience in premarital intercourse, will be found at Level III.

DESCRIPTIVE DATA

Motivations

Several motivations are apparently operative at Level III. They are intermingled, and become evident in varied ways from liaison to liaison. Curiosity, the desire for physical pleasure itself, the feeling that with intercourse one has achieved some important goal, are all in evidence. Some subjects seem to regard sexual conquest as a competitive experience; obtaining intercourse then becomes a sort of game requiring skill and persistence. A few case histories indicate that the subjects are seeking to satisfy some driving need through sex—some pressure that pushes them into experiences which they might otherwise forego. To decide with exactness which is the most important of these different motivations is impossible, but certain features of the case histories provide a good basis for inference.

Many excerpts from case histories could be cited to support the idea that a desire for the pleasure of intercourse is a prominent motivating factor. Boys say that they "enjoyed it," or they wanted the "pleasure" of intercourse. The subject in the following illustration, who became involved in his first sexual liaison between his freshman and sophomore years in high school at age fifteen, displayed this attitude:

> 13 During the summer M went to F1's house frequently to talk with her. Her mother was always away, so they started "playing around." Within a couple of weeks they had engaged in genital play several times. M foresaw the possibility of intercourse, was eager for it, and strove to obtain it. He asked F1 for intercourse several times, and even though she said "no" he continued to ask. F1 was not particularly desirous of having him fondle her genitals, but M would find a way of "tricking her" and getting her "very passionate." This was a part of his successful strategy of "wearing her down." The first time they had intercourse was after M had got her "really hot" during heavy petting. She was sort of a "rough girl." The first intercourse was almost a rape "like on the wedding night." He had heard so much about intercourse from older boys that he was over-anxious to experience it. It was about what he had expected and he had no feeling of disgust or disapproval after it was over with. M doesn't know how F1 felt. He wasn't at all interested in her. He was "sort of going with another girl," and wanted F1 strictly for intercourse. He would "sneak away and go to F1's house without anyone knowing about it."

One of the older subjects, age nineteen, said of his Level III liaison, "It was just an easy place to get sex, and that's what I wanted."

Another indication that for some subjects the main objective of maintaining the association was intercourse is that when it was no longer available the relationship was dropped.

> **20** One evening as M and F1 were returning to her home, F1 told M that she had "decided not to have intercourse again" until after she had married. There were "only a few words exchanged after that." The next day M wrote her that he "didn't plan to see her any more. We were through."

Another evidence of the concentration of the subjects on physical satisfaction appeared. This contrasted with a possible concern for the satisfaction of their partners, and was shown by their reply to the question, "Did your partner have an orgasm?" The common response indicated that the subjects were either unaware of or unconcerned with this aspect of the relationship.

> **13** "I didn't know there was such a thing as a female orgasm. So far as I know she never had one."

> **68** "I don't think she had an orgasm any of the times. I did nothing to help her."

> **91** "I don't know. I never paid any attention."

That the procuring of sexual intercourse was competitive and a game for some subjects has been suggested as a motive. This motive is apparent in numerous case histories which contain evidence of definite efforts of boys to equal or even surpass other boys in sexual achievement. These illustrations of rivalry and competition in obtaining intercourse are given below.

> **11** M and one of his boy friends each knew several girls who were said to be susceptible to sexual advances. They wagered $5.00 as to which would be the first to obtain intercourse. A third friend held the stakes.

> **53** M and his cousin were very close friends. Both were sexually uninitiated, but eager for the experience. One evening after M had gone to bed his cousin came to his home and aroused him, quite excited over the fact that he had dated a girl "with a reputation" that evening, and had had intercourse with her. He brought along her bra as evidence of his achievement. "I made up my mind that if he could get a date with her and have intercourse I could do it too" (as he later did).

6 M, who is now eighteen and sexually experienced, is "not as eager for intercourse as I was a year or two ago. When I was a junior and senior in high school, most of my friends and I were always on the lookout for a piece of tail. We have kinda cooled off now."

This attitude of rivalry and competition leads naturally enough to the indication that, for some of the subjects, the attainment of intercourse brought a real sense of masculine achievement. Evidences of this are found in a number of case histories.

177 The first time intercourse occurred in F1's home. M had a date with her at 8:00 P.M., but she called and suggested he come later. She also said that her folks were going out for the evening, and "Why don't we just spend the evening together at my house? The folks won't be home until quite late."

M thought, "Boy, this is it. Tonight's the night." After intercourse occurred M felt a real sense of triumph. "I remember thinking, 'this is what I have been wanting—to get into her. Now I have. I'll really have something to tell the boys.'"

68 M found the experience quite satisfying from the standpoint of his own ego. "It made me feel really grown up and a part of the gang."

49 M's friends, knowing he was hoping to have intercourse with F1, asked M if he had got intercourse. "I didn't tell them anything. I just let them draw their own conclusions." However, M knows that his behavior would have led them to the conclusion that he had had intercourse. He recognizes that he was using the experience as a status-gaining device.

Attaining intercourse seemed to be to some subjects an expectancy for males which they were ready to achieve. Thus, one subject who made several unsuccessful tries before obtaining intercourse, remarked jocularly, "but I'm a boy. I kept on trying."

Excerpts from some of the case histories, which led to the suggestion that sex was sometimes looked upon as a game, follow. One subject in particular (#52) used a phraseology which implied the element of pursuit and capture[1] throughout his discussion of twenty-one liaisons, most of them at Level III. He used

---

[1] The techniques developed by #52 for obtaining intercourse are related in the latter part of this chapter.

such expressions as: "I can usually tell on the first date if I can score."—"That was the night I got her cherry."—"I scored that time."—"I was in her in no time at all."—"I knew I was as good as in her."—"I had to work like a devil, but I was successful."—"I was able to make her on the third date."

Boys who wish to play at sex apparently can find girls who will play the game with fully as much zest as they do. The subject just mentioned gave several such illustrations in his case history from which three are given below.

> 52   M had dated one girl whom he "never has been able to make." He has tried and she has resisted until "it has got to be a game. I would try, and she would let me go only to a certain point." They used to laugh about it. Even after they broke up M would occasionally call her and she would invite him over to "see how far" he could get. This was all done in a pleasant, joking manner.

> During the summer M used to take F6 swimming at a resort lake where they played around in the water. They kept getting more and more intimate. "We would sometimes go out in the water and stand in it up to our necks and have a lot of fun down below." They would "feel each other's body and I would grab her at different places."

> M and F 10 sat side by side in history class in the back of the room behind everyone else. F10 would sometimes put her hand in M's pocket and reach down to stimulate him around the genital area, or rub the inside of his thigh. In one pair of his trousers she found a small hole, and from time to time, as she kept working her finger and hand into the hole, she widened it into a very large opening which would permit her to put her hand entirely through it. "She was always trying to do this to embarrass me or to make some kind of joke out of it." She would also unzip his trousers while driving and play with his genitals.

If the boys were seeking intercourse for their own personal objectives they evidently felt, to judge from their reports, that the girls involved with them were seeking just as much to satisfy their own personal motives.

The girls' objectives appeared to the boys to be those of getting a relationship established. They were eager, the boys felt, to get a boy friend, get engaged, or get married. Evidence to support the conclusion that this was the primary motive of the girl appeared in history after history.

This point, because of its importance, will be documented more fully than the preceding points have been. Even so the documentation could be tripled from the Level III case histories. As one reads the case histories the "boys want sex—girls want marriage" theme crops out over and over again.

> **6** M had had intercourse while he was a high school junior. After the first instance of intercourse F missed her menstruation period. She told M about it and they began a more or less frenzied (at least M felt so) exploration of possible courses of action. F1 wanted to get married. M agreed, but after a careful analysis of this possibility he concluded it was completely impractical. He had no money, no job, nor any prospects of parental support. It would have meant having to give up all his plans and tying himself down to a routine, futureless job. F1 finally agreed that marriage just wasn't practical. "It was interesting how quickly she menstruated after that."

A similar experience with a somewhat different outcome was related by another subject.

> **35** F3 was a virgin whom M dated several times before having intercourse. One evening she "let me go as far as I wanted." M used no rubber and did not withdraw. As a result of this single intercourse F3 thought she was pregnant. She told M, "now we will have to get married." M thought he was being forced into it and a quarrel ensued. F3 then told her parents and they came to see M. He denied ever having had intercourse with F3. About this time she left the state, leaving M with the impression she was going away to have a baby. After she left M saw F3's parents and asked them what the real state of affairs was. They told M that F3 was not pregnant. M thinks her parents believed him instead of her.

In the following excerpts, as the subject related the circumstances, the efforts of each person to take advantage of the other for personal reasons seem obvious.

> **123** F5 was a nineteen-year-old girl with whom M had intercourse when he was twenty. She was a home-town girl who worked in a restaurant and was physically very attractive. On the first date he found her a very willing necking partner. M figured

that he would be able to have intercourse with her on their second date, and he found this the case. In fact, F5 became very aggressive. She told M that "she wanted him" and from every standpoint she made it very clear that she wanted intercourse. She even stimulated his genitals, which took them immediately to intercourse.

M then realized that she was using sex to set up a relationship. After intercourse was over "I just let her talk. She was making a lot of plans about us. She wanted to date steady, and to really make something out of the relationship." The result was that "I just didn't go back. The relationship promised to get too complicated for me to be interested."

52   M would have continued going with F8 for he enjoyed intercourse with her, but she "kept getting more and more of this marriage stuff thrown in." As a result M quit seeing her altogether.

Two illustrations, both from the same subject, show how M and two different girls were trading on each other's desires for sex and a dating relationship.

40   In order to get F2 to accept intercourse M "fed her a line about how all the girls in college have intercourse." M also used another inducement. F2 noticed his fraternity pin, and immediately made it very clear that she would like to have the pin to wear. He finally gave it to her with the idea that if he did he could get intercourse. This, however, produced a problem afterward for M wanted his pin back. She said she had left it in the car. They searched the car but were unable to find it. Finally M went back into the house and found the pin on the sweater she had been wearing. M never saw F2 again, though she wrote him several times and for some time used to call his home hoping to catch him in.

One of M's friends had had intercourse with F6. She agreed to have a date with M at her home. Here M began to neck and make sexual advances. F6 was not resistant and in a short time "I had her stretched out on the bed, and figured 'here we go.'" It did not prove quite that easy, however, for she began to put M off with one excuse after another. She first said, "If I let you have it tonight, you won't come back to see me any more."

This seemed to be F6's big worry. She was not really resisting intercourse—she just seemed to be afraid that M would be dissatisfied with her, and would not return. "By that time, I was ready to say anything. I was pouring on a big line and told her she was just the kind of a girl I liked; I would surely be back and that I thought a great deal of her. It was terrible, the line I gave her."

This seemed to satisfy F6. She then indicated that she was ready to go ahead.

Some of the subjects quite frankly recognized that they had played upon the girl's desire for marriage.

168 "She was talking about marriage all the time, and I agreed with everything she said. But I didn't mean a word of it."

The next excerpt relates the involvement of a mother in a sexual relationship her daughter had entered. Was she attempting to help get M committed to marriage with her daughter?

17 M and F1 had been going together and having intercourse regularly during M's senior year in high school and his freshman year in college. F1 was very eager to get married. M mentioned several times in the interview how badly F1 wanted to get married. He thinks that this was one of the reasons she was willing to accept intercourse. During his first year at college he received a letter from F1 saying that her mother had realized from F1's physical appearance that she and M were having intercourse. F1 asked that M come to talk over their situation with her and her mother.

M thinks that it is quite possible that F1 told her mother. At any rate the situation upset M greatly. He went home, but before seeing F1 and her mother, he went to see his own mother, and talked over the situation with her. "This was a very hard thing for me to do, and I hated like everything to do it." M's mother, however, took an objective attitude toward what had been occurring. She told M in response to his question that she did not feel he was obligated to marry F1 unless she was pregnant. In that case the situation would be altered.

M went to F1's home and had dinner with her and her family. After dinner he had a talk with F1 and her mother. F1's mother was quite frank and straightforward about the situation. She "gave me three choices—one was to marry F1 now, two was to get engaged and definitely agree to marriage a little later on, the third was to drop the whole business and get out then."

M took the last choice. If M could have continued without too much involvement he would have been glad to do it. He liked F1 and they had been planning to get married, but he was just

beginning to get a taste of school and getting his eyes opened to
some possibilities he hadn't seen before.

The following case history illustrates a typical sequence in a
relationship in which the boy was interested primarily in sex, and
the girl seemingly in marriage.

> **33**   F5 is a girl with whom M is presently having intercourse. He
> started dating her for intercourse, but she was not as susceptible
> as he thought she would be. Intercourse occurred about one
> month after they started going together.
>
> M felt that F5 did not know very much about how to take care
> of herself. She asked after they had begun intercourse what
> would be done if she had a baby. M replied, "Don't be silly—
> you're not going to have a baby." Now that they are on close
> and more intimate terms, F5 has occasionally kidded that "Junior
> is on the way."
>
> M thinks, however, this is just a hint that she would like to
> get married and he pays no particular attention to it. So far as M
> can see the relationship is running down somewhat. He thinks
> this is because F5 has become more aggressive in trying to ar-
> range dates. "I think she needs security and wants to get mar-
> ried." The result is that she has been calling M up and arranging
> times for them to go out together. She has also been talking more
> about marriage. This talk usually occurs at the same time that she
> has been hinting about the possibility of pregnancy.
>
> She has also become more aggressive sexually. "She has got so
> now she just throws it at me. Sometimes she grabs my sex organs
> in order to excite me and crawls all over me." Not long ago F5
> telephoned M and asked him if he would like to come over and
> spend the week end with her. She said that her mother was leav-
> ing, and that no one would be there. M decided not to accept this
> invitation for she was getting too close to the time in her men-
> strual period when pregnancy could occur, and he also felt that
> she was getting too serious.

The intense drive toward marriage on the part of Level III girls
makes them particularly susceptible to exploitation. They want to
hear that they are loved, and they are willing to accept many risks
on the chance that a relationship will develop. They make themselves so vulnerable that the boys themselves often remarked that
the girls were "stupid," "dumb," or "suckers." One of the subjects
said:

105 "When will those dumb girls learn that boys will lie, steal, or cheat to get sex? If a boy has to tell the girl that he loves her to get sex, then he will tell her that."

Still another subject observing the same phenomenon said:

118 "She was so darned hot to get married that she would do anything to work that out. She was really working on it. Whenever you find a girl that way, you can get her to do almost anything."

Still other points of vulnerability may enable the boy to gain his objectives. An example is provided in the following case history:

169 M and his friend had set up a date for the day with two girls whom they had heard would "go all the way." Their objective definitely and solely was to get intercourse. They drove around during the day, parked, necked, swam and tried vainly to progress in the direction of intimacy. After eating in the evening, they went to a drive-in theater where they necked and petted. M's girl, F3, began "to get downright disagreeable" and said all boys wanted to do was "play around." After the show was over they went to get some beer. "We really weren't making any progress toward intercourse. When we got the beer, however, F3 began to brag about her drinking prowess. This fitted right in with my plans." M encouraged F3 and "she got pie-eyed."

After this they parked again. M tried to engage in intercourse, but F3 resisted. "I had to talk a long time." F3 was fearful about pregnancy, but M assured her it was all right. After a time F3 began to yield. At the very last F3 demurred, started crying, and wanted M to stop. He replied that having gone this far it wouldn't be good for them to stop. In response to another argument, M assured her that he wouldn't break her hymen so that she would still be a virgin at marriage.

In one case history the subject mentioned the use of sex in retaliation and revenge. The subject had been seduced by a somewhat older married woman whose husband was a teacher in the school he was attending.

68 "I was rather afraid for a time someone would find out what we had done, but I felt good about having put one over on her husband. I had never liked him anyway. I think this was one of the reasons she was willing, too. What she said made me think she was getting revenge by stepping out on him."

Not all boys respond promptly and willingly to the possibilities of Level III intercourse. The case histories that have been utilized, it should be remembered, are from subjects who accepted intercourse at this level—those who rejected the chance were automatically excluded from the study.[2] Of those who accepted the chance several responded unfavorably to their experience. The following excerpt indicates the reaction of one subject.

> **46** One evening M and F were on a double date. After the date was over she invited him in. He went in and they sat down in the living room and began a conversation. During the conversation, M "made several sly remarks" which led them into a discussion of what other kids they knew were probably doing sexually. Soon they were talking about intercourse, and F opened the way for the experience. She was so very open about it, and took the lead so actively that M was able to go ahead and accept the relationship.
>
> After intercourse was over they talked a little about it. Both were afraid of what had happened. The result was that M never went back to see F again. He figured he had "got into the wrong kind of a relationship," and he didn't think that was the kind of thing to continue.

Communication

If we accept the premise that good communication depends upon mutual respect and honest acceptance of each other by the participants, one thing becomes apparent almost immediately. Effective verbal communication in the sense in which it has been defined in this study is almost nonexistent in Level III liaisons. A number of illustrations of dishonesty and insincerity have already been given. The comments made by the subjects in regard to their Level III partners repeatedly included the phrases such as "I had no respect for her," or "I didn't care for her."[3] Deceitful approaches are commonly associated with disrespect, with attitudes

---

[2] Some were, however, included in another. See the reference to the study by Tebor (91) in Chapter X.

[3] Reiss (85) would attribute some of the expressions of masculine attitude to adherence to the double standard. Undoubtedly, many Level III attitudes were quite double-standardish. Reiss in an excellent discussion suggests numerous ways in which the double standard may affect masculine-feminine attitudes and interpersonal relationships.

of rejection, and with the creation of barriers. This sequence was very explicitly expressed by one subject:

98 "I had very little respect for her to begin with, and even less after we started having intercourse. I sorta realized that I was taking advantage of her and that made me feel a little guilty. But she was taking advantage, too. She was pushing all the time to get me to say that I was interested in marriage. I never agreed or disagreed with her marriage talk. I just listened and went along for the sex, but all the time I was respecting her less."

The data in Table 17, Appendix I, indicate that "argumentative-persuasive" communication was twice as common as "understanding" communication in Level III liaisons. After studying the case histories carefully the investigator concluded that even when "understanding" communication did occur it probably represented little more than a momentary concern, aroused by a disturbed or emotional reaction on the part of the girl. A genuine, prolonged effort to develop real understanding between the partners prior to Level III intercourse just seemed not to occur.

Some boys, on the other hand, become quite skillful in developing persuasive techniques. Seemingly they gave much time and thought to persuasive approaches, and got a great deal of satisfaction from their successful application.

114 M feels that the most interesting part of his relationships with prospective sexual partners is the discussions in which he tries to persuade them that they should have intercourse. M has become so expert in persuasion that he can use it with a great deal of success.

The discussion with F2 centered around right and wrong. M tried to make her see that she had no sound grounds for her objections. "I had it all down to a pretty good science by that time. I could take her ideas and make them appear that we both agreed on the same thing."

One subject commented:

146 "I never ask a girl if I may unbutton her blouse. I ask her if it unbuttons or unsnaps, or if it unbuttons in the back or the front. This way she has less chance to say no."

The persuasive procedures that are developed often play upon the girls' concern for love and for a relationship. The arguments advanced imply that the boy expects these will be realized if the sexual aspect of the relationship is accepted and developed. One subject said:

> "She simply wouldn't go ahead until I told her I loved her. Then it was all settled. She knew as well as I did there wasn't a word of truth in it, but she had to hear it."

Other subjects commented:

> "I told her I loved her, and all that baloney."

> "I said that I was sure intercourse would strengthen our relationship."

Sometimes the arguments will appeal to the girl's desire to appear sophisticated ("All the college girls are doing it"), or to her wish to be grown up and independent ("I asked when she would be mature enough to think for herself, rather than just swallow what her parents told her").

The arguments for sexual intercourse may also appeal to the girl's sympathy for the boy: "I told her I was going into the service next week"; or a sense of fairness, "I brought her to a climax with my fingers. Then I asked her if it wasn't only fair that I got some satisfaction out of it, too"; or "I said that having gone so far in petting, the only fair thing for her to do was to complete what she had started."

They may be designed to dispel fears on the part of the girl, "I told her that I knew about contraceptives and there was no danger of pregnancy"; or "I said no one would ever know."

Occasionally the interchange was more threatening[4] than argu-

---

[4] Evidence that there is a great deal of aggressiveness in a dating relationship as it relates to erotic experiences was found by Kirkpatrick and Kanin (64). They distinguished five degrees of erotic aggressiveness, i.e., "necking," "petting" above the waist, "petting" below the waist, sexual intercourse, and attempts at sexual intercourse with violence or threats of violence. They found:

> "Of the two hundred ninety-one responding girls 55.7 per cent reported themselves offended at least once during the academic year at some level of erotic intimacy. The experiences of being offended were not altogether associated with trivial situations as shown by the fact that 20.9 per cent were offended by forceful attempts at intercourse and 6.2 per cent by aggressively forceful attempts at sex intercourse, in the course of which menacing threats or coercive infliction of physical pain were employed. There is no reason to think that offended girls had

mentative in nature: "I told her that she knew what I wanted, and for her to come across."—"She delayed so long that I got disgusted. I told her I knew that she put out and that she knew what I wanted."—"I told her that line was getting her nowhere."—"I said I knew about her sexual relationship with my buddy, and if she didn't come across everyone in school would know about it."

Table 17 also indicates that in some three-fourths of the two hundred twenty-two liaisons verbal communication was either non-existent, or so scanty as to be non-classifiable. In fact, some subjects looked upon discussion as to the acceptability of intercourse as a threat to their objective. "If you begin talking you'll talk yourself right out of it."—"I never talk. Too many fellows make that mistake. I just work along slowly, but always go a little further each time."

The following is a typical situation.

> 17 There was no talk about it. We never said "boo" about sex. I just kept getting a little further each time. When she took my hand away I never resisted, but I'd put it back a little later, and go a little further if I could. It took me several months to get intercourse, but finally she put up no more resistance, and I just went ahead.

Relationships may develop which incorporate intercourse for a time, then the partners may separate for good—still never acknowledging by anything said that they have ever engaged in a sexual relationship. The following excerpt is an example.

> 192 "We never talked about intercourse, either before or after. We went together for several months, and had intercourse probably a dozen times. When we quit going together we still said nothing, though I think she got to thinking I was using her. At any rate she became more and more unwilling for intercourse. I still see her sometimes, but we do little more than nod as we pass."

Another subject said, "If you could read every word that was ever said between us you would never know that anything sexual had occurred between us."

---

merely a single unpleasant experience with one partner. The one hundred sixty-two offended girls reported one thousand twenty-two episodes. While for some girls offensive experience was no doubt trivial, considerable mention was made of fear and guilt reactions."

When a liaison is entered by two people whose interest is directly and openly sexual, there can be and sometimes is some very obvious (though not direct or verbal) communication. The actual subject of sex is still often circumvented by evasive references, or referred to only by implication. The way to intercourse may be opened very directly, yet no verbal statement could ever be quoted representing a direct commitment to participate in intercourse.

> **68** "She was as eager for it as I was. She left the room for a short time and a few minutes later came in in her nightgown. She said she was going to bed, and asked if I intended to come, too."

> **158** M and F1 went to F1's apartment after their date. They drank some coffee, talked a while and then turned on some music and began to dance. While they were dancing F1 said, "Now if this was a novel, at this point you would pick me up and take me into the bedroom." When she said this, "I picked her up and took her into the bedroom, and that is all there was to it."

> We (M and F2) did a lot of talking about sex on both a serious and a kidding basis. There was never any reference to a possible relationship between the two of us. Yet gradually we came around to the point where we both knew that each of us would find it perfectly acceptable. And that is what happened. We went on into intercourse without any direct reference to our own relationship.

A few couples talk about the sexual relationship very directly.

> **79** After we were through I asked her if she had had a climax. She said she had not, so we talked about it and about what was satisfying to her. Then we tried it again, and this time she reached a climax.

Several subjects used general sexual conversations as a way of leading toward intercourse. The discussion was used as a way of disarming the potential partner and getting her into a receptive frame of mind. Thus: "If you can get them talking and laughing about sex, it (intercourse) is easier to get."—"I always try to get some conversation started about sex. This gets a girl more used to the idea."

Other subjects indicated that if a dating partner herself began a discussion of sex, they regarded it as a possible indication of interest in intercourse on her part. One subject said, "When she mentioned sex I pricked up my ears, and led her on."

Some girls are aware of the various implications sexual conversations may have. One subject's fiancée told him that when, as they first began dating and he had started a conversation about sex, she asked herself, "What is he leading up to now?" Another sexually inexperienced boy told his dating partner that he was a virgin, and intended to remain so until marriage. He later learned that her reaction was "Oh, yeah! That's a different way of making a pass!"

Sometimes the discussion becomes not only open in its sexual nature but lewd and lascivious. The liaison referred to in the excerpt below seems quite clearly one in which all pretense of any other interest than intercourse had been abandoned.

> 146 During the time that M knew F2, he had intercourse with her about seventy-five times. Most of the time some other fellows were also present. Intercourse always took place away from her house. F2 and M were extremely free in their relationship. "We talked about styles of intercourse, our experience in intercourse, and just anything that came to our minds. Our talk was sometimes so gross you wouldn't believe it."

However, many persons involved in Level III liaisons would seemingly find it easier to engage in the actual sexual relationship, going through all the physical preliminaries, and through the act itself, than to make a direct verbal reference to the contemplated or actual relationship. This was vividly illustrated by the response of one subject who answered the question, "Did your partner in the relationship reach an orgasm?" with "Why, I don't know. I was interested in mine."

Then after a few seconds of reflection he said, "After all, I couldn't ask her a question like that. We weren't very close friends."

Actually, non-verbal communication is quite significant at Level III. As has just been noted, sometimes it completely supplants verbal communication. It is seemingly quite clear to both persons what is intended and what is about to occur without any verbal interchange. Subjects voiced such reactions repeatedly as, "We both knew what was going to happen."—"No one was fooled. She knew what I was after, and we both knew that the other knew."

This awareness may come through assenting and participating in certain kinds of arrangements.

158 F3 is a girl aged nineteen whom M met when he was twenty. One evening M and a friend agreed that they would like a beer date, so each called a girl and made arrangements for it. F3 accepted readily, and M invited her feeling that intercourse would be possible. The beer party itself was a well-laid plan on the part of both boys and the girls. Although there was no talking ahead of time about the possibility of intercourse, "everyone knew what was being planned."

Sometimes non-verbal communication leading toward intercourse takes place when one of the possible participants alters or changes a visible symbol in the environment. This is what occurred in the next two illustrations. The first excerpt also illustrates the kind of double-talk which never says anything, yet all the time moves the couple nearer intercourse.

124 F6 was a girl whom M had tried to date a number of times, but had always been turned down for some reason or another. Finally she agreed to go out with M. They went out, had something to eat, and drank a little. Afterward they drove back, and F6 invited M to her apartment. He went in and they sat down on the davenport to talk and neck. She had an "in-a-door bed" in the apartment. As they were necking M asked her if she "would like to pull the bed down and the covers back." F6 replied that she thought not. M decided that there was "nothing doing," so he went home shortly after that. He did, however, make another date with her for another evening when he was off work.

On this occasion they went to a night spot, ate some, danced, and drank a bit. When it was time to leave M asked F6 if she would like to go out and park. She preferred not to, but did suggest going back to her apartment.

As they entered the apartment, M noted at once that F6 had the bed down and all nicely ready. The davenport was covered with something which made it impossible for them to sit on it, while a scrap book was on the bed. There was a soft light beside the bed. M's immediate conclusion was that all this was an invitation for intercourse, and he became sexually excited. F6, however, was quite deliberate and composed. After she took her coat off she sat down on the bed and showed him her scrapbook. She had been "Queen of something, and the book was full of cheesecake." After looking at it for a time M pulled F6 over against him and began petting. She was still somewhat resistant.

After a time he suggested that she "model a kimono" which M had seen the first time he saw her. "It was a sexy number with a slit up the side." F6 demurred at this, saying that it was in the dirty clothes hamper. M urged, however, so she agreed. She returned a short time later in the kimono, and M admired her. She then returned to the bathroom, and while she was gone M undressed and got into bed. F6 came back in a robe which she removed and got into bed also. There was nothing said; they simply moved into intercourse.

49   M had met and had intercourse with F1 while he was a high school junior and she was a member of a traveling dance group which was visiting M's high school. M had met F1 while working backstage as property manager.

A year later F1's troupe of tap dancers was in town again, and had a rehearsal at the high school. M was released from classes to help the troupe to make arrangements for their show. M saw F1 backstage, and noticed that she had an engagement ring on. She seemed quite distant and not at all responsive to M's talking, so he felt there was not much chance to "get anywhere" with her. At the show that night, though, she had removed the ring and seemed more receptive. To M the removal of the ring "was the green light." From this point on M was able to proceed, without any talking, in such a manner as to gain intercourse.

Situations in which the subjects regarded what was said as "phony" or "said for convention's sake" were common.

42   "She always said she didn't want to do it, but she always gave in very easily. A little persuasion and a few pats—that was all that was needed."

97   "Most of these girls argue enough to be able to say that they have put up a protest. Once they have done that they are ready to go ahead."

54   "She protested, but you could tell she didn't mean it. You know what I'm talking about. When a girl says she doesn't want to go ahead, but then turns around and lays herself right out in front of you, you kinda get the idea."

In the preceding pages case history excerpts have shown how couples gradually become aware of what each is wanting or is willing to accept in the way of sexual advances. In the same way, still with no verbal communication, they became aware of each other's personal, self-seeking motives, and their true feelings toward each other.

"She never said so, but she thought I was using her."—"I never told her, but she knew I had no respect for her."

This growing awareness broke up most of these relationships. Had there been frank, honest communication most of them would have broken even earlier, for the relationships were not the kind that could stand openness and straightforwardness. The following excerpt illustrates this:

> 33 One evening F3 accused M of going with her for intercourse and no other purpose. "She said that was all I wanted of her." Because this was true, it produced a quarrel and hard feelings between them. That was the end of the relationship so far as M was concerned. He had no more dates with her.

To say that frank exposure of motives will produce an immediate break is not always true. In the following excerpt one can see the kind of desperate hanging-on which sometimes occurs in these relationships.

> 185 As intercourse continued F3's attachment for M seemed to increase. M did not respond. As far as he was concerned their relationship would never have continued if they had not been having intercourse. On one occasion F3 became angry and began to cry. She told M that she felt that the only reason he was going with her was for sex. "I spoke very bluntly and harshly to her. I said, 'You are absolutely right. That *is* the only reason I'm going with you.'" The next week M received a letter from F3 apologizing for what she had said and hoping that he would forgive her.

Effective communication at this level is quite frequently found between members of the male sex. In pairs or groups, boys at the late teen period with the predatory-recreational [5] approach to sex, have strong loyalties to each other—far stronger than any loyalty they are likely to feel for a Level III sexual partner. This loyalty shows itself in such circumstances as the following, all of which were found in Level III histories.

---

[5] Following a classification by Lindesmith and Strauss (68).

A. Boys knowing that one of their buddies has prospects of obtaining intercourse get out of the way in order to insure the "fortunate" boy the time and privacy needed to bring his efforts to fruition.

B. Boys will give friends tips concerning certain girls who they believe will be susceptible to sexual advances. They may even attempt to set up circumstances whereby in addition to attaining sexual satisfaction themselves they are able to include a buddy in the experience. Thus,

18 M told his closest friend that he had had intercourse with F3, "but I don't think he did anything about it. He was going with another girl at the time."

C. They may give overt assistance to a buddy who is dating a girl who might become his sexual partner. They may supply him with contraceptive devices, or brief him on the attitudes or resistances he is likely to encounter with the girl.

Protective Measures and Assumption of Responsibility

The level of protection which partners afford each other in Level III liaisons is very low. As a matter of fact, aggression, exploitation and advantage-taking are much more prevalent. Both male and female can expect that of the other. The very short period of acquaintance that exists in many of the liaisons, and the lack of any emotional investment or attachment which characterizes all of them, results in few persons' taking any thought for the welfare of the other.

In many of the liaisons no consistent or conscientious attention was paid to the use of contraceptives. Data in Table 26, Appendix I, do indicate that in 67.1 per cent of the Level III liaisons contraceptives were used at one time or another. This figure is misleading if taken as an index of effective protection, for all kinds of contraceptive measures are included—condoms, observation of safe period, withdrawal, douche. Moreover, contraceptive practices are frequently used under circumstances which add greatly to such ineffectiveness as already exists, e.g., in the back seat of a car, hasty application by inexperienced users. Ordinarily, the boy provides what protection there is, usually through withdrawal, or the application of a condom—one subject said, "an old one I had been carrying in my pocketbook for a couple of years." The couple may try in some kind of haphazard way to observe the "safe period." Often neither the male nor the female has adequate scientific knowledge as to the effective utilization of the "safe period." The girl may wittingly, or unwittingly, state her position in the menstrual cycle inaccurately. In many instances the couple lack facilities for douching. As one subject said, "douching requires plumbing facilities not found in the back seat of a car."

Some couples use contraceptives at the time they begin intercourse, but become more and more lackadaisical and careless as they go along.

> **63** M had condoms bought for him by a friend. He used these in the first few experiences in intercourse. These occurred in a car. Later instances took place at F's house without any attempt to use contraceptives. Nor did M attempt to withdraw.

> **8C** "I used a condom the first few times. After that I didn't use anything. Sometimes we tried to check on the safe period."

Another element of risk for the girl is that the boy feels less threatened by possible pregnancy than she does, and so may not use a contraceptive if she does not insist on it.

> **58** "We were both out for a good time, and neither of us fooled the other." When they were ready for intercourse, M asked F4 if he should use a rubber. She said, "It's up to you," so M used no contraceptive at all. "If she had got pregnant I wouldn't have married her, and she wouldn't have expected it."

> **146** "If she wasn't going to make a point of it (the use of contraceptives) I certainly wasn't. It was for her, not me."

Table 27, Appendix I, reveals the same lack of interest so far as planning for pregnancy is concerned. In a very small proportion (3.2 per cent) of the liaisons were any plans made for coping with a possible pregnancy. This probably reflects the decidedly lesser difficulties which boys face with possible pregnancy than do girls. They can escape the consequences of pregnancy more easily, and socially they are expected, more than girls, to "sow wild oats." Nor are the possible consequences of discovery or scandal as great for boys as girls. Harmful repercussions from gossip are less likely to occur with the boy than the girl. In the peer group knowledge of sexual involvement may actually gain the boy status with his fellows.

This cultural attitude appeared in several of the histories. Knowledge that the subject had been involved in intercourse was accepted as a joke by friends in the first instance, and by the family in the second. In the third instance the girl reacted more sharply to discovery than the boy.

> 94 The next day (after M's first experience in intercourse) he and a group of friends were talking about what had happened on their dates the preceding evening. A lot of kidding was going on. "How did you make out?" "Did you get any?" "Did you get your stick wet?" M very casually told them he "had made out" the night before. He was quite elated about it. "I thought it was a big deal, and that I was right in it, along with the rest of the guys."

> 6 M's family has heard about his sexual relationship also. It came out not long ago, when one of M's sisters married. A stag party was given for M's prospective brother-in-law the night before the wedding. At this party everyone was drinking, and began telling about their various experiences and episodes. M's father, and one of M's uncles, who had been a pretty wild fellow when he was young, were there. During the evening M told about his experience with F1. He told it openly and nobody seemed to mind. As a matter of fact his Dad thought it was funny. He went home and told M's mother, and she was "pretty teed-off." However, nothing at all has been said lately, and M knows that both parents have accepted it, and nothing will be made of it.

> 61 One afternoon one of M's boy friends came out to his home one afternoon when F1 was there. "The slug walked right in without knocking," and found M and F1 engaged in intercourse. F1 was highly embarrassed, and M somewhat so. He was also mad at his friend for the intrusion. His friend told a number of other boy friends what he had found, but there were no repercussions from it.

Clearly, promises to marry afford a girl at this level little or no protection. Illustrations of the unsubstantial nature of such promises have already been cited, but two more are added.

> 40 "She talked about our getting married and I went along with her. I didn't say I wouldn't but neither did I say I would. I just let her think what she wanted."

52 "I was wanting sex so much at that point that I was willing to promise anything."

The same frankly deceptive attitudes on the part of the women as are admitted by the men can not be documented by the data in this study. Some of the subjects, however, felt they were experiencing deception and duplicity, as well as practicing it.

131 "Both of us made a lot of promises, and neither of us meant to keep any of them."

8 F2 was a girl whom M had met during the summer when he was sixteen and she was fifteen. This summer there was considerable lovemaking between them. She told M, "She was nuts about me. She fed me quite a line."

The following summer F2 was back in town, and M again met her and had a date with her. After the dance they went out in M's car and he began to make advances. "The line she had fed me the summer before I fed right back to her."

Boys sometimes offer protection to each other. They may in so doing provide a certain amount of protection to the girl, but that, if it happens, is quite incidental. These are also further illustrations of male-to-male loyalty.

123 M had taken F2 to a dance on their first date. As they were leaving one of M's friends pulled him aside and handed him a rubber. "He told me that he had been out with her before and that I would need it." M had intercourse with F2 that night.

117 M spoke of a potential Level III liaison which he by-passed. A certain girl had been acting very seductively toward him. "My buddy told me that he had heard that this girl might be pregnant, and that she had said she was going to try to pull me in on it. Believe me, I stayed away from her."

105 When M was a high school freshman he struck up a sexual relationship with a freshman girl. He used condoms which he got through a senior boy, a friend of his older brother. This boy had heard M was having intercourse, and approached him about it. When he found it was true he gave M some rubbers. Later M went to him for more. "He thought it was a big joke, that I was getting into this girl the way I was."

Several subjects spoke of the readiness of boys to support a buddy who might get into trouble through his sexual activities. A common idea is that a boy who gets a girl pregnant is safeguarded by the statement of several others that they have had intercourse with her.

This protective attitude of males toward each other has important implications for a teen-age girl involved in a Level III liaison. She may easily have, and probably without knowing it, a fair-sized and quite cohesive male group lined up against her. Some boys will be spreading the word of her availability to others. Some of the older, more-sophisticated fellows may be urging the younger less-experienced boys on. In case of pregnancy she will almost certainly find everyone denying any responsibility. The readiness of the males to protect one another makes her situation doubly hazardous.

The lack of family supervision is a clear-cut characteristic of many liaisons at this level. Empty homes, parents away, teen-agers out part of or all night, use of liquor—all these circumstances appear in certain of the Level III case histories. In a society which has become organized so definitely along age group lines, and in which adult supervision is so rejected as in our own, how much adult-parental supervision can be exercised is questionable. There can be no question, however, but that the absence of such supervision makes such sexual liaisons as those discussed in this chapter more possible, and that additional supervision would have helped protect some who otherwise got into untenable situations.

In general, Level III relationships are devoid of personal attachment. This introduces another hazard, particularly for the female. Some girls are passed from one boy to another in somewhat the same manner as a piece of furniture. The most pronounced example of this involved the following circumstances:

> 40   M first knew of F6 when he heard from a friend that she was having intercourse with a friend of M's friend. Shortly after this M's friend's friend went into the service. He introduced F6 to M's friend, and she became his steady girl and willing sexual partner, according to what the friend told M. After several months this friend had to go away to school so he introduced F6 to M and she became his girl.
>
> M and F6 began intercourse on their second date. M was very pleased with the arrangement for a time, but gradually became disillusioned because he could never satisfy F6 sexually, and be-

cause she began pressing him to get married. "I got so worn out and so sick of it, I couldn't take it."

M's way out was to introduce F6 to one of his boy friends who knew the whole story, and who thought he would enjoy such an association. This transfer didn't last, though. It fell through after one week end, and F6 was back to M.

He then found himself involved in a desperate effort to get free of F6. Finally the only way out was a point blank refusal to see her again, even though she continued calling and writing him. At the time of the interview M had given F6's name and address to another interested fellow. M hoped that if he could start up a new relationship for F6, it might relieve him of her attentions.

The point was made at the beginning of this section that Level III liaisons were characterized by aggressiveness, exploitation, and irresponsibility rather than by protectiveness and the assumption of responsibility. One factor which led to this statement is the evidence that some boys become specialists in seduction. One example will be used; in this instance M, who reported twenty-one liaisons at three levels, made a careful analysis of the procedures he used in obtaining intercourse.

52 M, age nineteen, is a college freshman, an inactive church member, and a vocal and outgoing person. He talks readily and freely about his own sexual experiences and feelings. His first sexual experience came when he was fourteen years of age.

M realizes that he has a good bit more sexual experience than the average fellow. M thinks that he can tell on the first date "whether I will be able to score." If he takes a girl out and enjoys her as a social partner, finds her a good dancer, and a lot of fun, he will not discontinue dating her simply because he feels that he can not have intercourse with her. It so happens that there has been only one girl in his dating life with whom he has been unable to have intercourse. The rest of them have sooner or later become his sexual partners. If, however, he dates a girl and doesn't like her, but figures he can "score in a couple of times" he will continue to date her.

There are certain things which he finds are good indications as to whether or not the girl will become a willing partner in intercourse. For one thing M asks her if she will do something for him. If she "falls all over herself" trying to do what he asks, or to please him, then he figures that she quite probably will be willing to have intercourse if he urges it. He also thinks it indicative if a girl begins to flatter a boy. If she tells him he is a big wheel, or a smooth guy, it means that she is impressed, and will accept advances from him when she might not from other fellows.

With this in mind, M always tries to impress the girls he dates with how many persons he knows, and with his smoothness. He does this by having a speaking acquaintance with a great many other persons, and always speaking to them on a dance floor or at a party. He also makes a fair salary on his job. He is free to spend this on himself and his clothes. He has found that personal appearance is very important. Since he has worked in a clothing store, he is able to use his knowledge about clothing in such a way as to enhance his personal appearance. He has also made his car an important factor in impressing the girls he dates. It is not so much that the car is a new one, but that it is well-kept and fast. He does some racing, and has had a number of wins. This is a point that seems to impress the girls.

Occasionally he may use sex conversation as a way of stimulating an interest or a reaction in a girl, but never very often. In any event, he does not use crude conversation. If they go to a movie together and they see a passionate love scene, he may mention to the girl that, "That was passionate behavior," and imply what he thinks may result from it. If at a drive-in movie they see the car next to them rocking furiously, "I may chuckle and make some comment about what was happening in that car." M finds as he goes along that the girl gets more and more relaxed so that he is soon able to talk to her about anything he would like to. This usually comes about the second date.

M has found it effective when he begins petting to start kissing the girl on the ears, around the neck, under the throat, and in that way stimulate her physically. A very effective way is to rub the back of her neck. He puts his hand down her back and rubs it or rubs her buttocks. He never tries to stimulate her breasts because that means that his hand has to be between their bodies. That way he is not able to get close to her. M feels that he can practically always tell if a girl "has been made by someone else." Such a girl will usually act as though she wants him to stop and yet never really puts on the brakes. She puts up a kind of resistance for the sake of show, but it does not mean anything.

M has also found that the position he has been holding as a salesman in a women's clothing store has been an exceedingly advantageous place for him to meet girls. During the past summer when he was working there he met at least five or six girls with whom he was later able to have intercourse.

Some of the subjects used a process of rationalization seemingly as a protection against pangs of conscience. These rationalizations usually appeared as incidental comments during the interview. Examples of these are the following.

33 "I didn't work too hard on it. I didn't force F3. I have never forced a girl." However, once M had got the idea of having intercourse he continued to work at getting it. Though there was no discussion, after a couple of weeks he realized "it would be possible to have intercourse very shortly."

93 "I have never had intercourse with a girl unless she was willing. Sometimes I have had to argue like mad, but I've always got their consent before I went ahead."

18 "I always make sure that the girl enjoys it as much as I do. That makes it fair."

80 "It wasn't much of a relationship and I didn't enjoy it at all. I'm glad I didn't, for I felt better about it afterwards than if I had."

68 "I always make it a policy when I am with a girl to see that she goes to sleep before I do. So many times a fellow will have intercourse with a girl then go to sleep before she does. This makes her feel that he doesn't care for her at all."

Sometimes the couple manages to set up a situation in which conventional appearances can be preserved to a certain degree. This enables the couple to do what they want while affording them a certain protection against criticism, and possibly feelings of guilt. Actually both partners are probably aware of the deception and know quite well what is taking place.

146 M thinks that women like to have excuses to have intercourse. He thinks a good many of them use liquor as a pretext. On a couple of occasions he has had girls take a couple of beers, and then pretend to pass out. He knew very well that they were not as much under the weather as they pretended. It did afford them a chance to say that they didn't know what was taking place. He also knows that girls sometimes like almost to be forced into in-

tercourse. Thus, they can do what they would like to do, but at the same time they are able to say they had no control over the situation. A part of the reason for some girls talking before they accept intercourse is that they want to be persuaded.

One Level III subject did not observe the common tendency to tell other boys about a girl with whom he has had casual intercourse.

> **46** M had had one experience in intercourse with a girl when he was seventeen. He dropped the relationship and refused any further intercourse because he figured he had "got into the wrong kind of a relationship." He didn't think it was the kind of thing to continue.
>
> Later he was asked by some boys if he had had intercourse. When he said he had they wanted to know with whom. "I refused to tell them. I thought the least I could do to protect her was to keep her name secret."

It is interesting that this evidence of protectiveness came from an individual who was so near virginal status himself. Does the lack of experience make him more charitable in his judgments? Is there a basic quality of personality which has kept him both charitable in his judgments and virginal in his sex life? If he had more sexual experience would he lose this protective attitude?

EVALUATION OF SUBJECTS

A total of sixty-five subjects with Level III liaisons were questioned as to their satisfaction or dissatisfaction with intercourse at this level. No information or inadequate information was obtained from the other thirty-three subjects. The results from the ninety-eight who experienced Level III liaisons are as follows:

Number of Subjects	Reaction to Experience
28	Satisfactory
14	Mixed feelings
19	Unsatisfactory
4	"Just an experience—no feeling in particular."
33	No information

Most of those who expressed satisfaction did so on the basis of the physical pleasure derived from the experience. Those who found partners who seemed wholly or primarily interested in the sexual side, and who made no relationship demands on them, were more likely to express undiluted satisfaction with their experience.

Those who had mixed feelings and/or unsatisfactory ratings were often disgruntled because they found themselves involved in situations which threatened to entangle them more than they could tolerate. Some of those who rated their experience as unsatisfactory expressed a feeling of guilt over having become involved in such relationships.

> 42 The experience wasn't much, only about what M had expected, for knowing F1 he hadn't expected much. Intercourse occurred only one time for M never dated F1 again. "I felt kind of cheap about it afterward. That was the reason." F1 "was not a nice girl. I didn't like to be seen with her, and since I felt that way about her the less I was seen with her, or seen talking with her, the better."

All in all, there was relatively little direct expression of guilt by the male participants in Level III relationships. Resentment of what the subjects considered advantage-taking on the part of the girls, and as a result of unwanted involvements, was more common than expressions of guilt.

Some of the subjects who rated their experiences satisfactory with reference to short-term criteria (physical pleasure, excitement of conquest) would have rated it differently if they had been considering long-term consequences. For example, one subject who had five liaisons at Levels II and III and one at Level IV before becoming engaged to his seventh sexual partner rated all his experiences as very satisfactory. Yet in commenting on his engagement to F7 the subject remarked: "One of the reasons I'm glad about it is that I had begun to wonder if I had goofed off so much that it would always be that way. Would it always be in the back seat of a car, and nothing permanent?"

"Mixed feelings" sometimes meant in reality "satisfactory" on some points and "unsatisfactory" on others. The following is an example:

> 13 Up to the time M met F3 "it was sort of like I had been leading two lives. One was the life I led when I went with certain

girls for sex, and the other was the one I led when I went out with 'nice' girls. I liked the sex, but I have not liked the double life."

M also feels his experience in intercourse has helped him to know more about sex and how to treat his wife in intercourse. He now has more understanding of how they may attain mutual satisfaction.

GENERAL OBSERVATIONS

The quality of interpersonal relations found in Level III liaisons has been low and characterized by exploitive attitudes and behavior on the part of both the male and the female. The general impression seems to be that the boy is the aggressor in sexual relations found at this level. That this is far from being true becomes apparent from analyses of some of the Level III liaisons. Many females are apparently just as aggressive in seeking a sexual relationship as are the males.

Certainly, if the reports of these subjects are to be believed, marked aggressiveness is manifested by girls who seem to be seeking a dating and ultimately a marriage relationship. This aggressive effort on the girl's part seems to merit just as much concern in terms of its personal and social consequences as the boy's aggressive efforts to obtain intercourse.

Circumstances related in some of the case histories suggest that feminine aggressiveness stimulates, and from the male point of view justifies, masculine counter-aggression. Many men and women who have had unhappy encounters with aggressive conduct exhibited by members of the other sex are made bitter and rendered disrespectful in their conduct as a result. In other words, aggressive action produces an opposing reaction, and exploitation begets exploitation.

5

ANALYSIS OF LEVEL IV

LIAISONS

The plan of level classification (*see* p. 19) used for arraying the six hundred sixty-eight liaisons by levels of emotional involvement was devised to provide as clear-cut a distinction between levels as possible. The distinctions made between Levels I, II, and III held up well, but Levels III and IV case histories have presented fewer clear-cut distinctions, and the division between Level III and IV has been seemingly less satisfactory so far as providing descriptive data is concerned. The following distinction was made between these two levels in the level classification plan.

Level	Character of Partner	Degree of Attachment
III	Casual acquaintance who was perceived merely as a potential sexual associate.	Dating began definitely for purpose of obtaining intercourse. No affectional attachment on the part of the male.
IV	Dating partner who became a sexual associate before a strong relationship had developed.	The possibility of intercourse arose after dating began and before male became affectionally attached.

This differentiation presumably reflected the existence of friendly feelings in Level IV relationships, and possibly the beginning of emotional attachments. The expectation was, of course, that Level IV statistical and descriptive case history data would reflect differences in the sexual attitudes and conduct found at the two levels.

The distinction between Levels III and IV held up satisfactorily when it came to classifying the liaisons into levels. A boy might begin to date a girl because he thought she would have intercourse (Level III), or the possibility of intercourse might have arisen after he started dating her, and before any marked emotional attachment had developed (Level IV). This distinction was sharp enough to permit classification. The differentiations which appeared between Levels III and IV on the more intangible aspects of communication, motivations, attitudes toward protection and the assumption of responsibility, and the self-evaluations of subjects, were not as sharp, however, as those appearing between Levels I, II, and III.

Extensive citation of descriptive material from Level IV liaison histories seems unwarranted. Such an analysis would simply repeat illustrations and portray relationships very similar to those found in Level III histories. Therefore, only such features as indicate possible differences in the characteristics of the two levels will be discussed.

STATISTICAL RESULTS

Eighty-seven subjects contributed one hundred sixteen Level IV liaison histories. An extension of these data are contained in the following table.

Table 6

PARTICIPANTS AND LIAISONS—LEVEL IV

Number of Subjects	Number of Liaisons Reported	Total Number of Liaisons
69	1	69
8	2	16
9	3	27
1	4	4
87		116

Forty-three (49.5 per cent) of the subjects were virgins at the time of their first Level IV intercourse. The subjects judged thirty-nine (33.6 per cent) of their female partners to be virgins, sixty-three non-virgins, and fourteen of unknown status. This provides an interesting contrast with Level III. Here only five (2.3 per cent) of the two hundred twenty-two females were considered virgins by the subjects. Level III subjects evidently felt they were associated with women who were sexually more experienced than was the case with Level IV subjects.

An obvious difference between Level III and Level IV relationships is the amount of time invested in the relationship by the subjects before intercourse occurred. Data on this point are found in Table 12 and Figure A, in Appendix I. In almost one-third (31.1 per cent) of the Level III liaisons, intercourse occurred within a week after the subjects had started dating the girls. In another large portion of the liaisons (42.8 per cent), intercourse occurred in less than two months (though not within one week). This means that 73.9 per cent of all Level III liaisons occurred within two months after the couple started dating.

In Level IV liaisons, intercourse occurred in only 6.9 per cent of the liaisons within one week, and in 16.4 per cent in less than two months (though not within one week). Therefore only 23.3 per cent of the Level IV liaisons occurred within two months after the couple started dating.

DESCRIPTIVE DATA

Motivations

The motivations in Level IV liaisons, as they were judged, are very similar to those operating at Level III. Generalized comments will be relied upon mainly to provide the major points. A premeditated striving for intercourse was defined as characterizing Level III liaisons, whereas, by definition, it was excluded from Level IV liaisons as of the time the subject began dating the girl. Many of the subjects did, however, "begin to get ideas" very shortly after they began dating. As one subject said, "I didn't begin dating her with sex in mind, but from some of the things she said and did on the first date, I figured I could make her if I tried."

Characteristic comments from Level IV subjects who found an unexpected opportunity to participate in intercourse included these: "I never thought she would do it," "It was certainly a surprise to me."

The reports that opportunity for intercourse was unexpected raise an interesting point. How much of what Level III subjects saw in girls, and of what Level IV subjects did not see, was the result of what they were expecting to see? The behavior of the girls may very easily have been nearly identical, yet has been perceived one way by Level III subjects because they were seeking intercourse, and a different way by Level IV subjects because they were not.

A number of Level IV subjects also said they found their partners to be sexually aggressive. In the following instances no interpretation other than an aggressive move toward intercourse on the part of the girls would seem possible, if we are to accept the statements of the subjects.

> 121 M and F had been dating two months. One evening when he dropped by her house her parents were not home. As M began to neck with F he was surprised that she made no effort to stop him. He had no intention of doing anything, but F simply removed all of her clothing.

> 100 M and F3 had dated for some time. They did quite a bit of petting. One night they stopped and petted a bit, and F3 became highly excited. "I don't know what it is that girls get when they get excited, but whatever it is, she had it that night." She was "all over me" and "so eager that I did it out of politeness."

Sometimes the girls were quite blunt and direct in extending invitations to intercourse.

> "We were petting and she said, "God, M, tonight I'll give you anything."

> While we were necking at her home she suddenly stood up and said, "I'm going to bed; are you coming?"

> While we were necking she said, "It's hard to have intercourse in a car, but it can be done!"

> She said, with no provocation, "If I ever have intercourse with a man again, he's got to have a rubber."

The above excerpts might indicate that these were girls interested primarily in the pleasure aspects of the sexual relationship. There are, of course, other possibilities. Several subjects spoke of the apparent concern of their partners for getting some kind of deeper relationship established.

> **76** The thing which caused the relationship to break was that M began to feel the pressure to come to some decision about how serious he should be with F3. "I was so scared that I would have to get serious. I didn't want to be serious, or you might say, I wanted to be, but I didn't want to sign any contracts."

> **197** M figured that if she thought so much of him and was so eager to get married she would let him go as far as he wanted. This concern was clearly evident after a week of dating. "She wanted to get married and kept talking about and trying to get me to express an interest." Because of this M "knew she wouldn't stop me."

This desire on the part of the girl for relationship ties sometimes expresses itself in a seeming readiness to accept pregnancy.

> **76** The last time they had intercourse, F10 commented that she would like to become pregnant. She "would like to have a child by me." This has worried M "since he doesn't want to be tied down. She is getting too serious"—more so than M wants. He is thinking of dropping the relationship.

Further documentation could be given to these aspects of feminine motivation, but an elaboration would repeat much of what has already been written concerning the motivations of Level III partners.

Whereas no Level III subject indicated any reluctance in accepting an opportunity for intercourse, some of the Level IV subjects, even when intercourse appeared as a distinct possibility, went ahead only with some hesitancy. A single excerpt from one of several case histories will illustrate the occasional expression of reluctance on the part of some Level IV subjects:

> **173** During this period there was some petting and M had several chances to have intercourse with F2. "She would have given out any time." However, since he was "serious about her" he didn't want to. Later, his feelings for F2 were less ardent. At this time he decided to "get what I could."

Two subjects recognized that they had used intercourse as a weapon against female partners toward whom they felt some hostility. In the next excerpt M frankly acknowledged that he used intercourse as a form of retaliation.

63 M's first experience in intercourse with F2 occurred after about one year of "off and on" dating. The relationship had not been a satisfactory one in that F2 was pushing M too hard for a permanent relationship. This he did not want. Intercourse finally occurred because M was feeling resentful toward F2 for pushing him. Intercourse was a way of getting back at her, and of breaking the relationship, for he never went with her again after intercourse occurred.

Level IV subjects were very ready to acknowledge their interest in sensory pleasure; they also expressed a sense of masculine achievement resulting from intercourse. These same motivations were expressed by many of the Level III subjects.

By virtue of the definition which ruled out premeditated striving for intercourse at the time dating was begun, there was less evidence of rivalry and competition between Level IV males to secure intercourse than was noted at Level III. There also seemed to be less scheming and contriving by the subjects at Level IV than at Level III.

Communication

The slower progress into intercourse of Level IV subjects, as compared to Level III subjects, is reflected in the statistical data concerning differences in the amount and nature of communication that existed between the partners prior to intercourse at the two levels. These data are found in Tables 15 and 16, and their corresponding figures in Appendix I.

At Level III, Table 15 shows that 5.9 per cent indicated "much" communication prior to intercourse, while 16.2 per cent indicated "some" communication. Corresponding figures from Level IV subjects were, 6 per cent "much" communication, and 30.2 per cent "some" communication. Fewer Level IV subjects (36.2 per cent) than Level III subjects (45.5 per cent) indicated "no" communication prior to intercourse.

By examining the data in Table 17, Appendix I, we see that 41.6 per cent of all the argumentative-persuasive communication occurred at Level IV. Similarly, only 17.1 per cent of all the "understanding" communication, involving 8.1 per cent of all the liaisons, occurred at Level III, while 30.5 per cent of "understanding" communication involving 27.6 per cent of the liaisons took place at Level IV. This can only indicate a trend, but insofar as it is one, it may be attributed to two main factors. First, since Level IV subjects were less oriented toward seeking intercourse than Level III subjects, they were probably less disposed to argue, or plead for it. Second, female partners at Level IV, sensing the possibility of setting up a relationship, may have been more disposed to offer opportunities for petting or sexual intercourse than were Level III partners.

Larger proportions of both Level III and Level IV subjects indicated "no communication" following intercourse, than prior to intercourse. "No communication" following intercourse was reported by 71.6 per cent of the Level III subjects and 60.3 per cent of the Level IV subjects. "Some communication" was reported after intercourse by 7.2 per cent of the Level III subjects, and 26.7 per cent of the Level IV subjects. Only a small proportion of both Level III (2.3 per cent) and Level IV (3.4 per cent) subjects indicated "much communication" following intercourse.

Data relating to the nature of communication indicates that only a small and insignificant proportion of both Level III (3.6 per cent) and Level IV (2.6 per cent) subjects experienced argumentative-persuasive communication following intercourse. Since a good many of these relationships did not survive long after the beginning of intercourse, it is quite likely that tension and awareness of an imminent break prevented further arguing or persuading. The data are found in Table 18.

The difference between the two levels as it related to "understanding" communication following intercourse is again quite definite. Only 8.1 per cent of the Level III subjects indicated "understanding" communication, as compared to 22.4 per cent of the Level IV subjects.

As at Level III, non-verbal communication either sometimes contradicted or served as a substitute for verbal communication. Participation in petting, alluring behavior, ready acceptance of petting, or suggestive comments, served to indicate the girl's readiness to accept intercourse.

Possible marriage as a subject of conversation occurring at

Levels III and IV provides another indication of a greater tendency at Level IV to be aware of the possible implications of intercourse for the overall relationship. Possible marriage as a subject of conversation was raised by only two (0.9 per cent) of the Level III females prior to intercourse. The subject was not raised by any males, nor jointly by any of the couples at this level. Prior to intercourse no Level IV male raised the subject of marriage, and it was raised by only two (1.7 per cent) of their female partners. However, six (5.2 per cent) Level IV subjects, compared to none at Level III, noted that the subject had been raised jointly prior to intercourse. Table 21 contains these data.

The proportion of Level IV males and couples raising possible marriage as a subject of conversation following intercourse shows a difference in the same direction when compared with Level III subjects. Thus, no Level III male raised the subject after intercourse, but two (1.7 per cent) Level IV males did. Following intercourse, the topic was raised jointly by five (2.3 per cent) Level III couples and eleven (9.5 per cent) Level IV couples. See Table 22.

At Level IV one of the facets of communication presents a new phenomenon. We have already come across gossip centering about sexual experience, e.g., the gossip which goes on within a group of boys who have gone to a prostitute. Boys also gossip with each other concerning girls who are possible pick-ups, or they will give each other information on how far a girl will go, and how easily she will yield. There is a different kind of gossip at Level IV.

Level IV intercourse involves two persons who have become acquainted with each other and who date in a community of mutual acquaintances. In such a community where everyone knows everyone else many deductions are drawn. Some are based on observed behavior, and others are wild guesses. Some are shrewdly-timed "trial balloons" designed to tease out the truth from a mass of speculation.

The following excerpt illustrates the development of this kind of gossip.

> 6 M and F1 had intercourse at a party at M's home during their senior year in high school. Information concerning their relationship got out. It evidently came from the boy who was in the room with his girl at the time. What he could not see because of the dark he was probably able to hear, and he drew his own con-

clusions. At any rate, the story got around and M heard a good bit about it. He was known for a time among the other fellows as "lover boy." He still hears about the episode occasionally from friends who razz him about it. He doesn't mind their razzing, however, because he feels it is "all in good fun."

M and F1 later broke up. F1 then returned to a boy to whom she had been engaged earlier and married him. The marriage occurred not more than a month ago. Her husband knows that F1 has had intercourse with M because F1 told him. Later a certain girl, a mutual acquaintance of both M and F1, and one of her friends, pulled "a stinkeroo." The girls felt "it was up to them to tell the guy" that M had had intercourse with F1 so they wrote F1's fiancée a long letter giving the details. "Great friends!" M has found by experiences that high school gossip about a sexual relationship is pretty choice and spreads rapidly.

Protective Measures and Assumption of Responsibility

Level IV subjects indicate a greater interest in providing protection for their partners, and in assuming the responsibilities which might fall upon them as a result of their sexual associations, than was apparent among Level III subjects. The elimination of premeditated striving for intercourse as one factor in classifying the liaison without doubt has had much to do with this development. Even so the level of protection in Level IV liaisons is low, and attitudes of irresponsibility are much more the rule than attitudes of responsibility.

Some evidence of emerging concern of Level IV subjects for their partners is indicated by the fact that a larger proportion of them joined with the girl in talking about possible pregnancy as an outcome of intercourse than did Level III subjects. Table 23, Appendix I, indicates that whereas two (0.9 per cent) Level III men did this prior to intercourse, six (5.2 per cent) Level IV subjects engaged in such a discussion. After intercourse (see Table 24) only nine (4.1 per cent) of the Level III subjects participated in joint discussions about possible pregnancy with their partners, compared to twenty-two (19.0 per cent) of the Level IV subjects.

71 Intercourse began one evening when M was at F1's home. They were alone in the house and sat down on the davenport. They just gradually worked up to it together. After intercourse took place they talked about what they would do in case of

pregnancy and both agreed that they would get married if this happened.

Actual planning for possible pregnancy resulted in the data shown in Table 27, Appendix I. These indicate that seven (3.2 per cent) of the Level III liaisons compared to fifteen (12.9 per cent) of the Level IV liaisons contained plans for coping with pregnancy. Contraceptives were reported as having been used *at some time* during the sexual association by one hundred forty-nine (67.1 per cent) of the Level III subjects, and by ninety-two (79.3 per cent) of the Level IV subjects. This does not necessarily indicate greater consideration or protection on the part of the males, since contraceptives were often used only part of the time.

Some Level IV subjects were quite frank in disclaiming any intention of being responsible in case of pregnancy or discovery.

"If she had got pregnant I'd have tried to get her to a doctor for some shots, but I wouldn't have married her."

"I said to her, 'You understand that if you get pregnant I won't be here.' "

One subject, on the other hand, provided an interesting variation on the "running from responsibility in case of threat" approach. Instead of running he met the situation head on.

30   After intercourse occurred, F1 was extremely upset because M had not withdrawn, and she felt intercourse had taken place at the most fertile time of her menstrual cycle. She was so frightened about the possibility of pregnancy that her parents discovered that intercourse had occurred between F1 and M soon after she got home that night.

M was working in a downtown store the following morning. He glanced out the window and saw F1 and her parents driving down the street. He figured that she had told them, and that they were hunting him. "I just took off my jacket, and went out on the street to wait for them to return. I didn't intend to run. I was responsible for getting both of us into it, and I knew that she was in trouble. The only thing to do was to take the consequences." M went to his car which was parked at hand, and was met there by F1's father. M agreed at once that intercourse had taken place; the upsetting thing was that her father accused M of raping her. This matter was not pushed, and F1 herself told M later that she had not tried to make it appear that a rape had occurred.

F1's father after some threatening talk said to M, "I'm going to tell your folks."

"I said, 'You're not, either. I'm telling them myself.' I got in my car, drove off ahead of them, went home, and told my parents. I was certainly thankful when they said that while they wouldn't excuse me, they would help me."

M's attitude of accepting responsibility for what had taken place seemed to calm the situation. After some more threats about court action everyone calmed down. In a few weeks the incident had about blown over.

Level IV girls received more protection than Level III girls as a result of less gossiping by Level IV males. Level IV males were apparently somewhat less committed to the use of intercourse as an evidence of masculine achievement. They, therefore, tended to talk less in a boasting way to other males about their female associates.

100   Several of M's boy friends who knew that he was going with F3 had the idea that he and F3 had had intercourse. They asked M several times whether this had occurred. "I always just laughed and said, 'Oh, no!' "

Such an attitude would help protect a girl by preventing exploitive males from becoming aware of her as a potential sexual partner.

Some of the subjects did talk to other males in an attempt to work out problems they faced. They sought contraceptive information, advice on what to expect in the relationship, or to relieve a sense of guilt. This kind of talking has a protective overtone in it.

One way in which girls at Level IV endanger their position is to push or hurry the relationship too rapidly. They sometimes try to interpret the relationship as more meaningful than it is, or they try to move it toward permanency faster than the boy is ready to move. This may also reflect a stronger emotional attachment on the part of the girl than the boy.

Under such circumstances the boy may break the relationship, or come to feel resentment and hostility. An excerpt given earlier in this chapter illustrated how one boy acted out his resentment and hostility by using intercourse as a kind of a retaliation. Others who may have already formed some attachment for the girls, and who regarded their Level IV partner with more esteem than was evidenced at lower levels but who felt themselves being pushed, tried to break the relationship as gracefully as possible, and with a minimum of hurt to all concerned.

> **96** Ever since intercourse occurred about six months ago M has been trying "to shake" F. In fact he was trying to do that even before intercourse occurred. However, she is persistent in calling him, planning dates, and otherwise working to keep the relationship going. M has never come right out and told F that he wants to drop the relationship, because he doesn't want to hurt F. He is now going with another girl, and though he has never told F about it directly, he is sure she knows it. He hopes the relationship may "die out" within a few weeks without his having to end it.

Another aspect of some Level IV liaisons which interferes with the effective use of protective measures is the suddenness with which intercourse sometimes occurs. It may come with such speed that there is little or no chance for communication, and the couple may lack contraceptive devices even though they might have used them under other circumstances. The following excerpt shows how this may happen.

> **91** M and F had been dating for about one month before intercourse began. The first intercourse occurred in M's car. He was not prepared for it so withdrawal was the only contraceptive used. M "thinks" that he took the lead, but F went along very readily and at times was even ahead of him.

The loss of respect for their partners which some males experience after having intercourse is one of the hazards which appears for the first time in Level IV liaisons. This was not a factor before, since at Level I, II, and III the males had little or no respect for their partners in the first place. It is, as one subject observed, "impossible to lose something you never had." Twenty-three Level IV subjects reported that they lost respect for their partners, generally after the girl began to show a great deal of interest in marriage, or became possessive.

The masculine "loss of respect" for the sexual partner, so often said to be the consequence of premarital intercourse, may be a defense reaction. It appears to work as follows. The girl presses for some sort of commitment, or for marriage. The boy begins to feel threatened; he feels ensnared, entangled, or as is often said, "trapped." He responds by "losing respect." This enables him to justify the termination of the relationship and to do it without feeling guilty.

Another possibility is that the "loss of respect" is a projection or a displacement of the boy's own feelings of guilt. The possibility of this occurring would seem to increase with affection. Evidence developed in the various chapters of this study indicates, at least, that boys are more likely to feel guilt after experiencing intercourse with girls for whom they have affection.[1]

Nearly half of the subjects reported that they felt their intercourse experience did not change their feelings toward their partners.

EVALUATION OF SUBJECTS

Statistically precise and conclusive data relative to the subjects' evaluation of their sexual experiences cannot be derived from the Level IV liaisons. A relatively precise tabulation was possible at Levels I-III. This may have been the consequence of associations which were always brief, and expectancies which were rather exactly fixed in terms of physical pleasure. The associations usually involved only one or two experiences in intercourse. Reactions, under these circumstances, were probably less subject to fluctuation and to the ambivalences which arise so readily after many experiences and numerous periods of prolonged interaction.

At Level IV evaluations had to be given in terms of relationships most of which had existed for several months, and some even longer, and for which the subjects had had non-sexual expectancies in the beginning. Add to these factors the problems arising from changes in the feelings of the partners toward each other, the pleasures and tensions arising from a number of close associations, the reactions of parents, and still other influencing conditions, and the difficulties of pinning evaluations down to a single rating become apparent.

One tangible evaluation is the fact that twenty-three out of

[1] Reiss (85, Ch. 4) feels that the "loss of respect" on the part of the male is a very strong indication that that individual adheres to the double standard of sexual behavior.

eighty-seven subjects reported that they lost respect for their partners following intercourse.

Certain excerpts will indicate the range rather than the frequency of evaluative reactions voiced by the subjects. The first two express, on the whole, favorable evaluations. Although one or two subjects stressed the physical satisfactions of intercourse, most of the positive evaluations were related to psychological aspects of the relationship, and to affectional feelings for the partner. Personal gains are also mentioned by the subjects, as in the next two excerpts. These gains are more in terms of building self-confidence and assurance, than in terms of masculine achievement or group status, as was the case at the preceding levels.

> 37 M enjoyed this relationship, and feels that it had some value to him in that he gained sexual experience. He felt comfortable in the situation. It was not "a one-night stand"; it had an element of security in it. M and F2 had a definite liking for each other and F2 made him feel at ease.

> 12 As M looks back on his sexual experience he feels it did him a lot of good. It helped him to get over his bashfulness. "At that time I was very much an introvert, but after having intercourse the shyness seemed sort of to leave me." It was also helpful in that he came to know what to expect sexually. It brought sex to his attention, and as a result he began to inform himself about it. It was a beneficial experience.

A few of the subjects expressed mixed feelings over their experience.

> 45 M enjoyed the physical aspects of sex. He thinks he and F3 continued to go together longer than they would have had they not been having intercourse. At the same time he was sometimes disgusted with himself "for fooling around in a sexual relationship."

Others voiced dissatisfaction over their experience for other reasons than a loss of respect, as is indicated in the following two statements:

> 11 The more M reflected the more he felt the relationship had been unwise. The next day after intercourse M and F talked briefly. M, who plans to enter the ministry, told F that he thought that it had been unwise, particularly for him. Such an episode, if

it became known, might wreck his career. F agreed, but also responded that she wished the rubber had broken.

M's distaste for both the experience and his partner mounted. He had one date with F after his return to college in the fall. At this time there was some petting, but no feeling of closeness. M recognized that there was now nothing in their relationship to hold it together.

> 31   M hates to talk about his sexual relationship with F1. "I am definitely ashamed of it." One of the things which has bothered M somewhat is that after he had stopped going with F1, a couple of other fellows who knew that he had been having intercourse with F1 started going with her and tried for sexual relations themselves. "They said that they got no place, however."

An occasional subject voiced an uneasiness resulting from the sentimental attachment that had developed between him and his partner.

> 110   M felt a little regretful right after he and F2 began intercourse. She was a real nice girl, and he was not sure that he should have carried the relationship as far as he had.

The self-evaluations at Level IV, as well as data on communication, motivations, protective attitudes, and the assumption of responsibility, indicate that with the development of some sentiment and potentially tender feelings between the partners, changes occur in sexual attitudes and behavior. Positive evaluations tend to be made more in terms of the total relationship and its meaning to the subjects, and much less in terms of sexual pleasure and functioning. Expressions of dissatisfaction tend also to be made more with reference to the total relationship, and less with reference to physical sex. The picture becomes more complex and the analysis more involved.

GENERAL OBSERVATIONS

From the analysis of the liaisons in this chapter certain observations may be made:

1. The readiness with which some youths make promises to marry, or count on unreliable contraceptive methods to pro-

tect them from the consequences of intercourse, suggests either extreme heedlessness, or an abysmal ignorance on their part of the actual "facts of life." The suggestion is frequently made that accessibility to and widespread knowledge about contraceptives would lead to promiscuous behavior. An analysis of these liaison histories leaves the writer far from convinced that this is a valid argument.

Certainly some of these subjects were ignorant enough of contraceptive practices so that, if ignorance was a deterrent, they should not have appeared as subjects in this study. No one knows, of course, how many more individuals might participate in casual intercourse if contraceptive knowledge was widely available. But neither are we able to say that widespread knowledge is associated with promiscuous and exploitive use of sex. There are simply no data or any experiments which give us the answer; the poorly-informed are with us, but not the well-informed. The writer would be in favor of experimenting with a comprehensive educational program that looked at sex in all its aspects and ramifications, including contraceptive measures, their meaning and effectiveness. If this were done some sound conclusions as to how it affects behavior could be established.

2. Comparisons drawn between Level III and Level IV liaisons indicated that the chief distinction between these two levels is that in Level IV we are for the first time observing the development of sentiment and tender feelings in an association which includes sex. These feelings are in almost all instances just beginning and are inadequately rooted. Nevertheless, certain possibilities are suggested by the data:

a. A longer period of time before the beginning of intercourse elapsed in Level IV histories than was the case in any of the previous liaisons levels. This seems natural enough since the previous levels have dealt with prostitutes and pick-ups. Does this, however, hold the suggestion that if intercourse occurs very shortly after the initiation of a relationship, no affectional attachment will develop? Does the relationship, if it is to develop any real emotional ties, need cultivation for a period after its inception, free from the complexities and complications of a sexual relationship?

b. When an emotional attachment is developed it changes the approach to the sexual relationship. If the descriptive and statistical data utilized in this chapter are to be trusted the changes may include more communication for the purposes of developing understanding, more mutuality in attempts to communicate, more willingness on the part of boys to consider measures which will protect the status of their partners, and more concern for breaking a relationship with a minimum of injury. There is less tendency for boys to tell other boys that the girl with whom they have had intercourse, can "be had." Perhaps there is more readiness to use contraceptive measures. There may be less use of intercourse (and consequently of the girl) in rivalry with other boys, and for the purpose of gaining masculine status. Evaluation of satisfaction and outcomes seem also to be changing in character.

An examination of how attitudes and patterns of sexual conduct vary in relationships containing emotional attachments as contrasted to those containing none should be very important in further research. The liaison histories at Levels V and VI will also throw further light on this question.

6

ANALYSIS OF LEVEL V

LIAISONS

This chapter contains data on Level V liaisons—characterized by "considerable emotional attachment" before intercourse took place. This is the first level at which an acknowledged emotional attachment prior to intercourse has been included in the definition used for classification; in the liaison histories reported at Levels I-III emotional attachments were of no significance. Budding feelings were found in some of the liaison histories at Level IV, but these were not made a prerequisite to classification at that level.

STATISTICAL DATA

Data for this chapter were supplied by seventy-seven men who reported ninety-two liaisons. Of this group forty-one were virgins until their Level V experience. The range in the number of Level V liaisons as reported by individual subjects is given in Table 7.

In comparison with preceding levels, one interesting feature in the above data should be noted. This is the small range in the total number of liaisons reported by an individual subject. Only two Level V subjects reported as many as three liaisons. The largest number of Level IV liaisons reported by any one subject was four. The largest number of Level III liaisons reported by one subject was 13.

Table 7

PARTICIPANTS AND LIAISONS—LEVEL V

Number of Subjects	Number of Liaisons Reported	Total Number of Liaisons
64	1	64
11	2	22
2	3	6
77		92

These data suggest that as the degree of emotional involvement intensifies a decreasing number of liaisons are experienced at that level by any one individual. There may be several reasons for this. One is that as emotional involvement is heightened there may be less interest in and less willingness to enter a sexual relationship. There is evidence to support this point of view.[1]

A second reason for the fewer liaisons entered at Level V is that the greater the degree of emotional involvement the longer it takes for a sexual relationship to develop. An individual can obtain many Level I, II, III or even IV liaisons while developing one liaison at Level V or VI.[2]

DESCRIPTIVE DATA

Motivations

The circumstances surrounding the initiation of sexual liaisons at Level V suggest a somewhat different motivational situation than

---

[1] Evidence to support the idea that at levels of greater emotional involvement boys tend to be less aggressive in their quest for intercourse is found in Bell and Blumberg (8) and Ehrmann (27).

[2] A study using a random sample of individuals for the purpose of finding the extent to which sexual activities were confined to different levels, and the proportions of the entire number of liaisons falling into the different levels, would be a very useful study.

at the earlier levels. Subjects evidence concern for the overall relationship, and more interest in the personality of the partner. The physical sex act seems noticeably less important as an end in itself than was the case in preceding levels. Aggressive and open seeking after sexual experience is much less obvious.

In a certain sense aggressive striving is not necessary at this level. Accepted social arrangements for dating couples in our culture permit them much freedom in planning their own programs and, if they wish it, much opportunity to be alone. This is reflected in the liaison histories which indicated that the large majority of the Level V liaisons began after considerable petting, love-making, and sexual stimulation had taken place. In relating these experiences the subjects spoke of their being alone with their sexual partners in the subjects' or the girls' homes, at the beach, on picnics, or in an auto. As a result couples were able to move into sexual liaisons more leisurely, and with less obvious effort than was the case at the earlier levels.

An illustration showing how intercourse develops from much unsupervised activity and a great deal of intimacy follows.

> **34** Fl was M's first "real date." She lived in the same block with M. They dated between one and one-half to two years and M saw Fl practically every day, sometimes two or three times a day. They were quite compatible, and very happy in each other's company. M thinks the reason they got into intercourse was that they saw each other so much and were so close that it became almost inevitable. Necking, petting and physical lovemaking became more and more intense for a period of six to eight months prior to intercourse.

Excerpts from various Level V histories mention the sexual excitement and allure which builds up after prolonged petting and repeated stimulation. Such expressions as "we just got carried away"—"neither of us wanted to stop"—"we hadn't intended to go ahead," indicate that prolonged physical stimulation puts a heavy strain on rational controls.

In many instances a couple's movement into intercourse was a matter of progression. One petting experience after another would occur. After each instance the two found themselves a little nearer intercourse than they were before. There may have been urging and some pressure on the part of one of the partners, as in the first two excerpts, or the couple may have moved along as partners, as in the third excerpt.

77 During their second year of dating M began to desire sexual experience, but F1 resisted suggestions that they go ahead. She had been taught the "usual conventional ideas" about intercourse, e.g., she felt intercourse was something to be reserved for marriage; if anything went wrong the girl would be blamed more than the boy. As M continued to urge intercourse he could see that F1 began to consider the possibility. He argued that if F1 really loved him willingness to have intercourse would be proof of it. Finally M told F1 that if she would not consent to intercourse he intended to break off their relationship. This he did, and for a period of several weeks they did not go together at all. Then F1 saw M at school, and told him she was willing to resume the relationship on the condition specified by M, namely that they have intercourse.

With this understanding they resumed dating and about two weeks later they had their first experience in intercourse. They did not go ahead immediately because "I didn't want her to think that was all I was going with her for."

24 So far as intercourse was concerned M and F talked more and more about the possibility. M thought they should have no sexual relations before marriage. F seemed to feel that "nothing would be lost if we did, feeling as we did about each other." She was "definitely more ready for the relationship than I was." She did vacillate somewhat in her attitude toward it. Sometimes she would be for intercourse, at other times she would not be.

M feels that F probably wanted intercourse for the physical pleasure, and because, to her, it was an expression of being wanted and loved. She was in need of somebody to support and help her, for her life had turned out quite badly.

5 M and F1 began dating when he was sixteen, and she was fourteen. They had a strong feeling for each other from the first. So far as sex was concerned, they were innocent and "strictly on the purity side. Oh, that doesn't mean that I didn't think of it, naturally, nor that I was unwilling to try, but so far as my girl was concerned, I was determined not to press it."

Intercourse occurred after five or six months of dating. During that time things were gradually building up. M is sure that neither of them were trying for intercourse. "I know I wasn't. It was

a matter of expressing our feelings for each other through petting.
We never regressed. As each advance (in intimacy) rather lost
its thrill and became old, we moved on." The evening they began
intercourse "it was touched off" by M's touching F1's genitals and
her reciprocation. "We were just carried away."

Case history #5 suggests that this couple got into intercourse
as a part of the lovemaking growing out of their affectional attachment. "It was a matter of expressing our feelings for each
other . . ." About one-fourth of all Level V subjects made similar statements. Evidently the emotional attachments of Level V
couples contribute materially to their sexual involvement. Some
of the subjects recognized that sexual curiosity and a desire for
sensory pleasure were tied in with their emotional feelings. For
example, one subject said, "I loved her and wanted intercourse on
that account, but I found out what intercourse was like in the
process. I had always wondered about that."

Curiosity and desire for physical satisfaction as motivations still
show through the mantle of affection which surrounds the Level V
liaisons. A good many of the subjects mentioned these as motivations for themselves, and about one out of three indicated that
they thought this was a motive for girl friends as well.

One can see quite clearly from certain of the case histories that,
for some, movement into intercourse is premeditated, and the effort is persistent. In these cases desire for physical satisfaction is
probably a strong factor.

4 About a full year of dating went by before intercourse occurred. When it did M was seventeen and F1 was sixteen. They
moved into intercourse through necking and petting. M was not
sure they would have intercourse until it occurred, but as soon
as petting began he knew he wanted it. They went further and
further until one evening M was able to fondle F1's genitals. The
next evening he did this again, and this time broke the hymen
with his fingers. M was consciously trying to get intercourse, and
to stretch the hymen. He wanted to prepare F1 so intercourse
would not be painful.

Sometimes motivation, as the subject saw it, was quite complex.
In the following excerpt M was twenty-four, and sexually inexperienced. He had grown up in a family in which he had received
a strong indoctrination against premarital intercourse.

3 M and F1 had been dating for about a year before intercourse occurred. M liked F1 very much, and was strongly considering marriage. During the time they were dating F1 indicated her willingness to have intercourse, but M kept "stalling it off." Even now he isn't able to figure exactly why he went ahead. Probably there were several motives. One was that he had become angry at the continual razzing he was getting from the men where he worked, because of his sexual inexperience. His resistance to intercourse had been worn down, or eroded, by the comments on his virginity which he had received at various times.

Probably a more important motive was that he was quite upset emotionally over his relationship with F1. He was wanting her to settle down, but was unable to get any kind of an understanding with her. Probably his reason for initiating intercourse was that it afforded a revenge. For one thing, he used no contraceptive method. "I was quite ready to nail her down with a pregnancy if I could. I know that it was not a rational attitude or a logical answer to our problem, but I just felt that way." Pregnancy would have made her "cut out the running around" which was disturbing M. They had intercourse about six times over a period of three or four months. On all occasions M used no contraceptive. He was fully conscious of the possibility of producing a pregnancy. "I didn't give a damn."

The concentration upon achieving marriage as a probable feminine objective was mentioned by many of the subjects. This motive was attributed to over one-third of their partners by Level V subjects, but to only about one in ten of the subjects themselves. As the subjects saw the situation, many a girl saw in the development of a given relationship the possibility of marriage. These girls sought, often by methods poorly chosen, to achieve their purpose, to bring the relationship to the point of definite commitment, or even marriage.

94 M and F3 had talked about marriage a bit, a short time before they had intercourse. After intercourse the talk, particularly on F3's part, became more and more urgent. M agreed to some of it in a half-hearted way. He was really flabbergasted, however, when after he gave F3 an identification bracelet she had it engraved with the initials of her first name and his last name. "I thought, My God, what's got into her!" When M asked, she agreed that she had had it done because she expected to marry him. M protested that there had been no agreement, and she re-

plied that she had told all her girl friends that they were to be married. The relationship broke soon after.

17 M and F4 did not begin intercourse until they had been "going steady" for some time. M thinks that F4 thought more of him than he did of her. At any rate she was very eager to have him as a boy friend, and he thinks she was very desirous of getting married.

M thinks F4 may have agreed to intercourse because she feared if she did not he would leave her. M was aware of this concern, and now and then acted out or said something to heighten it. For example he used "that old gag about 'not buying a pair of shoes until you've tried them on.'"

18 M thinks F2 might have been thinking of marriage, though she never came out and said so openly. "She was very coy about it." However, after their second experience in intercourse she made references to marriage, and spoke of different friends who were getting married. M thinks "she made some assumptions" in which "I did not encourage her."

Several subjects felt that when friendship had begun to weaken the girls made intercourse more accessible than before, probably hoping to save the relationship.

94 F2 seemed to sense that M was drifting away and made special efforts to hold him. She was willing for intercourse, even more than before, and she also took an avid interest in M's hobby of hot rods.

An indication that sexual intercourse was being used to compensate for some personal difficulty or disturbance was noted in only three instances. Even in these instances, the evidence is conflicting. Certainly the indications of personal maladjustment were much less common at Level V than at Level II where sex appeared quite often to have been used as a compensation for some emotional difficulty or instability. Level II case histories were cited in which many of the subjects reported abject submissiveness and much self-debasement on the part of their partners. Some of the Level II subjects themselves appeared quite ruthless in their advantage-taking. Logically, there should be less of this at Level V, for the establishment of a relationship with any depth can hardly occur except when the persons involved are responsive to one another and, in our culture, meet each other somewhat on the level of equality. (If the reader wishes to refresh his memory concerning the points under discussion, so far as it relates to Level II liaisons, he should return to pages 63-70.)

The three instances noted at Level V did not involve self-debasement, marked submissiveness, or openly acknowledged advantage-taking as noted at Level II. In the first instance a boy, who gave a total of eleven liaison histories, became very deeply involved both sexually and emotionally with several of his dating partners. His sexual activities seemed related to a desire to prove himself, and find some security in his relationships. His case history contains the following statement:

> **47** M, age nineteen, came from an unhappy home. He had difficulty in getting along with his mother, and unhappy relationships with other children as he was growing up. He was scrawny, and had a bout with infantile paralysis which left him in poor physical condition. He never seemed able to do the things other kids did. He has always felt it necessary to prove his capacity. He is very proud, for example, of the fact that while smaller than average and not well co-ordinated, he had made the football team in high school. He did this through sheer grit and determination. At college he is also out for football, though "a lot of my friends think I'm through." M seemed defiant as he said this. He apparently has a deep sense of inferiority to combat.

The second illustration involves the subject in case history #52. This subject has been referred to several times previously. He gave a history of twenty-one liaisons distributed as follows: Level II, five; Level III, thirteen; Level IV, two; Level V, one. The Level V liaison had been broken at the time of the interview. Despite M's statement that this relationship involved genuine affection it appeared to the interviewer to be shallow, and meaningful to M mainly in terms of sex. Thus,

> **52** M found F3 very reluctant to enter intercourse. This probably stemmed from the fact that she was a virgin. When she finally agreed, M thinks that she did so in order to keep him happy and interested. He said to her on a number of occasions that he could get intercourse elsewhere, and that the only reason that he continued going with her rather than someone else was because he liked her. The implication was that unless she consented to intercourse she could look elsewhere for a boy friend. When she

finally agreed they had only two experiences at M's home. F3 cried a little after they were through. It was clear that she did not enjoy it, and M felt rather badly to have pushed the relationship on her. M is "not sure" whether intercourse caused them to break up, but it probably had some effect. He broke the relationship. He told her he had decided that to have intercourse was just hurting her, and therefore he felt it would be better for them to break, rather than to continue with sexual relations. He knows this hurt F3.

M gave information on his family background which left the impression that his parents had never paid much attention to his activities, or provided him any supervision. He seemed to approve of this very highly. Throughout the history, which covered a period of five years, the parents apparently never acted in any other than in a completely "hands off" manner. M spoke of week-end or all-night absences from home with no indication of parental concern, and in general indicated that his parents made no attempt to set limits, or provide direction. Quoting from the liaison history:

> 52 M's relationships with his family have been very good and quite close. He has a father, an older half-sister, a stepmother, a stepsister, and two full sisters younger than he is. He feels that one of the good things about the relationship is that they have treated him "like an adult." They have not tried to supervise or interfere with his affairs. The only thing they have ever made a point of is that he shouldn't drive while drunk. If he does come home drunk, nothing in particular is said about it. He doesn't know whether they know of his sexual experiences, but they do know that he stays out all night sometimes, and they must have a pretty good idea of what is going on.

The third illustration involved the oldest subject in the study.

> 24 M was twenty-eight years old, and had had sexual relations with one partner only. This occurred when he was twenty-six and she was twenty-five. The relationship has since broken. So far as M knows F1 was a divorcée with children. He is uncertain for she changed her story as they went along in the relationship. M thought a great deal of F1 at the time they began intercourse. Actually their relationship was quite a turbulent affair involving quarreling, some moodiness on the part of both, and apparent attempts to hurt each other's feelings. The relationship which lasted

for about eight months, broke up about three months after intercourse began.

Only two instances of intoxication at the time intercourse began were mentioned by Level V subjects.

These data can do nothing more than suggest possibilities. They do suggest that sexual behavior at Level V is less motivated by unconscious needs or marked emotional disturbances than was the case at Levels I-III. Such motivations, when present, may be of a different nature. Knowledge concerning the kinds of relationships and personalities most commonly found at the various levels would be most helpful in understanding the behavior and problems involved in premarital intercourse.

Communication

With an increase in the amount of affectional involvement in a sexual liaison the nature of sexual communication might be expected to change. Evidence can be presented to indicate that a change does occur. The statistical data in Appendix I permit a general, overall comparison of Level IV and Level V communication.[3] When this comparison is made several interesting facts are noted:

1. There is a considerable increase at Level V in the amount of communication prior to intercourse. This is especially noticeable when communication of an understanding nature is being considered.

2. There is a marked increase in communication for understanding following intercourse at Level V.

3. The amount of argumentative-persuasive communication shows a marked decline at Level V as compared with Level IV.

4. Efforts at mutual communication are more common at Level V than Level IV.

All these points indicate a trend in the direction of freedom and more thoroughness and mutuality in communication at Level V than was the case at Level IV.

Despite these trends there are still handicaps to effective communication. Some of these are suggested by details in the case

---

[3] Discussion of and tables and figures on communication are found on pages 257-84, Appendix.

histories. Thus, long-established barriers to free discussion may persist despite emotional attachments or mutual participation in physical intimacies. They are just too strong to be broken. The following three case histories illustrate this circumstance:

> 94 There was no talking about the possibility of intercourse. They just went ahead after about one and one-half hours. After they were through they went into the kitchen and got something to eat; they still made no verbal reference to intercourse. "It's funny, but I just can't talk to girls on matters like that."

> 15 M and F were quite free in all aspects of their sexual relationship. They engaged in sex play freely and experimented with different positions and procedures in intercourse. They were never able, however, to discuss their relationship with any degree of freedom.

> 60 M and F engaged in no discussion whatever before intercourse. After their first experience there was a little discussion of what had occurred "in subdued tones, but neither of us was able to come right out and say how we felt about it." They did get so they could discuss the safe period freely, and time their intercourse so as to observe it.

Sometimes a discussion will occur which, later developments show, are actually superficial and relatively meaningless. This probably results from an inability to voice real feelings on a subject so touchy as sex.

> 53 After their first experience in intercourse M and F discussed their feelings and how their behavior violated their teachings. This did not seem to stop their desire for intercourse and they engaged in it four or five more times. After the last experience they "really talked through" what intercourse was doing to them. "We really got down to talking." The result was a decision to drop intercourse.

The phrase "effective communication" has been used. Analysis of the communicative processes in Level V liaisons raises a question as to what constitutes "effective communication." Under what circumstances does it occur? Many of the subjects said that they had engaged in "much" communication either before or after intercourse, or that the purpose of their communication was to develop understanding. Yet in a number of such situations the couples were unable to reach or maintain satisfying decisions, their relationship moved along unsatisfactorily, or broke with one or both feeling distressed over the outcome. What caused these results? What interfered with effective communication?

Some efforts at communication took place at times when passions were so high that no effective discussion was possible. Attempts at communication under such circumstances were found by several subjects to be quite ineffective.

> 15 M and F have been involved in intercourse for several months, but they have had no effective discussion of their relationship. About the only time they have tried to talk is "when we are all heated up," and as a result their discussions "haven't amounted to much."

Sometimes frankness and honesty in communication is avoided because it threatens the objective of obtaining or maintaining intercourse. This point was made by several subjects.

> 8 M recognized that various issues centering about their involvement in intercourse had not been cleared up. However, M felt "it was better not to talk too much," or the opportunity for intercourse might be lost entirely.

> 62 "There was never any talk about what might be done in case of possible pregnancy. We just avoided that. It was too touchy."

Frequently, communication seems ineffective because the decisions reached are later breached. Apparently, this is often the result of one or both of the partners' agreeing to something about which they are not actually convinced. A number of subjects mentioned this circumstance.

> 26 M and F had been involved in necking and petting for four or five months before they had intercourse. They knew they were headed toward intercourse, so they talked about it in detail. They agreed that they didn't want to go ahead, but M knows that their real desires (at least his) never coincided with that decision. So finally, after several more conversations, they agreed to have intercourse.

> 42 F3 "liked to neck," and she and M kept going further and further until they were involved in intercourse "whether we had wanted to be or not." There had been a little talking to the effect

that "we shouldn't get involved in intercourse." Despite this agreement they found themselves still wanting intercourse. M kept "kinda pushing it," and F3 "just let me go ahead."

A number of the subjects mentioned situations in which their attempts to communicate got them nowhere. As one subject put it "we just talked in circles. We never really got anywhere." This indecisive, milling-around experience arose most frequently when the issue was whether premarital intercourse was "right or wrong." The difficulty at this point seemed to be that there were varying or vague ideas of "right and wrong" conduct. Some couples had no meaningful criterion for making a choice. Several subjects spoke of friends who "had to get married, and they seem as happy as can be." Another said, "We knew we were supposed to be against it (premarital intercourse), but we couldn't see exactly why—especially since we loved each other." Still another one said, "We did a lot of half-hearted talking about *not* doing it, but none at all in which we recognized our desire to go ahead."

The following excerpt relates an experience of indecisive communication. It shows how far some couples go sexually while being unable to discuss or to decide upon some very important aspects of their total relationship.

8 M and F3 talked on a number of occasions about the possibility of intercourse, but their conclusion about it was always indecisive. After the first experience there was no further discussion though M recognized that the issues had not been cleared up. However, after a time and several more experiences, M and F3 did talk and decide to put some limits on themselves. Their limits were that they didn't want intercourse too often, and particularly they wanted to avoid pregnancy. M has never asked F3 if she has felt guilty about the experience although at times he thinks that she has been tense and worried, probably because of the possibility of pregnancy. Soon after intercourse began they agreed to marry in case of pregnancy. They also talked about the possibility of marriage although they have not reached a definite decision. There has been some talk about the possibility of each of them dating other persons.

Sometimes the whole effort becomes so frustrating and so obviously futile that the couple give up the effort entirely.

17 M and F1 made no effort prior to intercourse to understand how each felt about the possibility of entering a sexual relation-

ship. After they began intercourse, however, "we talked it all over at length several times." On each of these occasions they decided "absolutely to stop it." However, their resolutions never held up, so now they "have forgotten it," and accept intercourse as a part of their relationship.

One subject discussed his experience in a situation in which he and his girl friend had striven futilely to reach a decision in regard to their own sexual standards. He suggested four reasons why the two of them "never really got anything decided":

1. "We didn't have enough background to know what we were talking about. We had never studied sex and we had no knowledge to go on."
2. "We knew too little about anyone else's experiences to get any help in that direction. We were just working in the dark."
3. "Our only standard for deciding right and wrong was what we had been told were accepted social beliefs. But that didn't help when we knew there were really different beliefs, and that they contradicted each other."
4. "In spite of the fact that we were pretty free in our discussions, sometimes my girl friend found it difficult to talk. I had to carry the ball most of the times. This made it one-sided."

One suspects also this subject might have added that effective communication about such matters as sex must be approached from many sides, and requires repeated conversations. A couple will ordinarily need to talk through issues again and again, before they arrive at a consensus which is really secure, and fully understood by both.

According to many subjects, effective communication has several benefits when it occurs. It may help them cope with disturbing feelings, as in the following excerpt, or to arrive at decisions which will stand, as in the second excerpt.

> 30 M and F2 got into intercourse without discussing the possibility. After two experiences they were both feeling so guilty that they had to get their feelings out. Once they broke the barrier they found that they could talk quite freely. As a result their situation has improved greatly. They have been able to handle their guilt feelings quite well, and M finds that openness and freedom in talking make it much easier for him to manage his

own feelings. If the two of them get aroused now, they recognize frankly how they are feeling, and decide whether they wish to have intercourse. There is some talk of marriage but they are not engaged, and M isn't sure they will be.

163 M became involved in intercourse without any discussion of the possibility. Intercourse occurred about seven or eight times over a period of about two months. During this time M and F3 got into prolonged discussions about sex as a part of their relationship, and decided that it would be a good thing for them to drop intercourse. This they did about six months ago. That way they would not be so deeply involved—not so closely tied to each other while they still aren't sure whether they want to be.

At this level, as at other levels, there were a number of instances of exclusively non-verbal communication, and also instances in which non-verbal communication contradicted and superseded verbal communication.

34 After M and F1 got to her home, she went to her room and dressed in her pajamas. "I knew then that she was willing to go ahead." They went to the kitchen, got something to eat, then sat on the davenport where they began petting. There was no talking or discussion, nor any urging one way or another. "I think you could say it was mutual."

77 F "kept saying that she didn't want intercourse but she certainly didn't resist me in any way. She let me move as fast as I wanted to. In fact, by the way she acted I think she was as desirous of intercourse as I was."

74 Intercourse occurred one evening after M and F9 had been visiting at her home. On the way back they parked and started petting. Sexual desire mounted sharply, and M partly undressed F9. He tried to get her girdle off, but could not. This calmed him down a bit, and he said to her, "If this is going to happen, you will have to be a party to it, too." At this point M got out of the car and went for a walk, debating with himself as to what he ought to do. When he came back "she had her girdle off," so they had intercourse.

The point in petting at which the girl is willing to touch or fondle the male genitals is an important non-verbal cue. It suggests to most boys that intercourse is not far away. Several subjects mentioned this as being the particular circumstance which caused them to decide that intercourse was possible.

Illustrations have already been given in this chapter of argumentative-persuasive communication. Several subjects spoke of threatening that they would find another dating partner if intercourse was not forthcoming. This occurred even though the subjects had expressed affection for their partner.

Sometimes the communication took the form of urging the girl to go ahead by offering reassurances that the subject "knows what to do" and that "nothing would happen," as in the following excerpt:

> **51** M found F2 reluctant to begin intercourse. "She didn't want to go through with it, but I urged her to. I told her that it would be all right, and that nothing would happen. I knew how to take care of things." M assured F2 that he loved her (she seemed to fear that intercourse would make a difference in his affection for her). "She did it because I wanted her to." After they were through intercourse F had "tears in her eyes." M thinks this was because she was both angry and frightened.

Protective Measures and Assumption of Responsibility

More evidence of concern for protective measures and of a willingness to assume responsibility are found among Level V subjects than has been found at any previous level. This doubtlessly grows out of the affection existing between partners in the Level V liaisons. Even so, there are still marked gaps when what was done is compared with what could be done.

References to the use of contraceptive methods are found in at least half of the liaisons at this level, but their use is accompanied by a good many hazards which increase the chances of pregnancy. Three methods, withdrawal, condoms, or observance of the safe period, were used in almost all instances. These methods were far from being consistently applied. The subjects often indicated that in the beginning they made use of some contraceptive device in all instances of intercourse, but ended by admitting that "there were a few times when I didn't."

Irregularity and carelessness in the application of contraceptives sometimes gets couples into difficulty. The following excerpt relates such a situation.

77 For the first year, M was quite careful to use a condum as a contraceptive measure. Then he and F1 began having intercourse without a rubber, but observed the safe period. They sought to confine their intercourse to times just before and just after the menstrual period. M had obtained his knowledge about the safe period from reading he had done in some of his father's books. Gradually M and F1 became more and more lax in their contraceptive measures. They began to encroach more and more upon the mid-menstrual cycle days which they had first decided to avoid. Late during the second year F1 became pregnant.

The uncertain, erratic use of contraceptives occurring in some of the liaisons is illustrated in the two following excerpts:

5 M tried a rubber a few times, but it "diminished the sensation so much," and one broke, "so I had no trust in them." Their main reliance was on withdrawal, and observation of the safe period. M would always withdraw except for "just a few days before or after menstruation." They avoided intercourse except during the presumed safe period.

F's menstrual periods have always been irregular so at first they were always worried about pregnancy. However, "I finally just got so I didn't worry. If it occurred, outside of the shock it would have been to our families, we were ready to let it happen. I would have married her at once."

38 The first intercourse occurred in M's car and no contraceptive method whatsoever was used. M and F had intercourse two or three times a week over a period of more than two years. A couple of times they carried on intercourse throughout the entire menstrual month using no contraceptives of any sort. On a few occasions M used condoms secured from a friend. "I guess you might say we lucked out. As I look back we were pretty lucky not to get a baby. It makes you wonder if one of us might have been sterile."

Inconsistency in the use of contraceptives is not the only hazard in these liaisons. Lack of knowledge is another. Thus, in one interview a subject said he had been observing the "safe period" but revealed that he understood the safe period to be midway between menstrual periods. Another said that he "always used rubbers except during the safe period when it was *perfectly safe* not to." Other subjects indicated that their contraceptive knowledge was hazy, and that such knowledge as they did have was obtained from other boys.

Sometimes, as several of the subjects observed, nature seemed to provide the protection. Either the couple "lucks out" while engaging in normal sexual activities, or they may be "just plain sterile." Thus, two Level V subjects related long and extensive histories of intercourse without pregnancies. One subject (#4), age twenty-two started dating his fiancée when he was sixteen and she was fifteen. They began intercourse a little over a year later and continued it regularly thereafter up to the time of the interview. The other subject (#58) reported a history of regular intercourse over a period of fifteen months. They had had intercourse "over two hundred times." Their reliance had been on condums, observation of the safe period, and withdrawal.

One subject mentioned his amazement at the lack of knowledge about sex, which he found in his girl friend, and her implicit faith in his knowledge about what was safe and unsafe in contraceptive practices. "She never asks any questions, but relies on me and what I tell her. She never seems to have any doubts."

The contraceptives themselves were often obtained from or through boy friends. Some of the subjects were so young at the time they were engaging in intercourse that they did not have the courage or poise needed to purchase the contraceptives themselves. One subject spoke of having bought two packages of condums which he later gave to friends "who needed them, and wanted to borrow them from me."

A third hazard is that the contraceptives were often applied in circumstances that would increase the chances of their being ineffective. A hurried application of a condum in the confines of a car seat, by relatively inexperienced persons, means that the chances of failure are much increased.

Although some subjects made no plans as to what would be done in case of pregnancy, many more expressed their intention of marrying their girl friends in case of pregnancy. Such comments as these were made repeatedly by Level V subjects:

> "We agreed in case of pregnancy we would get married right away."

> "I'd have married her just like that."

"I'd have married her if she had got pregnant. That's the way it is done in our community."

"No question about it, we will get married."

Others planned for marriage reluctantly, e.g., "Oh, I suppose I'd have married her. There wouldn't have been anything else to do." One boy found himself getting cold feet so far as marriage was concerned so he changed his plans to an abortion, but without conferring with his girl friend.

Sometimes the resolution to marry grew proportionately feebler the longer the relationship continued. Several subjects suggested that although they had considered marriage seriously at first they grew less and less sure of this decision as they went along. "I suppose I'd still have married her, but it would have been quite reluctantly." Many times these changes in feelings were not mentioned by the subjects to their girl friends.

Two subjects mentioned the use of masturbatory exchange[4] as a method for obtaining sexual gratification, and at the same time avoiding the risks of pregnancy. "You can get into a whole lot less trouble that way."

The protection provided the girl by the boy's refusal to talk with other boys about their sexual relationship was markedly more evident at this level than at earlier levels. Passing information along to other boys so they might have intercourse with the same girl was wholly absent. A number of subjects said specifically that they told no one of their sexual relationship with their girl friend. If it was told, the most likely circumstance was to do so quite some time after the relationship had been terminated. On other occasions two boys who were aware that each was engaged in similar relationships, might exchange information in hopes of understanding their situation better.

Several subjects related instances in which they had tried to keep knowledge of their sexual relationship from close friends or other persons.

66 . . . No one ever knew M and F were having intercourse, though a number of M's friends thought they were. "You know how they talk about any couple that is going steady." M did not make any point out of their talk one way or the other. A friend

---

[4] Comfort (21) supports this as a method of premarital sexual expression.

who bought him contraceptives occasionally knew, of course, he was having intercourse somewhere, but "I would tell him that I was finding pick-ups and taking them out, or something of that sort."

During this time M and F had a talk with one of their high school teachers about their dating relationship, but no mention was made of the fact that they were having intercourse. "We were afraid that he might tell some of the other teachers. You know how teachers talk back and forth in a small school."

In another instance, one of the subjects refrained from initiating intercourse at a time when he felt it might have been disadvantageous to his girl friend.

62 M and F3 had been attending a party and both had been drinking. Actually, F3 was considerably under the influence of liquor. During the evening, M and F3 went out to a secluded place on the lawn, sat down together, and began petting. After a while M realized intercourse was possible. F3 made no resistance. In fact, she moved into a position that made intercourse very possible. M recognized, however, that she was very drunk, and he thought it was better to avoid intercourse. Accordingly, he took her back into the house. Later they talked about their experience quite openly, and came to the decision that it would be all right for them to have intercourse, since both of them were agreeable.

Not all subjects were as gallant as those in the two excerpts above. Another subject (#94), who was very carefree himself (and quite double-standardish), commented that his girl friend did not think it wrong for them to be having intercourse. "Her sex education fell down very badly."

Another hazard in these relationships was the numerous one-sided emotional attachments which were reported. Usually these unequal attachments involved more girls who became attached to their boy friends than vice versa. Although this picture of one-sided attachment was obtained from masculine reporting, actual experience in working with young couples prior to marriage indicates that subjects were reporting accurately. The frequency with which one-sided emotional relationships develop raises the question as to why this should occur. This issue will be examined briefly in the section General Observations.

Still another complicating factor potentially affects the outcome of youthful associations involving sexual intercourse. This is the extent to which many teen-age youths are still dependent upon their parents, and the decisions their parents make. They are not the free agents, particularly in a time of crisis, they believe themselves to be. Several excerpts illustrating this point follow.

In the first, M, who was sixteen at the time of the sexual association being described, misjudged his feelings, and would almost certainly have found a pregnancy more difficult to cope with than he anticipated.

> 94 At first M thought "this was true love" and that intercourse "sort of bound us together." M and F2 talked some about what they would do if she became pregnant, and they agreed that she would go to a doctor to get some shots. Toward the end of the one and one-half months during which they had intercourse M began to drift away from F2. He just "sort of lost interest in her."

In the next case history M certainly misjudged his capacity to stand up against the will of his parents. His intention to have the premarital pregnancy involving him and his girl friend culminate in marriage was short-lived after his father took control of the situation.

> 77 After M found that F1 was pregnant they decided that they would be married at once. Both were nineteen years old at the time. M went home, told his parents, and said that he and F1 were planning marriage. This news turned out to be highly objectionable to M's father. At the same time F1 told her mother that she was pregnant and obtained her consent to marriage.
>
> The two families were in different social classes. M's father was quite a well-to-do businessman, and F1's mother was a single woman who was supporting her daughter and herself by her own efforts. M's father went to see F1's mother to insist upon an abortion. The mother consented, though F1 resisted this change in plans as long as she could. In the end, however, the abortion plan was followed and M's father stood the expense.

Some of the experiences couples have in carrying forward actual liaisons are quite nerve-wracking and tension-arousing, if we are to believe the data supplied by the subjects. The following excerpt is a case in point.

> 55 M and F had intercourse the first time in M's car. No contraceptive method was used, not even withdrawal. Both M and F

were scared over what had happened. Neither of them felt right about it. They continued, however, and had a total of twelve to fifteen experiences in intercourse before they stopped. During that time they had been frightened a couple of times for fear that F was pregnant. The last time M was very frightened. "I could picture myself leaving home with the seventy dollars I had saved, or having to go to my parents with the problem. They wouldn't have gone for that." So far as precautions were concerned, they always watched the safe period, though M never used rubbers or withdrew.

They decided to cease intercourse because of their fear of pregnancy, and because neither believed it to be right. They never were free or easy in their sexual relationship.

Many of the promises to marry, so common among the subjects involved in these liaisons, seemingly represent immature decisions. Some of the promises are made as a response to the pressures they feel to be grown up, and to the desire to gain the sexual experiences which they associate with maturity. Youths who are sixteen, seventeen, or eighteen, still dependent upon their parents, without job experience, and who have yet to complete their education, are in a difficult situation so far as marrying and supporting a family is concerned, even though their motives are honest and relationship-centered. Some who have never held a job and lack effective vocational competencies are involved in sexual situations which could very suddenly result in their having to assume the roles of husband and father if their promise to marry were to be fulfilled. That such marriages are hazardous is indicated in divorce statistics which show a higher rate of marital breakup for teen-age marriages.

Several subjects recognized that in becoming sexually involved they had got into more complexities than they had bargained for.

"We were too immature. We just got in over our heads."

As M looks at it now he "knows that we were both just too immature" (to be involved in intercourse).

Immaturity and lack of readiness were used by one individual to stave off intercourse. The following excerpt was given by a subject who had had previous sexual experience. At the time of the interview he was dating a girl of whom he was quite fond, but with whom he had not had intercourse.

15 M and F enjoy each other and have been contemplating marriage. In fact, this is somewhat of an issue between them right now. M feels he is not ready for marriage but his girl is taking it for granted they will get married after she graduates from high school in a few months. M has pointed out possible financial and housing problems, and what they would be up against if they had a pregnancy soon after marriage. "That slowed her up for about three months, but lately she has started to put the pressure on again." Intercourse has been a possibility for a long time, and as M sees it, the possibility has been encouraged by F. He, however, is not particularly-interested.

EVALUATION OF SUBJECTS

As at the previous levels, Level V subjects were asked to express their feelings toward and their attitudes of satisfaction-dissatisfaction concerning their sexual experiences. As at Level IV the replies tend to be diffuse, and it seemed impossible to categorize them in a meaningful way. Certain features stood out, however.

Only a small proportion of the seventy-seven subjects expressed unalloyed satisfaction or dissatisfaction with their experiences. Most of them had both positive and negative comments to make; they had found both favorable and unfavorable features in their relationship. An example of such a mixed evaluation follows:

47 M has no real regrets about having had intercourse with F1. He thinks they would have been better off if they hadn't, but at least they learned they were suited to each other. Intercourse has been pleasurable, and M thinks it has brought them closer together. They have especially enjoyed the physical intimacy. After they started having intercourse there were a number of little quarrels and arguments between them—not about sex, but other little things. M blamed their arguing on sex. That is all over with now, and they are getting along fine. M thinks that F1 has no regrets, and would do it all over again if she had the opportunity.

One of the most interesting and significant features of Level V evaluations is the extent to which subjects expressed dissatisfaction concerning personal or relationship aspects of their sexual associations. Only one subject expressed dissatisfaction with his experience in intercourse as a sensory experience, and even then only as an incidental phase of his evaluation. Over half of the Level V subjects expressed some kind of negative personal feelings concerning the effect of premarital intercourse. The most common expression was one of guilt. This feeling was voiced again and again by the subjects. They were guilty in relation not only to their girl friend but sometimes to others as well. Such expressions as these were common.

"I felt like I was taking advantage of her."

"I realized I had pushed her into it."

"I felt ashamed when I thought of my parents and what they would have expected of me."

"I had a hard time facing her parents."

These guilt reactions provide an interesting contrast to the feelings of resentment and hostility so often expressed by Level III and Level IV subjects. At levels of minimal emotional involvement male participants apparently react antagonistically toward their partners more often than they feel guilt. As they become emotionally involved feelings of guilt become more common. This hypothesis needs further testing.

The data indicate still another hypothesis for study. They suggest that if the same information for women were available, Level III and Level IV girls would express more guilt than Level V girls. At Levels III-IV a good many girls are apparently taking a more or less calculated gamble on establishing a more binding relationship through permitting intercourse. At the same time, they realize they are violating conventional standards on two scores. First, they should not be engaging in intercourse at all. Second, they should not be using it as a lure. Their awareness of these circumstances causes them to feel guilty.

At Level V, however, it would appear that love has been used by the girls to rationalize and sanctify the use of sex. Several subjects mentioned an attitude of this kind on the part of their partners:

"She said she couldn't see it but that it was all right, feeling toward each other as we did."

"She was quite ready to go ahead. She felt it would be all right since we loved one another."

Ehrmann (27)[5] reached a conclusion in his study on premarital dating behavior which supports this observation. He writes:

Female sexual expression is primarily and profoundly related to being in love and to going steady. . . . Male sexuality is more indirectly and less exclusively associated with romanticism and intimacy relationships . . . males are more conservative and the females more liberal in expressed personal codes of sex conduct and in actual behavior with lovers than with non-lovers. In other words, the degree of physical intimacy actually experienced or considered permissible is among males *inversely* related and among females *directly* related to the intensity of familiarity and affection in the male-female relation.

Other negative feelings were expressed by the subjects also. One subject and his girl friend were "very angry with ourselves for letting it occur."

One Level V subject (#77) who got into a very complex relationship involving a premarital pregnancy, an abortion, and an unwanted break between himself and his fiancée said that he had "noticed a tendency" since this occurrence to be "very much more cautious" in extending his affections to anyone else.

On the positive side references were made to the feeling that intercourse produced a sense of closeness and better understanding. Three subjects indicated that sex kept the couple together until the relationship had developed other strengths. (The results in these cases may have justified the hopes of the female partners.) One married subject felt that premarital intercourse helped the couple get sexual adjustment out of the way before marriage. Several others spoke of the physical pleasure which they experienced in intercourse.

A study of the case histories leaves the writer feeling, however, that some of the evaluations reflect the subjects' need to rationalize, and an inability to face what actually occurred. One of the best illustrations is the history of subject #77, just cited. After the

[5] Ehrmann (27) has done a careful and comprehensive study on premarital dating and sexual behavior. This work deserves a much more extensive analysis than can be given in this publication. Persons who are seriously interested in this field will find Ehrmann a source of valuable information.

premarital pregnancy, the abortion forced by M's father, and the break between himself and his fiancée, M says in evaluating his experience:

> "If I had it to do over again I think I would not do it differently. I think F would say the same thing. With all the trouble it caused us, intercourse was still an expression of our love for each other." M adds that he would be willing to accept the desirability of premarital intercourse for his own or other children if they were in love.

This seems a paradoxical view to take. Perhaps M is speaking for himself alone. Certainly there are some other persons not represented in this appraisal—F, her parents, M's parents, and the families of each from whom we need to hear. In spite of M's willingness to accept this experience as desirable, does this really mean that it was desirable for the others involved? Heavy costs, financial and psychological, were incurred in this particular experience.

GENERAL OBSERVATIONS

This chapter portrayed the efforts and experiences of couples, most of them teen-agers, who have attempted to utilize sex as an aspect of a dating association in which there is a definite affectional attachment. Four observations which are in the nature of interpretations remain to be made.

1. Some time has been devoted to relating illustrations of measures the subjects used, or failed to use, to protect their partners from untoward consequences of premarital intercourse. To those mentioned the writer suggests still another measure to be added—that of time investment. In analyzing the liaison he has come to think of the investment of time as a sort of all-embracing factor which conditions the nature of the total relationship. It could, and probably would be quite important in reducing the exploitation evident in most of the premarital intercourse experiences already analyzed.

   The investment of time would provide an opportunity for the development of effective communication. This in turn could result in the clarification of purposes and motives. If the couple were not compatible, time would give them a chance to discover it and break up before they became involved in exploitive premarital sexual relationships. If they were compatible they would have reached a point in their relationship at which they would put the value of the relationship above simply sensory satisfaction. They would be more nearly in a position to think with some objectivity on these questions: Can our relationship sustain and be improved by intercourse? Is it worthwhile to try to integrate it into our relationship? How will it affect our other relationships, and are we ready to meet these possible consequences?

These questions are not easily answered for there are many unforeseen factors which may influence the outcome. Nevertheless, if, rather than relying upon dogmatic answers, we are giving objective consideration to the issues of premarital sex standards, these questions must be asked.

The investment of time has been suggested as a protective measure, but it can also be a hazard. As time increases the affectional attachment in a relationship it increases the potentialities for hurt. Whether it is sex that is under consideration or something else, the stronger the emotional ties, the deeper the injury is likely to be if erroneous decisions are made.

This thought raises an interesting question concerning the extent to which we should seek to embed premarital sexual expressions in the context of love. Or, more accurately, perhaps the question is, to what extent and by what processes should premarital intercourse be tied to love? Can it be tied to sentiment and tender feelings in such a way as to decrease exploitiveness without considerably increasing psychological injury and distress when intercourse does occur, or a relationship breaks?[6]

2. Immaturity, with its accompanying lack of judgment and in-

---

[6] Christensen (18) raised a question somewhat akin to these in an article in which he compared premarital norms in three cultural settings, Denmark, Utah, and Indiana. He felt that fewer negative psychological consequences resulted from premarital intercourse in the most permissive culture, i.e., Denmark. Blood (10) has suggested that only if sex is associated with love can we expect the development of tender and sentimental associations between men and women.

capacity to deal with potential outcomes, would appear to be one of the most serious hazards in relationships involving premarital intercourse. Although one must guard against the assumption that immaturity is automatically correlated with age, still it seems to be a very real issue when the persons involved in premarital intercourse are as young as were many of the subjects in this study.

Some of the subjects are very clearly neither aware of what responsibilities may be involved in premarital intercourse nor of their capacity, or lack of it, to cope with them. They imagine themselves free to make decisions, and to carry out plans which are actually beyond them. They are financially more dependent than they realize, and emotionally, volitionally, and sometimes legally, still under the control of their parents.

Neither have they the experience needed to judge the depth and stability of their relationships, or what these relationships may demand of them. They speak of love, yet avoid communication for fear it might spoil the chance for intercourse. They feel sure they are experiencing "true love," or that "I know how to take care of the situation." They are swept away by the excitement and elation of being chosen by someone, of being in a close relationship. They confuse sexual passion with love. They are unaware of the time investment needed before an affectional relationship has depth, and emotional expressions become consistent and placid enough to live with.

Teen-age youth can, of course, develop affectional relationships with maturity and depth; many have done so with parents and friends. But here a time investment has occurred, and made a meaningful relationship possible. The years involved in establishing a strong, affectional relationship with parents contrast very sharply with the few months, or even weeks, which some of these youths have spent in their dating associations. Many youths would completely reject the validity of an analogy which equates parent-child and male-female love, but to the writer the parallel seems sound. Relationships that can stand the gaff of everyday life and the seering intensity of human interactions are not built as quickly as youth (and some of the rest of us) would like to think.

3. An earlier reference was made in this chapter to the numerous dating associations in which girls seem to be more deeply in-

volved emotionally than boys. Several reasons could be advanced to explain this. The writer suggests the following possibilities.

a. The pressure to marry, and the marked emphasis on romance and marriage, produce a psychological set which helps to convince a girl she is in love in almost any relationship that has any promise. This condition promotes the "falling in love" phenomenon which is so common in our culture.

Boys have not been conditioned so much in this direction, but as more responsibility for rearing them and for structuring their environment is falling to the mother, this condition may be changing. This assumes that women are more romantically inclined than men, and that they imbue their children with romantic values as they rear them. If this is so, could this explain the increasingly large number of boys who are now considering marriage, and are marrying while still in their teens?

b. The insecurity felt by a girl involved in premarital intercourse leads her to want to buttress her position as carefully as possible. Whether she consciously realizes it or not, a strong emotional attachment with her sexual partner seems her best security. She, therefore, presses to intensify the emotional involvement as much as possible.

4. A psychology of relationships is needed. We have spent much effort in developing individual psychologies, but we now must spend more time in learning how relationships grow, flourish, and/or decline. Further discussion bearing upon the psychology of relationships is found in Chapter VIII.

7

ANALYSIS OF LEVEL VI

LIAISONS

Level VI liaisons include those in which the partners were engaged to be married at the time sexual intercourse occurred. A formal announcement of engagement was not a requirement for a Level VI classification; a mutual understanding that marriage would occur was considered as constituting engagement.

STATISTICAL DATA

Each of twenty-eight interviewees* reported a single Level VI liaison. Thus, Level VI liaisons constitute only 4.2 per cent of the total of six hundred sixty-eight liaisons. Several factors probably account for the small number of Level VI liaisons. First, the method used in selecting subjects probably did not provide ready access to men with Level VI experiences. Most of the subjects were college undergraduates and, in all likelihood, the group the

---

* After IBM computations were completed, and content analysis was begun, an error in classification of three liaisons was discovered. Three Level VI liaisons had been included as Level V liaisons. This error appears in Table 10, Appendix.

investigator reached did not include a high concentration of affianced individuals.

Second, individuals do not volunteer for Level VI interviews as readily as for interviews concerning liaisons at a less intense level of involvement. At Level VI there is much more concern for protecting the girl's position and reputation. This makes interviews somewhat more difficult to secure.

Third, because of the time needed to develop an engagement relationship, it seems logical that there would be fewer sexual liaisons at the engagement than at the pre-engagement level. An individual could engage in many Level I, II or III liaisons in the length of time required for a Level VI relationship to develop into a bona fide engagement.

The average age of the subjects at the time their Level VI sexual liaisons began was 18.7 years. Four were seventeen years of age, eight were eighteen, eleven were nineteen, two were twenty, and three were twenty-one. This means that most of the engagements had occurred at the high school level, or within a short time thereafter, and while the subjects were relatively young. Had these engagements culminated in marriage these might have been regarded as "early marriages." Eighteen of the twenty-eight subjects reporting Level VI liaisons were sexually inexperienced prior to their experience in Level VI intercourse.

At the time the subjects were interviewed the status of their engagement associations was as follows: Four subjects were married to the fiancées with whom they had had intercourse. Sixteen subjects were still engaged to the fiancées with whom they had had intercourse. Of this group, five couples had given up having intercourse. One subject was experiencing an unstable engagement with the fiancée with whom he had had intercourse. Seven subjects had broken their engagements with their liaison partners. None had any intention of restoring it.

DESCRIPTIVE DATA

Motivations

In the analysis of the case histories it soon became apparent that "being engaged" meant very different things to different persons.

One couple may enter an engagement in great seriousness, and regard it as a relationship that will involve them in important responsibilities, offer them essential personal satisfactions, and carry them into marriage. This is, of course, what we like to think engagement means to couples. On the other hand, an engagement may be contracted because that seems "the thing to do," or for the romance involved, or because it provides a cloak under which certain other purposes may be achieved. Moreover, the reasons may differ for each partner, and may change for each as the engagement progresses.

The impression gained from some interviews was that the subjects regarded engagement as a way of leading into intercourse. Such statements as the following led to this conclusion:

> "When I wanted to persuade her (the fiancée) to have intercourse, I would say, 'as long as we're going to be married, I can't see anything wrong with it.'"

> "I didn't want to mention my uncertainties about marriage for fear of losing intercourse."

The following excerpt from the description of a short-lived engagement involving two high school seniors is an illustration of an engagement maintained as a cloak for sexual desires.

> **164** As intercourse continued M's feelings for F changed from certainty to uncertainty, and he gradually lost respect for her. At the same time his interest in the sensory side of sex was increasing. As M put it, "It was like she was a female dog in heat, and I was the male dog." The idea of intercourse occupied his thoughts a great deal. . . . When F talked about marriage, M agreed with what she said because, "I couldn't let easy stuff like that go. I was afraid she would get mad and leave me, and I wouldn't get intercourse."

Two other subjects recognized that their engagements resulted from having been sexually attracted to their partner, without being attracted in other ways. The awareness emerged, seemingly, after intercourse actually began.

> **159** M and F became engaged after an acquaintance of about three months. Intercourse began as soon as they became engaged, occurred almost daily thereafter. Gradually, M realized that his interest was sexual, and that he felt little interest in the character

and personality of his partner. More and more they began to move directly into intercourse when they dated, and to make sex the central and most significant part of their relationship. The engagement was broken after several months of this kind of association.

With awareness of the diverse reasons for contrasting engagements, and the differing concepts of what engagement means, the course followed by a relationship in its growth or decline is no longer so confusing.

On the other hand, the self-centered motivations which have appeared at previous levels are seemingly tempered at Level VI by much more concern for the partner and her feelings. To a much greater extent than at earlier levels, motivations in mature, bona fide Level VI relationships appear to be mutually shared. Engaged partners, having invested much time and feeling in their associations, seem to desire the relationship to remain strong. The maintenance of the relationship becomes the paramount objective, and behavior directed toward personal, individualistic satisfaction is frequently renounced when it becomes apparent that it may damage, or disrupt the association. When motives are at cross-purposes Level VI partners seem more able than was the case at levels of lesser involvement to sympathize with the other's situation, and relatively willing to make efforts to reconcile the differences. This concern for maintaining a strong relationship seemed to make management of sexual desires easier for most of the subjects. Thus, one subject had had intercourse with three different girls prior to becoming engaged. In each instance he felt that the sexual relationship had resulted in loss of respect for his partner. When he became engaged, therefore, his decision was definitely to avoid intercourse. "It isn't difficult because the relationship means so much to me that I wouldn't do anything to endanger it."

Another subject who regarded himself as very responsive sexually, spoke of an instance in which his fiancée became so aroused that "she pulled me over on her, and wanted me to go ahead. I just held her close to me until she calmed down."

Several subjects said that the strong affectional attachment engaged partners feel for each other was the reason for their participation in intercourse. Their desire to be physically close, and to enjoy each other fully, produced sexual desires that led them into intercourse. The point of view expressed in the following excerpt is typical, though plans for marriage were not always so far along as in this instance.

> 187 M and F had definitely set a wedding date and their plans for marriage were well under way when intercourse occurred. "It wasn't that we really intended to start intercourse, but we had built up such a desire for each other. We were so much in love we would begin to express our affection for each other, and this would create sexual desires. It just naturally led to intercourse." M and F agreed that it was mutually acceptable. They had no regrets, and once intercourse began there was no attempt to avoid further experiences.

Deep affectional feelings undoubtedly produce a longing for physical closeness, and this in turn leads to situations in which sexual arousal occurs. This is not the whole story, however; other motives are present, also. Their frequency and relative influence can not be ascertained, but the subjects themselves recognized their existence.

Since eighteen of the twenty-eight subjects were virgins before entering their Level VI liaisons one might expect curiosity to appear as one of the important motives. These expectations were confirmed. Curiosity combined with a strong feeling of affection is suggested by some subjects as a mixed motive for intercourse. This may be a rationalization on the part of the male, however, to avoid the appearance and feeling of selfishness.

> 66 M thinks that his purpose in having intercourse was his feeling for his girl friend, though in the process he found out what intercourse was like. He had been curious about it.

Several of the subjects stated that curiosity, uncomplicated by other objectives, was their motivation.

> 164 M feels that he learned something of value from having intercourse. He is no longer curious. He is not always asking, "What is it like?" He now knows. This has been valuable information for him because his parents never told him a thing.

Quite often, curiosity and the desire for physical pleasure were intermingled.

> 168 "I couldn't control myself. . . . Oh, I really knew what I was doing. I just wanted to try it so much that I couldn't stop. It was a wonderful experience."

Three of the subjects said that the movement toward intercourse was largely the responsibility of their partners. These men maintained that their fiancées asked for intercourse verbally or by suggestive actions. The following excerpt exemplifies this situation.

> 10 M thinks that F was more ready for intercourse than he was. M argued that they might as well wait until marriage. This would enable them to avoid possible complications. F agreed, but continued the actions which resulted in heavy petting, and which were exciting and stimulating. Although intercourse finally occurred M wasn't trying for it.

Three subjects felt that some of the impetus to enter intercourse came from outside sources. They stated that discussions and a seeming social acceptance of premarital intercourse within their living groups and elsewhere helped them to overcome their hesitancy toward it.

> 168 M feels that the idea of intercourse with F became more acceptable as he heard talk about sexual experience among the boys in his living group, and participated in open discussions about sex in classes. This made him feel less inhibited and less hesitant.

The complexities of motivation are further illustrated by one of the subjects who reported that he and his fiancée had intercourse twice in the month preceding their marriage.

> 14 "We had held strongly all during our courtship to what we regarded as a Christian pattern of sexual conduct, that is, avoidance of premarital intercourse. We had been going together for over a year and were wanting to get married. I was eighteen and my fiancée the same age.
>
> "My parents were opposed to our marriage, and we were just 'spinning our wheels.' We were right up against a brick wall with them. Then my father relented, and said he would give his permission for me (an under-age person) to marry. As he was about to sign, my mother renewed her objections and he refused.
>
> "It was at this point that we went into intercourse. As I look back at it—it was about a year ago that this happened—I think

I can see several reasons for what we did. We were so frustrated and blocked that intercourse did two things for us. First, we needed to be close to each other, and this was the way we could get the closeness we wanted. Second, it helped me feel that in spite of the objection of my parents we were moving toward marriage. Actually, in a certain Christian sense, we were already married after intercourse. Then, perhaps there was an element of spite against our parents in what we did. It is all very complex.

"Later we went to my minister, and he got my parents to give their consent to our marriage."

Communication

Analysis of the communication between the subjects and their partners in Level VI liaisons, when contrasted with communication at levels of lesser involvement, revealed several interesting characteristics. Level VI communication generally appears to be more objective, more purposeful, and to have more weight in determining decisions, than has been the case at earlier levels. The discussions seem to center more about what the partners want, and how decisions on sexual conduct will affect them and their relationship. The discussions are more extended, both in range of points discussed and in the amount of time devoted to them, and sometimes are more leisurely and relaxed. There is more pointedness in the discussions—less going-in-circles, and getting nowhere. There is less contradiction between words and acts. Even so, all these characteristics, particularly the last one, were contradicted from time to time in Level VI liaisons.

Of the twenty-eight subjects involved in Level VI liaisons, eight reported no discussions on intercourse prior to its initiation. Twenty reported extensive discussions. Of the twenty couples ten agreed to begin intercourse and the other ten decided to avoid it but did not.

Why did the latter couples not hold to their decisions? The close physical contact involved in love-making and petting aroused sexual desires which overthrew their decision. Thus, we have situations in which verbal objectivity is overpowered by physical desires, or put another way, the feelings developed through physical contacts contradict and override decisions made verbally.

The possibility of physical desires overturning a prior decision to avoid intercourse is increased by virtue of the relatively light taboos against petting. Though all the subjects seemed aware of the social restrictions on intercourse, they did not seem to feel a similar restriction on the experience which leads to intercourse, namely, petting. Time after time the subjects discussed petting in a manner which indicated that they considered this a part of a normal relationship. They exhibited little or no hesitancy or guilt feelings about petting, though some of them felt guilt over intercourse. Yet it was petting that eventually led these couples into intercourse.

An increasingly strong affectional attachment, then, may work in opposing directions at the same time. It may on the one hand dispose couples to wish to behave considerately and thoughtfully toward each other; in such circumstances many conclude that they should avoid premarital intercourse. On the other hand, it may create a desire for physical closeness and a psychological unity which propels them toward intercourse. These opposing desires create the dilemma of the engaged couple.

The following case history is typical of those who entered intercourse after extensive deliberations.

> 28 M and F were very close from the beginning, and never had secrets from each other. They discussed everything, and confided everything. There was never any tension or conflict. M and F discussed their feelings toward their experiences in intercourse freely. They saw no wrong involved. They regarded sex as sacred, and not as a forbidden pastime to be indulged in surreptitiously, or at the earliest moment. "People should talk things through and come to their own conclusions as to whether they will have intercourse. If they can't do this, they certainly haven't any business being involved in it."

Two couples first decided to avoid intercourse, then reversed this decision when they felt they had made a decision which was damaging to their total relationship. One of these reversals is related in the following excerpt.

> 23 After M and F became engaged there was an increasing amount of physical intimacy with a growing awareness of sexual desire. There was some petting, but they talked it over and agreed to avoid intercourse. In an effort to do so, they frequently said good night early so as to avoid sexual arousal. This resulted in spoiling their week ends, and not accomplishing much in the

way of reducing sexual desires, either. After working this way for a period they talked it over again. They decided that the program they had been following had not accomplished much. They then decided to go ahead and have intercourse.

Ten couples decided against having intercourse but were unable to live up to their resolution. The following illustration is typical.

48   After a year of steady dating some petting began. It soon became quite intense. M and F recognized this, and talked about it to the extent of agreeing that they must not go too far. They had no intention of becoming involved in intercourse. Yet, after some heavy petting, they had intercourse one night. "It sounds funny to say it, but we couldn't seem to stop. At least we didn't."

Practically all subjects agree, however, that once verbal communication is established, it is very helpful in dispelling many of the unexpected troubles that may result from intercourse. The ability to discuss freely seems very important in keeping the relationship strong. If communication barriers arise after intercourse, they are apparently more easily dispelled by couples who have established good communication prior to the event, or who believe in the importance of good communication. The following example is a case in point.

21   Intercourse occurred between M and F with no previous verbal decision concerning it. There was nothing said after it was over, and no intercourse occurred again until about two months after the first time. During this period a feeling of embarrassment and guilt existed. "Because she was important to me," M finally opened a conversation by saying he felt their experience had created a feeling which ought to be cleared up, and he hoped that they could reach an understanding. Once they could talk about it they began to understand each other better, and were brought much closer together.

Actual experience in intercourse may have varying effects upon the capacity for communication. Two men who experienced intercourse with their fiancées, despite a mutual decision to avoid it, reported that after intercourse occurred the partners' ability to talk freely broke down. Until then verbal communication had been excellent.

> **7** M and F enjoyed each other's company and were always har-
> monious in their associations. They discussed everything freely
> and frankly up to the time intercourse occurred. After intercourse
> a barrier grew up which made it impossible for M to talk to F
> about his concern that sex might be the focus of their relationship.
> Nor could he speak of his feeling of guilt or find out how F felt
> about the sexual part of the relationship. He still wishes they
> could have a frank talk about the sexual part of their relationship.

Other subjects found the barriers to free discussion removed
less dramatically, but still removed.

> **132** M and F had intercourse about seventy-five times. Sexual
> relations have produced a great closeness between them. Inter-
> course has released their feelings and they have discussed and
> confided things to each other that they would never have men-
> tioned otherwise. At the same time, there is a certain tenseness
> resulting from a fear of the possibility of pregnancy.

Other subjects found, as will be illustrated in case histories cited
later in this chapter, that intercourse destroyed communication.
Feelings of guilt may make a free exchange of ideas quite difficult,
often impossible. Persons who experience such consequences may
be individuals who have been taught very strictly and severely
about sex, or who are frightened and upset by the idea or by actual experience.

Freedom in the physical aspects of the sexual relationship may
develop even while the capacity for verbal communication declines. One subject remarked, "We have been quite free in our
undressing and our sex play, but we have become less and less
able to talk with each other."

Thus far the evidence relating to the values of what can be accomplished with communication and its relationship to premarital
intercourse is contradictory. Some seem to find communication the
solution for their difficulties; others talk and reach decisions but
still find themselves behaving contrary to their wishes. Evidently
communication is not enough; it needs to be supported in some
way if the decisions reached through communication are to have
substance.

At this point the experience of couples who began intercourse
and then decided to renounce the relationship is enlightening. Six
couples made reference to such circumstances in their initial inter-

view. What experiences did these six have in renouncing sexual intercourse?

In five of the six instances what had originally been perhaps half-hearted decisions to refrain from intercourse became, for one reason or another, firm decisions to abstain. This was accomplished by getting all aspects of the situation out in the open, and by the development of a new perspective on the relationship. Three of the six also referred to efforts to set up arrangements that tended to support or implement the decisions made in free communication.

In the first history (#193) M was able to approach communication from a new vantage point, and thus achieve an openness which he had not been able to obtain before. At the same time his upsetting emotional experience had brought him to a firm decision that they should abstain from further intercourse. The same effect of an upsetting emotional experience is seen in history #168.

> **193** M and F went together for about two years in high school, and on several occasions became very deeply involved in petting. They were never able to talk freely about sex or their petting relationship. They got into intercourse one night when M simply "didn't stop." Afterward, both he and F were very upset. This happened four months ago. M and F are still unable to discuss their feelings. The tension between them has steadily increased. M has found F withdrawing from any affectional advances. F has met any attempt to talk over their sexual experiences with a rebuff. She seems to feel, whenever M opens the subject, that he may be attempting to secure intercourse again. Her statement is, "I just can't go through with it. We just mustn't let it happen again."

After the research interview M had a long conversation with the investigator on possible ways of improving communication between himself and F. After the conversation M felt confident that he could talk with F. He felt both of them had been jittery, tense, and fearful, and that this feeling upset them when they started talking. He set up the conversation on a new basis, and later reported that communication was improving. He regrets that intercourse occurred because it has had such an upsetting effect upon their relationship. He did not find it particularly satisfactory, especially since it created so much tension. He would have much preferred that it had not occurred, but he feels sure now that they understand each other, and that there will be no more intercourse.

> **168** After the initial intercourse F was very upset. M decided that he and F must talk through their feelings thoroughly. M felt that as a result of their talking they were closer together than ever. M felt that it was not the intercourse itself that had brought them closer together, but that the experience of having intercourse "shook us up so that we had to talk it through, and we came to a real understanding." They decided that they would forego any further intercourse before marriage.

In the next history an upsetting emotional experience seemingly led M to a new concept of his own behavior. This helped in developing a firm decision on his part as to what should be done.

> **167** M had tried for intercourse before he and F became engaged, but "she wouldn't let me." After they were engaged M pressed for intercourse with more determination. F always demurred, but M "kept on necking and petting until she gave in." Intercourse occurred five times, but each time after the same arguments, and after M had exerted the same pressure. Each time F said that she didn't want to engage in intercourse any more, and she wished that M would not push her for it. M has acceded to her requests, and does not try any more. He is sorry for his actions and feels very guilty for having pushed F the way he did. He has told her that he is sorry for having "forced" himself on her. F has told him that she understands.
>
> M now feels that his attitude toward sex has been immature. He wants to revise it so that it represents greater maturity. He grew up in a home which "lacked closeness and affection," and he feels this may be a part of the problem. M and F have now avoided intercourse for a year. M does not find this hard now, but at first "it was quite a struggle." They plan to be married within another year (as they were).

In the next case history an upsetting experience led to a firm decision which was implemented by a program to help the couple sustain it.

> **182** When intercourse finally did occur it came at a time and under circumstances which "left me wondering how it happened that we went ahead." M and F were "just out parking and petting and the first thing we knew we were involved it it." Right after they were through they talked about the fact that intercourse had occurred. M in particular was concerned to know how

F felt about what had happened. She was not upset but they still decided "that we would not do it again." However, the second experience in intercourse occurred within the same week. After this experience F was late in her menstrual period. That frightened them both and they were quite disturbed until she did menstruate. They did not have intercourse again for about a month and then had one other experience. This time "we decided definitely against it." They have dropped heavy petting as well, and have agreed to avoid situations in which petting or intercourse might occur. M has been able to keep the decision "without much difficulty."

In case history #23 neither M nor F seemed disturbed by their sexual experience, but absorption in planning so involved them that they "sort of forgot" intercourse.

23 After their fourth (and last) experience in intercourse, M and F became very absorbed in planning their wedding "and sort of forgot" intercourse. However, M has no regrets or any feeling of shame over his experiences. He thinks it had little effect on their relationship, but if any it was to improve it. M thinks F feels about it as he does.

In the sixth case history M and his fiancée decided after beginning intercourse that more risk was involved than they cared to take. Tensions and frustrations were arising over possible pregnancy and ensuing complications, so after considerable discussion it was decided to forego further intercourse.

6 "This was hard at first, but we have managed to stick to our decision, and now it isn't so very difficult. The first thing that helped was getting the whole matter out in the open and talking about it from every angle. The thing that really clinched it though was when I decided that if tensions and resentments were not to weaken or wreck the relationship we had to give up premarital intercourse. Once I had made up my mind to this it was much easier.

"Then we talked over what we could do that would help us hold to our decision. We decided we should plan a program of activities that would not throw us too often into tempting situations. Also we wanted situations which permitted us to express our feelings for one another and provided interesting things to do.

"We gradually developed a program which had a number of features in it. We decided or worked out these things:

"1. We made our physical expressions of affections briefer, and let them occur at times and places when we couldn't work into long petting sessions.

"2. We enjoyed playing cards or sometimes visited and talked with our respective parents. We had done this before, but we stepped up this activity.

"3. We would go to either her home or mine where we would go into the kitchen together and prepare something to eat or drink.

"4. We took long drives together. This was especially helpful because we were alone, close together, and could get a real sense of affection and intimacy through talking. Still we were in a situation which didn't permit petting.

"5. We both like to dance so we agreed to go to dances and stay until the dance was over, then go home.

"6. We knew several other couples who were probably in the same situation as we were. So we made arrangements to engage in various activities with them. We went on picnics, wiener roasts, and got together and sang. We usually had a lot of fun.

"7. We attended more movies, and other events which were not too costly but still enjoyable."

Analysis of the preceding six case histories makes it evident that there is no single program, in terms of specific features, that will fit every couple. What is done needs to be in keeping with the unique circumstances of a situation and with the personal qualities and characteristics of the individuals involved.

The analysis also suggests that communication in and of itself is not enough in the management of sexual impulses. Decisions made in the communicative process need some kind of support, if they are to be maintained. Although a blueprint of specific actions can not be offered certain features or principles in the management process do suggest themselves. These features are:

1. *Thorough and open discussion of as many aspects of the situation as possible.* These discussions are probably most helpful if they are engaged in a number of times, and on occasions when the will to help and understand one another is high. A time when the two are highly aroused sexually does not constitute such an occasion.

2. *A firmly based decision as against a half-hearted one.* The abil-

ity to reach a firm decision is usually helped, it seems, by some rationale for the decision which is accepted by both.

3. *The avoidance of situations which would tempt them to engage in heavy and prolonged petting.*
4. *Opportunities to express affection in ways which involve a minimum of overt sexual stimulation.*
5. *Participation in programs or plans which carry the couple toward mutually accepted goals.* This probably has the effect of helping to avert tensions and frustrations that arise when a couple feel their relationship is not progressing. These tensions and frustrations are likely to be relieved through sexual participation.

Another of the communication problems facing Level VI subjects is what to do about telling fiancées about previous sexual experiences. An elaboration of this point would duplicate the treatment of the same issue in a later chapter. The reader is referred to Chapter IX for this discussion.

Protective Measures and Assumption of Responsibility

Protective measures and responsible attitudes toward premarital intercourse are more in evidence at this level than they were at the preceding levels. Even so, much improvment is still possible. Contraceptive practices are generally quite inadequate, and frequently non-existent. Seventeen subjects reported either that they considered withdrawal an adequate protection against pregnancy, or that they used no protective devices at all. Six of the twenty-eight subjects mentioned confining intercourse to the "safe periods" of the menstrual cycle. On the whole, the knowledge of the subjects about contraception is limited. The subjects at this level are less experienced sexually than the subjects at the preceding levels. We must remember that sixty-four per cent of the subjects were virgins, and the average age of the entire group was 18.7 years at the time of their Level VI intercourse.

Some of the subjects seemed little concerned with preventing pregnancy, perhaps because they were planning to marry anyway. In any event, the fear of pregnancy seems to have been of little or no concern. Only three men stated that the fear of pregnancy weighed heavily in their decisions as to what to do about intercourse. Ten couples had discussed the possibility of pregnancy and developed the firm intent to marry in the event of such an occurrence. The other eighteen couples had no definite plan in the event of pregnancy. Five of the eighteen subjects assumed that they would marry their fiancées immediately if pregnancy occurred, and one assumed they would have an abortion. The remaining twelve subjects presented no evidence or said they had not thought about what to do in case of pregnancy.

The subjects were also asked whether they had taken measures to safeguard privacy, and to prevent discovery of the couple while engaged in intercourse. Two subjects said that the movements of persons who might discover them were carefully noted, and two others indicated that they were always fearful of discovery. These four persons were the only ones, however, who mentioned any pronounced concern with possible discovery. This can not be taken to mean that the other twenty-four couples lacked any fear of discovery, but the concern was of so little moment that it was not mentioned in the interview.

A definite concern was evident on the part of the subjects, however, to protect the reputation of their fiancées. The relating or even boasting by subjects, of their achievements to contemporaries which was observed at previous levels, is non-existent at this level. Eleven of the twenty-eight subjects made a special point of stating that they told no one that they were involved in intercourse with their fiancées. Seven subjects told either their best friend or brother, but usually for the purpose of securing information or advice from them. Nine subjects offered no information on this subject.

Several of the subjects hesitated to enter the interviews until they had obtained the permission of their fiancées. Several actually checked with their fiancées to get their reaction and acceptance. The following paragraph illustrates this hesitancy though the subject resolved it himself in this instance.

192   M was hesitant during the initial interview about discussing his relationship with his fiancée. He was concerned because he didn't know how F would feel about it. After some discussion concerning the purpose and conditions of the research, M decided that going through the interview would not be violating his confidential relationship with his fiancée.

Level VI liaisons sometimes provide another protective measure which can be very valuable to the relationship. Engaged persons seemingly have a greater willingness and capacity to reopen discussion, or to keep talking about their situation in case feelings and attitudes change. This is another evidence of concern for each other's welfare found at Level VI.

A final important protective measure is the utilization of time. A relationship between time spent in the total relationship and liaison level has been demonstrated.* The average length of time the partners had spent with each other prior to intercourse increased as the liaison levels moved toward deeper and deeper affectional attachments. The time factor, though an obvious one, is important only in that time is necessary for the building of a relationship. The capacity for full and honest communication, and the trust and confidence that make one value the worth of his relationship, are not built by wishing. Motives become similar and each-other centered only as a couple build an understanding of each other, and this takes time. This, the writer believes, explains why those liaisons in which intercourse occurred in a shorter period than six months are practically always Level IV or lower. They have not had the time to become anything else. This also explains why they break so easily, and many times suddenly. The couple thrust upon their total relationship the strain of an emotional experience which the relationship is not strong enough to bear. As a result, the relationship may collapse like a toothpick structure.

This is not to say that if a couple have spent enough time they can engage in premarital intercourse, and their relationship will support it. What counts is whether the time has been used to nurture a firm, well-grounded relationship.

Level VI subjects also seem concerned with the satisfactions their partners experience in intercourse. Nineteen subjects indicated such a concern. Of this number, fifteen reported that through discussion they became aware of ways in which they could help their partners achieve physical and mental satisfaction in intercourse. This concern with the experience of one's partner, according to the subjects, generally has the effect of strengthening the overall relationship.

---

* See Table 12, Appendix.

192 M's fiancée was very ignorant and unaware of sex. She was responsive, however, and they gradually worked into a deeper relationship. He is quite sure that she was a virgin. He has asked her if she has received the satisfaction she wanted, and has engaged in the kind of foreplay which would build up her sexual desires. From time to time M has asked F what she thinks about intercourse, and if she feels that anything is wrong in it.

EVALUATION OF EXPERIENCE

As each subject was interviewed, he was asked if he was satisfied or dissatisfied with his Level VI sexual experience. A tabulation of the replies from the twenty-eight participants follows:

Number of Subjects	Reactions to Experience
10	Satisfied
6	Mixed feelings
3	Dissatisfied
4	Neutral
5	No information

The main reason for the expressions of satisfaction on the part of the Level VI subjects arose from the fact that they had found a woman whom they respected and loved, and with whom they had effected a warm and successful intercourse experience. The consensus seemed to be that intercourse had heightened the sensation of intimacy and satisfaction between the liaison partners.

One subject stated that his experience in intercourse with his fiancée had the effect of making him feel more relaxed around women. This was quite important to him.

137 So far as the total experience is concerned, M is "glad he had it." "I had never gotten out and done much before, and the experience sort of rounded out my personality. It gave me a feeling of assurance, and an awful lot of confidence around girls."

The evaluation of mixed reactions to a Level VI liaison seems to stem from the fact that many of these couples, despite all other satisfactions, still feel that they are doing something wrong. These feelings of guilt and regret were stated, or strongly suggested, by a third of the subjects.

Sometimes the guilt or regret is simply a general feeling. The source or precise nature of the feeling cannot be defined, even by the subjects, yet it is strong enough to limit or destroy their total satisfaction.

> 7   One of the most satisfying things about the sexual experience for both M and F was that they felt closer and more unified as a result of their experience. M would have enjoyed the relationship more if he had had less fear of pregnancy (though he wasn't really worried), and a lesser sense of guilt. "I felt we should have been married, though I didn't feel either of us were doing anything wrong. We loved each other and intended to be married."

Most of the guilt feelings were associated with thoughts of parental disappointment or disapproval. One subject felt that he had violated parental teachings, and thus had failed his parents personally. ("Deep down, intercourse out of wedlock does seem wrong. I guess this is the way my mother taught me.")

A disturbed feeling on the part of the Level VI partners seemed sometimes to occur, even when the parents have built a free and relaxed atmosphere around the subject of sexual intercourse.

> 28   Neither M's nor F's parents were aware of the sexual relationship between M and F. Though M's parents had always been very frank and open with M about sex and told him anything he wanted to know, M feels sure that they would have been disappointed in him had they known. F's parents might have sent her away to some school if they had known. M thinks this may have worried F some, though she never said it has. Both felt that though they regretted hurting their parents they had their own life to live, and they would have to go ahead in the way they thought right. M's parents have always given him much responsibility for making his own decisions.

Three individuals who expressed dissatisfaction with the Level VI liaisons had either experienced failure in sexual functioning or had unexpected, disturbing reactions to intercourse.

One subject reported that his sexual experience had created a concern over his sexual capability. This was very important to him for he feared he would be unable to provide his partner sexual satisfaction.

> 182   As a result of his experience in intercourse M wondered if he would be able to delay his climax sufficiently to give his partner sexual satisfaction. In all three instances he discharged very

quickly, particularly the last time. In their discussions about their relationship he and F decided that the reason F did not reach satisfaction was that M was too quick to ejaculate.

One subject maintained that because he placed faith in an unsuccessful engagement in which he had had intercourse, he had become distrustful and suspicious of women. He now finds it difficult to believe in other relationships.

159   M does not want any intercourse relationship with the next girl that he intends to marry. He feels sure that one result of his experience was to make him more suspicious and less trusting of women. He feels that it is now harder for him to trust in a relationship. He has come to believe the quality of the relationship is the important thing, and sex is secondary.

Another subject describes a personal traumatic reaction to intercourse for no apparently explainable reason.

157   When F broke the relationship M was hurt quite badly. It especially hurt his ego and for a time he was glad he had had intercourse with her, for he had at least ruined her for another man. He realized now that his feeling represented an attitude of retaliation and a spirit of revenge. He doesn't feel that way now. M remembers once after intercourse he "laid right down and cried." He never did understand why this occurred and it bothered him.

One of the interviews during which the subject expressed mixed feelings concerning his experience turned into a counselling relationship. M felt quite a definite disturbance over what had happened in his relationship as a result of intercourse.

89   M had had intercourse with his fiancée very largely, he felt, as a result of his insistence and persuasion. There had never been any free discussion of this aspect of their relationship. Tensions and irritations had developed in their total relationship to the extent that F had terminated the engagement. This had been and still was very upsetting to M. He had wanted the engagement to continue but now feels that any resumption of the relationship is hopeless. He was bothered even more by the feeling that his actions in urging intercourse had been the cause for the break and that probably F held this against him. "More than anything I'd like to get rid of the feeling that I took advantage of her."

As a result of the discussion M decided to write F a letter in which he made no attempt to restore the relationship but simply expressed his regret at what he had done and asked her pardon, if she felt resentful toward him. He expressed the hope that she might consider him a friend as they went their separate ways. After a couple of weeks F replied to this letter by saying that she had harbored the kind of feelings M suspected, but, as she now saw it, the responsibility had to be shared. She said to M that she accepted his desire for friendly feelings, and assured him that such was the case on her part.

F's reply was a real relief to M. His comment was, "I'd like to have had her back, but at any rate I can now go on without feeling upset about the experience."

GENERAL OBSERVATIONS

Premarital intercourse has been successfully integrated into some Level VI liaisons while others are seemingly weakened or destroyed by it. This we know. Why this occurs is not positively known, but the data of this study suggest five factors which probably have considerable bearing on the outcome.

First, the outcome depends upon the partners' capacity to build a relationship, and the extent to which they have created a relationship between themselves before intercourse occurred. Thus, the ability to develop a relationship in which communication is free and honest has much to do with the success a couple has in coping with the stresses and strains that are often the consequence of premarital intercourse. The extent to which motives are mutual in nature and each-other centered, as against self-centered, divergent and opposing, provide important clues to how intercourse will affect a relationship.

Second, the meaning the engagement has to the persons involved is a significant factor in determining the effect of premarital intercourse on the relationship. Is the engagement based upon a strong, soundly-based attachment between two people, or is it an immature relationship contracted because of social pressures, and because, to some degree, it suits the convenience of the persons involved to be engaged? An engagement may mean a very different thing to one couple as compared with another.

Third, the kind of teaching the individual received about sex has much to do with determining his reaction to premarital intercourse. Some are burdened with guilt and a feeling of having violated moral principles; others accept participation in intercourse as normal, to-be-expected conduct. The former undoubtedly get into the category of the premaritally sexually experienced less frequently than the latter, but when they do their mental distress is also undoubtedly greater.

Fourth, the general maturity level of the couple is probably an important factor in determining their capacity to integrate premarital intercourse into their total relationship. Ability to face and cope with damaging consequences of premarital intercourse, when they arise, is undoubtedly a correlate of maturity. A person with a relatively high level of maturity is probably able to put sex in perspective, see how important it is in relation to other values, and exercise better judgment as to its management than a less mature person.

The population of subjects reporting Level VI liaisons is certainly quite heavily loaded with youthful and probably immature individuals. How much different, one wonders, would the picture have been had these subjects been four or five years older? Certainly a maturity factor is involved here. How does it affect the impact of premarital intercourse on interpersonal relationship?

The *fifth* factor is sheer luck. Some of the relationships which terminated quite to the satisfaction of the participants might well have ended otherwise, given a different set of circumstances. Premarital pregnancy, discovery, or awareness of sharp criticism over their conduct, could easily have altered outcomes, and the evaluation of the participants. In a certain sense, participation in premarital intercourse is like driving a speeding car on a crowded roadway; the consequences of the experience can be known for certain only after the course had been run.

8

DOES PREMARITAL INTERCOURSE

STRENGTHEN RELATIONSHIPS?

The central purpose of this research has been to provide data concerning the effects of premarital intercourse upon the interpersonal relationship of the participants, and an important aspect of this issue is whether premarital intercourse tends to strengthen or weaken this relationship. This has been raised quite pointedly by comments from a number of the subjects who reported sexual experiences with partners for whom they felt some affection. These subjects often referred to the "strengthening" or "weakening" effects of premarital intercourse on their overall relationship. The data obtained through the interviews indicate the need for a separate chapter dealing with the general effects of premarital intercourse on the overall relationship.

The idea that premarital intercourse might strengthen the relationship of those involved in it has been injected into discussions of premarital sexual standards by the findings of Burgess and Wallin (15). These data are found in their research on engagement success and failure, as reported in *Engagement and Marriage*. Burgess and Wallin asked those of their subjects (eighty-one men and seventy-four women) who reported experience in premarital intercourse if they felt the experience strengthened or weakened their relationships. Some 92.6 per cent of the men and 90.6 per cent of the women indicated that they thought it had strengthened their relationship, and only 1.2 per cent of the men and 5.4 per cent of the women thought the experience had weakened it. The remainder noted no effect one way or the other. The findings of these studies were publicized in newspapers and magazines, and have found their way into numerous books. They have been interpreted by many as proving that premarital intercourse strengthens relations. This idea has become an important part of the thinking of young people and deserves careful analysis.[1]

---

[1] Burgess and Wallin (15, pp. 371-72) comment on their finding as follows:

". . . This finding could be construed as testimony for the beneficial consequences of premarital relations, but with some reservations. First, couples who refrained from having premarital intercourse were not asked whether not doing so strengthened or weakened their relationship. They might have reported unanimously that their relationships had been strengthened by their restraint.

"Such a finding could be interpreted as signifying one of two things: (a) that both groups are rationalizing or (b) that given the characteristics, expectations, and standards of those who have intercourse the experience strengthens their relationships, and, similarly, that given the standards of the continent couples the cooperative effort of couple members to refrain from sex relations strengthens their union.

"Second, for some couples, at least, the "strengthening" of their relationship may not be in their long-run interest. The experience of intercourse could conceivably give a temporary and spurious solidarity to unions which might otherwise properly succumb before rather than after marriage. Third, couples having sexual intercourse may not be unbiased witnesses of its consequences. They may be moved to rationalize and justify their behavior by affirming its positive effect, for if good can be said to have resulted from what they have done, there is less reason to feel guilty about it. Fourth, statements made in the engagement interviews by men and women strongly suggest that more persons found their sex relations to have a disturbing effect than is indicated by their questionnaire responses. Finally, the engagement success scores of persons who had intercourse tend to be lower than the scores of those who were continent. This is not necessarily incompatible with the strengthening effect imputed to intercourse by those who had it, but it at least suggests that continence may have the same effect in greater degree."

ANALYSIS OF DATA

In our study the subjects were asked how their feelings, and the feelings of their partners, changed as a result of experience in intercourse. The subjects were also asked to evaluate their sexual experience. That is, were they satisfied or dissatisfied with it, or did they have mixed feelings?

On the basis of data derived from these questions liaisons in which there had been a change, so far as affectional attachment was concerned, were isolated. The purpose was to throw light on the question, "Does premarital intercourse strengthen or weaken a relationship?" For example, did a relationship which began as a dating relationship, but in which intercourse ensued before there was any feeling of affection, i.e., Level IV, strengthen until it became a relationship with marked affection, or even an engagement? Or, conversely, did a Level V or VI relationship deteriorate to a relationship of lesser emotional involvement?

Weakened Relationships

Initially, an effort was made to isolate relationships that weakened following the beginning of premarital intercourse, but after a time this attempt was dropped. So many complicating factors were involved that a clear-cut classification was impossible. At levels of minimal involvement there was no relationship to weaken. Level I and II subjects had no intention of establishing an interpersonal relationship with their sexual consorts—in fact, barriers were erected against an attachment. Consequently, there were no weakened relationships to report; the experiences were simply episodes. For all practical purposes the same thing was true at Level III. In other words, a relationship of some depth must be in existence before it can be weakened emotionally.

At Levels IV and V some relationships broke without any period of decline or weakening being noted by the subject. Sometimes the girl was responsible for the break, and the subject did not know whether premarital intercourse had anything to do with it. In a few instances Level IV-V subjects noted that their overall relationship had already begun to weaken before intercourse occurred. In at least one instance, according to the subject, intercourse was entered with the hope that it would strengthen the flagging association. This hope was not realized.

Two relationships were reported broken by the pressure of parents, and several others broke seemingly as the result of separation.

The interviews also suggested that many of the relationships which might have been classified as "weakened" were weak and flimsy to begin with, quite apart from any consequence that might have arisen from sexual involvement. They were probably heading for a break, and premarital intercourse merely revealed, perhaps to the long-run benefit of everyone concerned, that the relationship had no vitality. This possibility is suggested by such comments as "Oh, we didn't have much in common, anyway"—"I guess we probably would have broken up even without intercourse"—or "I knew after intercourse that our relationship was based entirely on sex."

For these reasons the idea of isolating a group of "weakened" relationships was abandoned.

Strengthened Relationships

The effort to isolate relationships which, the subjects felt, had been "strengthened" by intercourse was more successful. Thirty such associations, or 4.5 per cent of the total of six hundred eighty-eight liaisons, were found. They have been grouped as "S" or "strengthened" relationships. The original liaison level and the extent of the movements in these thirty liaisons is indicated in Table 8.

A highly interesting feature of Table 8 is that in twenty-five of the thirty "S" liaisons intercourse was initiated in relationships in which the partners were already strongly affectionate, or were engaged. Of the other five liaisons three originated at Level IV, and two originated at Level III, that is, only 16.7 per cent of the thirty originated at levels of weak or minimal emotional involvement.

The two liaisons which originated at Level III both culminated in marriage. The first one involved a teen-age couple who were married after pregnancy had occurred. When the subject (#50) found himself involved in a premarital pregnancy he remembered the research interview, and returned to talk with the writer. His attitudes seemed positive, and both he and the girl desired to go ahead with the marriage. Several conversations with M after marriage, and the arrival of the child, indicated a reasonably strong marriage with apparently a good chance of surviving.

Table 8

MOVEMENT OF LIAISONS WHICH STRENGTHENED FOLLOWING INTERCOURSE

Number of Liaisons Showing Movement	Original Liaison Level	Moved to:
1	III	Affection and forced marriage
1	III	Marriage
1	IV	Marriage
1	IV	Strong affectional attachment
1	IV	Engagement
18	V	Engagement
4	V	Marriage
3	VI	Marriage

The second liaison originating at Level III involved an older couple. Here the writer also became involved in a counseling relationship with both the subject and his fiancée after the research interview. This time the outlook was less favorable. Even a week before the wedding the couple were in such serious conflict that in the writer's judgment the marriage would be threatened. He felt that both persons were involved in definite personal difficulties so disturbing that they were likely to disrupt the marriage. Following marriage the couple moved, and the writer has no knowledge as to the final outcome.

The qualities of the three liaisons which originated at Level VI are indicated in the next two excerpts.

36 M was twenty-three at the time he met F4, who was an office worker, and a divorcée. Though they began having intercourse within a month after they met, they went together eighteen months before they were married. Their relationship progressed slowly but steadily toward marriage, and gave evidence of a mature, thoughtful couple coming to a decision. For example, during the early part of their engagement they talked over F4's first marriage with a counselor to see if their was any evidence that this experience would have any effect on their own marriage.

M, in the next excerpt, indicated that he felt that "intercourse strengthened our relationship" and that he and F2 had "rather accepted the idea of marriage without discussing it." What he has to say, however, raises serious doubts as to the accuracy of his observation. Despite M's favorable appraisal of the relationship which placed the liaison in the "S" group, the writer hazards two interpretations. First, M is disturbed by a presumed sexual inadequacy, and is attempting to prove his capacity to himself. Second, he is confusing the pull of sexual satisfaction with a strengthening of the overall relationship.

126 M has never discussed their sexual relationship with F2. He has wanted to ask her if she has been sexually satisfied, but has never brought himself to the point where he could. He does not know, for example, whether she has had orgasms, though he thinks she has. He hesitates to speak to F openly about it, since she might say that he has not been able to satisfy her. That would bother M greatly.

M wanted to find out what sex was like, and was interested in the physical pleasure of it. Another factor was that he was uneasy about whether or not he could respond sexually. His inability to reach a climax bothered him, and he was concerned as to whether he was normal.

The next excerpt relates to a Level IV liaison in which the subject moved into engagement. This excerpt shows how very complex the situation involving a couple can be, and the many factors which must be weighed by a subject in judging how premarital intercourse has influenced a relationship. It also indicates, as do several other excerpts, that judgments about the consequences of premarital intercourse on the total relationship would differ according to the time when the judgment is made. The favorable judgment which the subject expressed at the time of the interview could hardly have been possible while intercourse was occurring.

172 At the time M and F2 began having intercourse they had been dating two years. M was eighteen, and F2 was sixteen. F2 was considerably worried about the possibility of pregnancy. Once she was late in menstruating, which frightened F2 and startled M. They then agreed upon marriage in case of pregnancy. F2's chief concern was the possible negative reaction of their folks and others. M was concerned because she was con-

cerned. Once she told M that she could not marry him if she became pregnant, because then she would always feel he married her out of a sense of obligation. F2 sometimes becomes quite emotional. Once she said if she became pregnant she would commit suicide. M assured her that he intended to marry her whether she got pregnant or not. She also said on several occasions that she was fearful that M would lose respect for her.

Twice after intercourse she broke down crying. She finally said she just couldn't go on being frightened at the end of every menstrual period, for fear she might find herself pregnant. So M and F2 talked it over and agreed to have no more intercourse, an agreement they have adhered to for about nine months. They haven't found it particularly hard, though both sometimes become frustrated. On an occasion or two, M has had an ejaculation while petting.

M feels that intercourse "definitely cemented" their relationship. It made him look at F2 from the standpoint of marriage. As he looked at her in that light he liked what he saw. When they began intercourse, there had been talk of marriage. Shortly after ceasing intercourse they became engaged. Intercourse speeded the maturation of the relationship considerably.

We will now turn to an examination of the twenty-two "S" liaisons which originated at Level V and the three which began at Level VI. Of the twenty-two liaisons at Level V eighteen became engaged and four were later married. The three Level VI subjects had had intercourse with their fiancées, and were married at the time of the interview.

An examination of these "S" liaisons shows that these subjects reported more direct and open communication than was the case in most liaisons. Their discussion seemed to go more directly to the heart of the issue: Should they have or should they avoid intercourse? Each partner seemed able to convey his feelings to the other in a meaningful fashion. Sometimes this communication came before intercourse occurred, sometimes it came afterward. Sometimes it resulted in a decision on the part of the couple to continue intercourse, sometimes to abandon it. In a number of instances it seemed induced by the fear of pregnancy, a consequence for which the males now seemed much more ready to assume definite responsibility than was the case at the preceding levels. The following excerpts illustrate the facility of these couples for communication.

48 While both M and F enjoy the physical pleasure of intercourse the most satisfying thing is the feeling of intimacy and
closeness coming from it. They fully trust each other and are able
to share and talk about their feelings. After intercourse they have
a very real feeling of closeness and intimacy. Their experience
has been as much or more than either of them could have hoped
for.

150 M and F feel they get along much better as a result of
having intercourse. It has helped them to be frank. They have
no secrets from each other. They have overcome "the hurdle of
embarrassment and feel very much closer than we did before."

140 M feels that his relationship with F3 has been notable for
one thing and that is the complete frankness and candor with
which they can discuss anything. "We know each other better
after a couple of months of going together than many persons
would in going together for a year or more."
    They have discussed what they should do about their sexual
relationship. M was not in favor of continuing intercourse for
he feared in view of his experiences with a previous girl friend
that it might damage or possibly ruin their relationship. However, he found F3 more ready to accept the relationship than he
was, so after discussion they arrived at a decision to continue
with intercourse. F3 told M she had had one experience in intercourse, and M told F3 of his previous relationships.

The "S" subjects also made frequent references to the fact that
their "respect" for their partners increased, or that they "respected" them.

152 M thinks he gained some respect for F7 during their relationship, and that his concentration on sex probably decreased
during the time they went together. He wondered at times,
though, if F7 wasn't becoming increasingly interested in the sexual part of their relationship. She took a more active role in intercourse, and discussed their sexual relations more.

Affectional attachments seemingly engendered a concern in
some of the subjects which caused them to value the maintenance
of the overall relationship more than they valued sexual satisfaction. As the following three excerpts show, for some subjects this
resulted in a greater capacity to communicate, an increased readi-

ness to protect the partner, and a concern for her feelings. The subjects seemed willing and able to order their sexual behavior to meet the apparent requirements of maintaining the overall relationship.

187 M cleared with his wife before agreeing to go through the interview. He expressed very strong disapproval of men who were so one-sided in their relationships that they were willing to talk to others about their sex experiences with their girls or fiancées without their consent.

5 At about the end of two years (over a year ago) M and F became dissatisfied with their sexual relationship. They seemed to be "running it into the ground." Each time they went out they took it for granted that intercourse would occur, and the excitement and anticipation was dying down. M began to wonder if their relationship was being held together for sex only. Also M felt it unfair that he was always getting satisfaction, and F was not. He felt as though he was "sort of taking advantage of her."

As a result they discussed the matter, and in a "very mutual" way agreed to cease intercourse. "We were very pleased and proud of ourselves." M was also pleased to find that he was not upset over the omission of intercourse, and that he still cared for F as much as ever.

They continued going together, but later decided to test their relationship further by ceasing to date for a time, and to date others. This they did, but found that they desired to return to each other. They are now engaged and plan to be married in about five months. (They are now seemingly happily married, with two children.)

190 M and F agreed that in case of pregnancy they would get married. M realizes as he looks back that this decision would have had many difficult features about it. They probably would not have been able to handle it financially, and it is almost certain that their parents would have objected. "It would have been hard." M and F also talked about other aspects of their sexual relationship, and finally agreed to drop it because of their religious convictions. They have had intercourse a couple of times since they came to this agreement, but M feels that they will not have any more before marriage.

Two of the subjects felt that intercourse held them together until their relationship strengthened enough so that sex became secondary. The following excerpt is used as an illustration.

> 4 M and F6 are engaged, and have been for a couple of years. M is twenty-one and F6 is twenty. M feels that sex helped to keep them together in the first part of their relationship. They enjoyed each other as persons from the beginning, but it is only in the last couple of years that sex has become subordinate to the total relationship. They have now reached a point where they are completely free and easy with each other. Not long ago they were laughing at how shy and bashful M was with his early sexual advances.

Several subjects suggested that intercourse provided them with a sharing experience. The following excerpt is an example:

> 48 As a result of intercourse (or during it; M isn't sure which) there has been a great deepening of their relationship, and a constantly improving understanding. There is "an increased unity of thought." M thinks that intercourse may have helped him understand F better. At least intercourse established another sharing relationship between them.

The question needs to be raised concerning the extent to which subjects in general, or a particular subject, rationalize their situation when they state that intercourse has strengthened the dating association. Was M in the following excerpt rationalizing the beneficial effects of intercourse? Or is this liaison moving into the "strengthened-weakened" category, next to be discussed?

> 171 M has felt that intercourse has been beneficial to his association with F5, but lately he has been considerably bothered over what may be the outcome. He doesn't want to lose respect for her and have this relationship turn out as the one with F1 did. He would like to stop intercourse right now, but he feels that stopping will be much easier talked about than done. For one thing he is concerned about what F5 thinks about his reluctance to continue intercourse. She has already interpreted his hesitancy to continue as an indication that he is losing interest in her. He can feel a restraint building up between them, and is aware of an inability to talk freely. M wishes they could break this barrier and really talk, since the relationship means more to him than sex.

Strengthened-Weakened Relationships

Eleven subjects reported liaisons in which, following intercourse, there was an initial feeling that the relationship had strengthened, only to be followed by a definite weakening, and in some instances, a collapse of the association. Those liaisons have been classified as "S-W" or "strengthened-weakened" relationships.

Of these eleven "S-W" liaisons three began as Level III experiences, six as Level IV, and two as Level V. This provides an interesting contrast with the "S" liaisons in which five-sixths originated at Levels V and VI. A rather typical pattern emerged with an analysis of the "S-W" case histories. The "strengthening" feeling was ordinarily quite a strong upsurge which followed closely upon the initiation of intercourse. The comments of the subjects left the impression that probably this was a sort of infatuation based upon sexual attraction, and sustained by the physical pleasure and excitement of intercourse.

> **164** "That was about all I thought about! I had her picture in the cab of the truck I drove. I would look at it and think of being with her that night. . . ." This relationship weakened, however, when M began to find "what kind of a girl she was." "Like some of my friends said, she was fine if you could get through the Coast Guard guys who were always flocking around her."

> **140** . . . M thinks now that his attraction to F2 was primarily sexual. He noted how after they had intercourse a few times, he began to see a number of faults and shortcomings in F2 that he would not want his wife to have. She was quite narrow-minded, and pretty much of a "party girl." When M was under the stress of sexual passion, however, "she looked pretty good." Actually, as M went along he lost respect for F2, though he thinks she became more and more attached to him.

Excerpts from other "S-W" liaisons would add little. The picture has already been drawn and is essentially as follows. The initial surge of feeling seems to be based mainly on sexual attraction. When the initial thrill and excitement has worn off other considerations emerge which begin to undermine the relationship. They include such things as the boy's fear that he is becoming over-committed ("being trapped"), and/or a loss of respect for his partner. This "loss of respect" may be a defense enabling him to break the relationship, or it may be a projection of his guilt onto his partner.

When a relationship begins to weaken some girls apparently make themselves more accessible sexually than they were before. At least some of the subjects felt this. Though sex may hold some of the men for a time it makes them more wary, for they are likely to feel the girl is using sex as a snare.

In two of the "S-W" liaisons the girls broke the relationship. These subjects felt this happened when the girls found more likely candidates for marriage than they were proving to be.*

In summarizing this chapter certain statistical data should be added. We have already noted that 83.3 per cent of the "S" liaisons originated at Levels V and VI, while an almost equally large proportion of the "S-W" liaisons originated at Levels III and IV.

Table 9 shows the lengths of time of the overall relationships for the "S" and "S-W" liaisons prior to the beginning of intercourse. This might be called a measure of time investment. The significant fact is that whereas only two of the eleven "S-W" couples has dated as long as six months before intercourse occurred, in almost two-thirds of the "S" liaisons the couples had dated this long or longer. Even then, the one "S-W" liaison which existed a year before intercourse occurred fell in that category through a technicality. In this instance, M and F had dated "on and off" while they were in the early years of high school. Then they broke up for a couple of years, and started dating again after high school graduation. They began intercourse "within a few dates" after they resumed their association.

In contrast, almost two-thirds of the "S" couples had dated for at least six months before intercourse occurred. This represents a considerably greater time investment. Apparently this is importantly related to the strengthening or weakening effect of premarital intercourse on the total relationship.

Finally, the average age of the "S" subjects was computed as of the time they had intercourse in the "S" liaisons. This was found to be 19.4 years. The average age of the entire two hundred

---

* A series of what might be regarded as "weakened-strengthened" relationships, particularly histories 21, 193, 168, 167, 182, and 6, are found in the communication section of Chapter VII (Level VI). Here the importance of communication in determining the direction a relationship will take is apparent.

subjects at the time of their first experience in intercourses was 17.6 years. This is a difference of 1.8 years. This may indicate that a maturity factor is operating here. This factor may enable the subjects (and the couples) to handle their sexual affairs more maturely than they are able to when they are younger. If this is so, then maturity becomes an important factor in determining the capacity of a couple to handle the impact of premarital intercourse on their relationship.

Table 9

TIME IN OVERALL RELATIONSHIP PRIOR TO INTERCOURSE AND TYPE OF MOVEMENT IN LIAISONS

Time in Overall Relationship Prior to Intercourse	Type of Liaison MOVEMENT		TOTAL
	Strengthened "S"	Strengthened-Weakened "S-W"	
	N : % down	N : % down	N : % down
Less Than One Week	0 :	2 : 18.2	2 : 4.9
% across	:	100.0 :	100.0 :
One—Two Weeks	1 : 3.3	1 : 9.1	2 : 4.9
% across	50.0 :	50.0 :	100.0 :
Two Weeks—Six Months	10 : 33.3	6 : 54.5	16 : 39.0
% across	62.5 :	37.5 :	100.0 :
Six Months—One Year	7 : 23.4	1 : 9.1	8 : 19.5
% across	87.5 :	12.5 :	100.0 :
Over One Year	12 : 40.0	1 : 9.1	13 : 31.7
% across	92.5 :	7.5 :	100.0 :
TOTAL	30 : 100.0	11 : 100.0	41 : 100.0
% across	73.1 :	26.9 :	100.0 :

GENERAL CONCLUSIONS

This analysis leads the writer to believe that the effect of intercourse, in and of itself, on the strengthening or weakening of a relationship is indirect and minimal. Movement, it would seem, may be more adequately and meaningfully explained by an examination of other factors which are a part of the relationship than by simply noting whether intercourse has or has not occurred. Intercourse is an overt and distinguishable event to which various consequences can be attributed, yet the data suggest that much more than this is involved.

In some instances the effect of intercourse in changing the nature of a relationship may be quite direct. It may have, for example, developed a symbolic significance which can produce a very real change in the overall relationship. When a man has been taught all of his life, in accordance with one kind of double-standard practice, that "nice girls" have nothing to do with sex, he may find his relationship with a girl markedly changed by intercourse. At the same time, such a high value may have been placed upon virginity itself that when it is lost it changes the man's appraisal of the woman. Some women undoubtedly regard intercourse as an expression of love which changes the nature of the relationship for them.

Also, intercourse is sometimes used as a defense against a deeper involvement, or as an excuse for avoiding commitments. A "loss of respect" for their partner has been reported by a number of boys as a consequence of their experience in premarital intercourse. This was suggested in Chapter V as being sometimes a countering reaction to the pressure the girl is putting on the boy for specific commitments, or deeper emotional involvement. Intercourse helps to solve this dilemma for the boy very neatly. It opens the way for a "loss of respect," thus providing a ready-made defense against becoming too deeply involved, and an excellent excuse for breaking an undesired relationship.

Some ideas concerning factors that condition the development of a good interpersonal relationship between dating partners have developed during this study. It seems appropriate to mention them here. The writer suggests that the following factors have a bearing upon the establishment of a strong interpersonal relationship:

1. *The willingness of each person to permit the other freedom in deciding how far he wants to go in and how much he wishes to make of the relationship.* When one of the partners tries to entangle, snare, or tie down the other the relationship is weakened rather than strengthened. Relationships which contain the emotional satisfactions desired by those who are parties to them, are not created by persuading, threatening, or forcing individuals into them. The reaction of an individual who feels he is being possessed is to reject the one trying to possess him.
2. *The establishment of mutual respect.* This may be attained in several ways, but essentially it must rest on the ability of the couple to be their true selves before each other, and still be respected. Misrepresentation of motives, and dishonest expressions of interest and attachment, will eventually be seen for what they are. The expression of dishonest motives and intentions in sex, for example, is eventually recognized. When they are they take a toll in mutual respect and weaken the relationship.

   The concept of reciprocal respect needs to be extended to others than those involved in the primary relationship. Sometimes serious damage is done a primary relationship when one or both of the partners feel that the need for secrecy has walled them off from persons important to them in other relationships.
3. *The various aspects of the relationship must develop on a somewhat even front.* Each relationship rests upon a number of qualities and capacities which are utilized by the parties to the relationship, as they react to one another. Examples are the capacity for confidential interchange and communication, a feeling of trust, expressions of affection, emphatic feelings, and interest in intimate experiences. Some of these qualities, for example, emphatic feelings, can be developed only gradually. Others, i.e., attempts at confidential sharing, or sexual intimacies can be engaged in long before the other relationship qualities have been developed. Thus, one or another quality sometimes forges far ahead of the rest in its development. Since the qualities are related to one another, an attempt to move too

fast with one while the others lag is likely to endanger the whole relationship. In such instances a couple is likely to find their relationship thrown into disorder, and wrecked by this inco-ordination.

4. *Simultaneous involvement is important.* When the involvement of a couple in a relationship is about equal, and has advanced at about the same pace, the two tend to give and expect about the same things from each other. When one outpaces the other, this produces an inco-ordination. The more deeply involved person is likely to make heavier demands on the partner than he is ready to accept; the less involved person may wittingly or unwittingly exploit the one more deeply involved.[2]

5. *The capacity for effective communication.* Communication has already been mentioned in this listing but it merits special reference. The value of good communication, and the difficulties that result from poor communication, have been illustrated repeatedly in this and preceding chapters.

6. *A capacity for self-direction and self-government.* A relationship free from exploitation and possessive directiveness needs as parties to it people who are willing to discipline their own impulses. This might be called the need for self-governorship. Thus, if each person is to experience freedom in the relationship, but at the same time the relationship is to be maintained, then each must at times curb his own impulses and desires. This holds true in the field of sex as well as in other things.

7. *Consistency and predictability of reaction and behavior.* It is most difficult to build a relationship with another person, or persons who are erratic and unpredictable in the major aspects of their behavior. Two things in particular, it would seem, help build predictability and consistency into a relationship. One is effective communication. The other is an explicit formulation of our basic assumptions and beliefs about ourselves, other people, and things in general. Obviously the latter can never be fully achieved, but to the extent it is behavior becomes more predictable and consistent.

8. *The nature and extent of involvement in other relationships.*

---

[2] Reiss (85, pp. 136-44) has developed a "wheel theory of love" which emphasizes from a different approach the importance of simultaneous involvement.

Relationships cannot be neatly separated and compartmentalized. Many young people have found this to be true of their sexual relationships. Their assumption that no one but themselves is involved proves erroneous when they find themselves trying to cope with some untoward consequence arising from the sexual relationship. Discovery, pregnancy, emotional disturbance, or some other difficulty, may very quickly involve numerous other persons, and developments in these relationships may markedly affect the primary relationship between the sexual partners.

The listing of these factors should not obscure the fact that risks will be encountered in all relationships, just as risks are inherent in all of life's activities. Experimenting and trial-and-error learning will inevitably take place as relationships flourish and wither, and this is to be expected. Some associates will be poorly chosen, and some relationships will rest on weak, unstable foundations. Many may be better broken—even though some hurt may be involved—than permitted to languish. What we must hope for is honesty and sincerity in motives, and openness in recognizing the problems and circumstances as they exist.

I began and will close this chapter by referring to the Burgess-Wallin (15) study which bore upon the question of whether premarital intercourse would strengthen or weaken a relationship. These writers suggested the need for "some reservations" in construing their findings "as testimony for the beneficial consequences of premarital relations." Summarizing the same point as Burgess-Wallin, i.e., the likelihood that intercourse will strengthen the relationship of couples who are deeply affectionate, I would put it this way:

Some deeply affectionate couples have, through the investment of time and mutual devotion, built a relationship which is significant to them, and in which they have developed a mutual respect. Some of these couples are relatively free from the customary inhibitions about sexual participation. Some couples with this kind of relationship and background can, and do, experience intercourse without damage to their total relationship. The expression "without damage" is used in preference to "strengthening," for it seems that in practically all instances "non-damaging" intercourse occurred in relationships which were already so strong in their own right that intercourse did not have much to offer toward strengthening them.

The test of even these strong relationships comes when some untoward or unwanted event arises. Sometimes this is pregnancy, or open knowledge among family and/or friends that the relationship is occurring, or more often, subtle changes in feelings of the pair toward each other, e.g., growing possessiveness, resentments, upsetting guilt, or tensions arising from an inability to communicate. It is these events, when they occur, which often stamp the decision of the couple to proceed with intercourse as unwise. Such consequences produce stresses and strains which make it clear that a certain maturity factor is involved, and must be taken into account when considering possible outcomes. For example, coping with the strains which come with an unwanted pregnancy in our middle-class culture tries the adultness, not only of the couple, but of those associated with them.

The important condition in understanding the meaning of sex and its significance in strengthening or weakening a relationship is to avoid fastening our attention upon sex, or making the determination of whether or not a specific act has occurred our major concern. We need instead to be concerned much more broadly with relationships and the various factors and circumstances which make them meaningful, or destroy their meaning for those involved in them.

9

PREMARITAL INTERCOURSE AND

MARITAL ADJUSTMENTS*

Does premarital intercourse have beneficial or harmful effects on general marital relationships or marital sexual adjustments? This is a common question this research was not designed to attack. In a separate project, however, some data have been obtained from married men relative to their experience in premarital intercourse, and their evaluation of the effects of these experiences on their marital adjustments. Also, many of the two hundred men who participated in the study reported in the preceding chapters have since married. Some of these have visited the writer, and evaluated the significance of their premarital experiences so far as general marital adjustments and marital sexual adjustments are concerned.

These data, therefore, seem to warrant some discussion of the possible significance of premarital intercourse for marital adjustments. This discussion may help stimulate further research and determine its direction.

---

* The help of Dr. James Mabry in the development of this chapter is gratefully acknowledged.

SURVEY OF OPINION

Before examining these data it will be helpful to survey briefly authoritative opinions on this question. Some opinions are based on research and others are simply opinions. A respectable amount of literature on the subject has accumulated, for writers and researchers, no less than laymen, have been concerned with the effect of premarital intercourse on marriage relationships.

Speculative opinions range from one extreme to another and are easier to find than opinions based upon research. Some authorities regard premarital intercourse as essential to successful marriage whereas others regard it as highly damaging. We will do no more than to quote opinions from these extremes.

An illustration of the view that premarital intercourse is highly beneficial is found in the following quotation from Reich (84, pp. 26-27):

> Not long ago, it was considered a moral crime, calling for drastic punishment, when a couple who intended to be married, became sexually acquainted with each other beforehand. Today, quite spontaneously, and in spite of the influence of church, scholastic medicine, and puritanical minds, the view becomes more and more general that it is unhygienic, imprudent and possibly disastrous if two people bind themselves without having first convinced themselves that they are matched in the basis of their life together, that is, in their sexual life.

A good many writers advance the contrary view that premarital intercourse will have harmful effects on general marital adjustments or marital sexual adjustments. In this connection Reiss (86) has been critical of the statements made by the authors of several of the marriage textbooks. He offers the following quotations from two of the widely used textbooks. The first is from Duvall and Hill (26) and the second from Bowman (12):

> (1) Unfortunately the history of couples who establish full sex relationships outside of marriage is not encouraging to read. Even engaged couples who have agreed on marriage plans find full sex relations bring unanticipated consequences . . . there are many indications that their idealized images of one another may be shattered thereby, that the sense of mystery, the aura of holiness, will vanish.

(2) Modern young people who pride themselves on being informed and sophisticated ought to be keen enough to see that, up to date, premarital intercourse has never produced better marriage. . . . It is never good preparation for marriage. It is never necessary preparation. Most marriages succeed better without it. None require it. Many are damaged by it.

Reiss then adds:

These statements are far too extreme to be justified by the available research evidence, e.g., Terman and Hamilton did find a slight correlation between pre-marital intercourse and such failures but these men clearly stated that this was not to be taken as proof of a causal connection. The slight correlation may be the result of the fact that unconventional people have less objection to breaking an unsatisfactory relation and also less objection to engaging in pre-marital intercourse. This entire area is very much undecided at the present time. Even the definition of the terms "success or failure" have not been clearly settled. There may be some unconscious association of conformity with success, thus biasing the results.

Research on the relationship between premarital intercourse and marital adjustments has been conducted by Davis (22), Locke (70), Terman (92), Burgess and Wallin (15), and Kinsey (57, 58). Reevy (83) has related premarital petting behavior of girls to their scores on a test predicting marital happiness. In the main these research workers have developed statistical correlations which relate sexual experience to ratings of marital adjustments, rather than illustrative materials which describe the nature of the impact of premarital intercourse upon marriage.

Burgess and Wallin provide excerpts from case histories which indicate how the experience of premarital intercourse affects the relationship of engaged partners. No excerpts are included, however, which relate experience in premarital intercourse to marital sexual, or non-sexual marital relationships. Burgess and Wallin (p. 366), after analyzing their data and those from other research projects, comment upon the significance of premarital intercourse for marital sexual adjustment. They conclude that

. . . statistical findings on premarital intercourse and sexual success in marriage do not support the theory that coitus before marriage has an adverse effect on the sexual relationship after marriage. In certain individual cases premarital intercourse possibly does have the negative aftermath which some speculation imputes to it. In the main, however, it may be that persons who would be most harmed by premarital relations because of acute feelings of fear, guilt, or anxiety are by the same token least likely to engage in them.

Burgess and Wallin (pp. 370-71) also summarize research findings relative to the relationship existing between experience in premarital intercourse and general marital success (when marital success is measured in terms of the achievement of happiness). This is their conclusion:

> Summarizing roughly, the results of the different studies, although not decisive, support the conclusion that husbands and wives with no experience of premarital intercourse have the higher probability of marital success, whereas couples in which husband or wife had premarital relations with spouse and others have the lower probability. Between these extremes in premarital experience, the evidence is not altogether consistent as to whether the chances of marital success are better for persons who restricted their sex relations to other individuals.
>
> As to the interpretation of the relation between premarital intercourse and marital success we agree with Terman.
>
> Premarital strictness in regard to sex may or may not be the cause of the greater happiness. It [marital happiness] may, instead, merely tend to select the persons who by ideals and personality have greater natural aptitude for successful marital adjustment, while laxness before marriage may tend to select those with less of this aptitude. . . . The relatively small prediction weights warranted by our data on sex experience prior to marriage are in striking contrast with the importance attached by moralists to premarital chastity.

The second Kinsey report (57) provided data not available to Burgess and Wallin when they made the summarization just quoted. Dr. Kinsey cited data from which he concluded that there is "a marked, positive correlation between experience in orgasm obtained from pre-marital coitus, and the capacity to reach orgasm after marriage" (p. 328). He then concluded (p. 329):

> These correlations may have depended on selective factors, or they may have depended on causal relationships. The most re-

sponsive females may have been the ones who had had the largest amount of pre-marital experience and, because they were responsive, they were the ones who had most often reached orgasm in marriage. The females who had abstained before marriage may have been the physiologically less responsive individuals who, therefore, were the ones who had most often remained chaste, both before and after marriage.

But there are several reasons for believing that such selective factors could not have accounted for the whole of these correlations. There are psychologic and sociologic data which show the importance of early experience in establishment of habits of thought and attitudes which are very difficult to alter or counteract in later years.

Hamblin and Blood (47), however, took the data used by Kinsey in arriving at this generalization and in a re-analysis reached the conclusion that

> Two spurious factors (generalized scruples against all sexual pleasure and internalized taboos against the use of reliable contraceptives) are consistent with and presumably account for the observed relationships. In combination, the results cast doubt on the validity of the hypothesis that premarital coital experience *per se* facilitates the wife's sexual adjustment as measured by orgasm rates. It should also be pointed out that the notion that pre-marital coital experience *per se* hinders the wife's sexual adjustment is also doubtful if orgasm rates are used as the measure. Rather, experience or inexperience in pre-marital intercourse seems to bear no consistent causal relationship to the wife's sexual adjustment.

Kinsey (58) also introduced another rough measure of the effects of premarital intercourse on the marital adjustments of individuals. Both male and female interviewees with premarital experience were asked whether they had any regrets concerning their sexual participation. He commented on the masculine response to this question as follows (p. 562):

> It is sometimes asserted that all persons who have pre-marital intercourse subsequently regret the experience, and that such regrets may constitute a major cloud on their lives. There are few males whose histories seem to indicate that they have so reacted to their pre-marital experience, but a very high proportion of the

thousands of experienced males whom we have questioned on this point indicated that they did not regret having had such experience, and that the pre-marital intercourse had not caused any trouble in their subsequent marital adjustments. It is notable that most of the males who did regret the experience were individuals who had had very little pre-marital intercourse, amounting in most cases to not more than one or two experiences.

The attitude of regret as expressed by married women was (57, pp. 316-17):

> . . . some 77 per cent of the married females, looking back from the vantage point of their more mature experiences, saw no reason to regret their pre-marital coitus. Another 12 per cent of the married females had some minor regret. These figures differ considerably from those usually presented in public discussions of such pre-marital activity. They illustrate the difference between wishful thinking and scientifically accumulated data. There are, of course, more cases of regret among disturbed persons who go to clinicians for help.
>
> The regret registered by a portion of the sample appeared to depend on the nature of the pre-marital experience. For the most part, those who regretted it most were the females who had had the least experience.

When the quality of interpersonal relationships is used as the criterion for evaluation important reservations seem necessary in accepting "no regrets" as a satisfactory standard for measuring the significance of premarital sexual intercourse. This is, first of all, a measure of individual satisfaction rather than appraisal of the total relationship situation. A person with "no regrets" may be one who has become quite incapable of setting up a relationship. He may feel little or no concern for the welfare of others. Such an individual might damage many other persons, and disrupt many relationships in the process of gaining personal satisfactions for which he would express "no regrets."

Furthermore the effects of premarital sexual experience on later adjustments, especially when not extensive, are hard to determine. Separated by time, confused by memory lapses, and diffused by the impact of numerous other influences, cause and effect relationships cannot be clearly distinguished. This is especially so when the person making the evaluation is asked only to express satisfaction or dissatisfaction with no accompanying analysis of the situation to which he refers, nor any clear definition of his evaluative criterion.[1]

The opinions which have been cited relate the effect of premarital intercourse on marital sexual adjustment or on general marital adjustment in a highly generalized, overall way. The data that have been developed are not much more specific. They relate premarital experience (or lack of it) to happiness ratings which the individual has given his marriage, to his own expression or regret or lack of it, or for women, to the capacity to achieve orgasm in marital intercourse. Little is available which affords us a clear insight into exactly how premarital intercourse affects marital relationships.

DATA FROM THIS STUDY

I will now return to a discussion of the data collected in my own investigations. The approach will be wholly descriptive, and more concerned with demonstrating possible relationship consequences than in drawing conclusions. The data which are used are based on case histories secured from twenty-seven married men with experience in premarital intercourse, fortified by insights developed from long experience in counseling.

Of the twenty-seven subjects ten had their intercourse experience with women other than their wives. Of the ten, seven said that they attempted intercourse with their fiancées, and were refused. Two of the remaining three had intercourse once at the casual level as an experiment, found it unsatisfactory, and made no further attempt to secure intercourse with anyone prior to marriage. The third member of this trio had had intercourse with three persons prior to meeting his wife. He would have liked it with her, but he was aware that she was opposed to premarital intercourse, so he made no advances.

Six of the seven men whose fiancées rejected their advances had had extensive intercourse experience prior to engagement. One who was devoted to casual sexual experimentation estimated that

---

[1] The writer found in some of his studies, for example, that the criterion many sexually experienced men used in expressing "no regrets" was that they succeeded in avoiding pregnancy or embarrassing, complicating entanglements.

while in the military service he had had intercourse with one or two different girls every week, i.e., experience with something like one hundred fifty persons before he married. The least experienced of the six had had nine partners.

For each of these individuals the refusal of his fiancée to participate in intercourse enhanced his respect for her. As one of them said, "I don't think I would have married her if she had been willing."

Another said, "It increased my respect for her when she refused. I have always more or less lost respect for a girl when she entered into intercourse."

Still another commented on how much his respect for a girl dropped "when she is too easy to make. Then I don't care for her at all. The girl who stops you is the kind I respect." This proved to be an accurate description of the conduct which attracted him to his wife.[2]

Of the seventeen men who had intercourse with their fiancées only two had confined their sexual experience to their fiancées only. Although this group is too small for generalizing, the men who participated in this study were very clearly unlikely to limit their sexual activities to one partner, or strictly to their fiancées. Experience in intercourse with other women was a common prelude to intercourse with a fiancée.

The Burgess-Wallin data on married men who had had premarital intercourse are of interest at this point. These data were obtained from three hundred and ninety-three subjects who had had experience in premarital intercourse. Of this group 25.7 per cent had had premarital intercourse with spouse only, 41.2 per cent had had sexual experience with spouse and others, and 33.5 per cent had had it with others than the spouse.[*]

These data suggest several questions which should be examined in further research. If a boy has premarital intercourse how

---

[2] Kanin (55) who has done considerable research in premarital sex behavior suggests "the female's rejection of erotic exploitation [may] pave the way to marriage. That is, calculated male exploitation can encounter resistance and rebuff which, for some males (perhaps middle class males in particular) signifies 'wifely material' and, hence, again the possibility of emotional involvement and marriage."

[*] The figures were derived by the writer through recomputing the data given in Burgess and Wallin (15), Table 28, p. 330.

greatly does this enhance the chance that he will seek (and obtain) intercourse with his fiancée? Does premarital experience on the part of a boy mean that in the engagement period the maintenance of chastity (if it is maintained) becomes almost entirely the responsibility of the girl? What proportion of those boys who have casual sexual intercourse react by feeling that the only girls they can respect are those who reject their advances? Does the attitude of a sexually experienced man toward his fiancée, and toward intercourse with her, depend upon the level, or levels (i.e., prostitute, pick-up, casual acquaintance, dating partner) at which he has experienced intercourse?

The data upon which the remainder of this chapter is based will be presented under two headings. First, the reaction of the spouses to the fact of premarital intercourse will be explored, and second, the self-evaluation of the subjects will be noted. The chapter will conclude with some general observations.

INTERSPOUSAL REACTIONS

A common concern of individuals who have had premarital intercourse with persons other than their spouse is whether the spouse should be told of these experiences. "Should I tell?" is a question which arises repeatedly with sexually experienced men approaching marriage. This issue might well affect the marital relationship. The concept of romantic love, which in our culture is subscribed to by many persons, usually carries with it the desire for a kind of exclusive, possessive association. Confidential discussions are a way in which this feeling of exclusive belonging is created. Monogamic sexual association is a phase of behavior which has much power in building this feeling.

Burgess and Wallin (15, p. 267) found in their study of engaged couples that approximately 30 per cent of the men and 23 per cent of the women reacted to references concerning former dating friends with whom their fiancé(e)s had had affectional attachments with "reticence, tension, or emotion." Burgess and Wallin regard this as an indication that

> . . . many young people have not as yet accommodated themselves psychologically to the changes which have been taking

place in courtship practices. Men and women no longer necessarily become engaged to and marry the first person with whom they are at all intimate.

So, when honesty in confidences would require the individual to reveal previous sexual experience it is not surprising to find evidences of concern and uncertainty. Some solve this dilemma by deciding not to tell at all as was the case with some of the married men in our study.

> M had intercourse with three girls before meeting and marrying his wife. He thought it unwise to tell his wife about these experiences. She knew of F3 with whom M was quite emotionally involved, but she did not know of their sexual relationship. Even so she was "kind of mean" in her attitude toward this girl.

> M's wife doesn't know about his premarital sexual experience. This bothers him a little bit. He has thought about telling her but doesn't know whether he should or not. He is inclined to keep it to himself, since he feels that this experience in premarital intercourse has had little effect one way or another on his marriage.

The greatest hesitancy in revealing these experiences are seemingly displayed by men who have had the fewest liaisons.[3] Thus M who has had one experience "which has always bothered me," is also bothered because "I've always felt I should tell my wife, but I've never done so."

When the male attempts to tell, the fiancée or wife may prefer not to listen.

> 14 A few months before he was married M who had had two partners in premarital intercourse started to tell his fiancée of his experience. Before he could "come right out" and tell her she told him she was not interested and "so I shut up." M would have liked it though had he been able to tell her. He would rather tell her than to keep it from her. He wanted to be completely honest and has told her everything about himself. This is the one thing that he can't talk about to her.

When the fiancée (or wife) is told several reactions are possible. The reaction may be unfavorable, accompanied by hurt or anger.

---

[3] Some observations from Kinsey (58), quoted on page 206 of this chapter support this statement.

M told his wife that he had had intercourse with two girls before they were married. "She was pretty mad about it for a couple of days, but she soon got over it." M is glad he told her for "there is nothing hidden between us now."

A more common reaction appears in the following statements.

M's wife knows about F (his only premarital sex partner other than his wife) and that M had intercourse with her, but "it doesn't bother her."

M told his wife before he was married that he had had intercourse with several different girls. She seemed mildly interested and curious, and said something which implied that "girls expect this of men."

"Before we were married I told her of my experience in premarital intercourse. She accepted it all right and didn't seem to mind at all. The only thing she said that I remember in particular was 'Well, I may not be the first, but I'd better be the last.'"

Several wives regarded their husbands' premarital experiences favorably.

M laughed at the questions, "Does your wife know you have had premarital experience? If she does what is her attitude?" M had had a single, unsatisfactory and unsatisfying casual experience before marriage. He told his wife before marriage that he was not a virgin, and she construed this to mean that he had had considerable experience. This pleased her, because now he 'would know exactly how to proceed on the wedding night.' M left her with her illusion and he thinks it did help her to be more relaxed and to feel that she was in experienced hands in their initial intercourse.

M and his wife both had intercourse with each other and with other persons prior to marriage. Each knew the other to be a sexually experienced person when they began dating. The result was that they had nothing to hide from each other, so on a number of occasions both before and since marriage they have exchanged notes on their experiences and laughed about events which occurred in these relationships. Both feel this has been very beneficial for they have worked out an excellent sexual adjustment in marriage and are perfectly free in their sexual relationship with each other. Each feels completely free to say how he feels and what he wants in the relationship.

In the next instance the wife exemplifies still a different reaction to the knowledge of her husband's sexual experience. May she have been using the prying behavior her husband reported as a means of disturbing or "getting back" at him?

> M had had premarital intercourse with twelve different persons as well as with his wife-to-be prior to marriage. He told her about his earlier experiences, and now she raises the subject "about every so often and tries to pry details of these earlier experiences out of me. She seems to find it amusing, but I don't." M rather regrets having had these experiences; at any rate he regrets having told his wife about them.

Burgess and Wallin (15, pp. 348-50) also report on women's reactions to hearing of their fiancé's sexual experience with others. They found favorable reactions on the part of 11 per cent of the fiancées, neutral reactions by 45.1 per cent, and unfavorable reactions by 35.6 per cent. The responses of 8.3 per cent were unclassified.

Burgess and Wallin observe that

> These percentages seem to indicate that women of the type who make up the Burgess-Wallin sample do not react favorably on learning of the sexual experience of their engagement partners. Their reaction as judged by the latter is far more likely to be unfavorable or at best neutral and it should be remembered that at least some who ostensibly reacted in a neutral manner may not have been wearing their hearts on their sleeve.

Perhaps as more and more men experience premarital intercourse the trend toward social acceptance of such experience for men will continue. In this case, more and more women will probably display neutral attitudes toward premarital sexual experiences on the part of their fiancés. The shrug-it-off attitude ("what else can one expect of men") will likely become increasingly common. Also, if an increasing number of women experience premarital relations one can anticipate a more ready acceptance of premarital experience on the part of men as well.

SELF-EVALUATION

As each of the married men was interviewed he was asked to evaluate the effect of premarital intercourse on his general marital, and his marital sexual adjustment. Possible relationships between experience in premarital intercourse and marital sexual adjustment were commented upon much more pointedly than the effects of premarital intercourse on general marital adjustments. The definition of "sexual adjustment" was left to the individual subject. Whether the wife would have defined sexual adjustment in the same way, or would have agreed as to the degree of adjustment if she had, can not be determined.

Positive consequences for marital sexual adjustments arising from premarital intercourse were cited more frequently than neutral, or negative consequences. Those who cited positive consequences felt that premarital intercourse meant that the couple had either completed, or had taken long strides toward a satisfactory sexual adjustment prior to marriage. The two comments which follow are typical.

> M feels that their experience in premarital intercourse was good for him and his wife in that they had no problem of sexual adjustment in marriage. Immediately after marriage they stepped up the frequency of intercourse, but they very quickly settled into a mutually acceptable pattern of sexual relations. They have been married eleven months and feel that they get along very well.

> So far as M can see his experience in premarital intercourse was perfectly satisfactory. Neither he nor his wife has ever expressed any regret. What it all amounted to was that by the time they got married their "sexual adjustment was sort of out of the way." They have been married over a year.

The reports of these subjects find some support in a study by Kanin and Howard (56). They tried to ascertain from women whether experience in premarital intercourse was related to ratings of individual sexual satisfaction as achieved on the honeymoon. They say:

> At the end of the first two weeks of marriage, only 7.8 per cent of the women with premarital coitus report their sexual activities

as unsatisfying, in contrast with 24 per cent of the women without such experience. Women with premarital experience appear to achieve sexual satisfaction in marriage more readily. This capacity for earlier sexual responsiveness may be due to more premarital coital experience and, perhaps more important, personalities which are to some degree free of inhibiting normative controls, as evidenced by the lack of religious interests.

One subject felt that his experience in premarital intercourse helped him to remain "faithful" to his own marriage.

M had three partners in sexual intercourse prior to marriage. He thinks these experiences were good. "I don't have to sit around now and wonder what intercourse with other girls would be like. It helps to keep me faithful to my own marriage. It lets me know that I can derive the same satisfaction from my wife, as I could from others."

Another of the subjects who seems less securely anchored, escaped an extramarital liaison by calling up the image of his own marriage.

M's wife spent two weeks with her folks. He was left at home pretty much on his own. On a business trip to another city he called a girl he had known prior to his marriage, and they went to a party together. There was quite a bit of drinking. Then he took her home, and although he had not had sexual relations with her before marriage, she was ready and he could have had intercourse. M was physically ready, but thoughts of his wife came to mind and he did not go ahead. This hesitancy surprised him quite a bit when he thought of his premarital behavior. (M had had three pre-marital partners.) He has not told his wife about this experience. He would rather she didn't know how "he had almost slipped."

Still another subject says that in premarital intercourse he learned

". . . how to treat a partner during intercourse, and how women reacted and felt during intercourse. It cleared away barriers to discussion, gave rise to discussions on religion and valuable discussions on other subjects."

Several men felt their experience had been neutral in its effects. "I can't see that it made any difference."—"It made no effect that I could see."

One subject who had intercourse with his fiancée, expressed mixed feelings.

> "I think intercourse brought us closer together. It gave me the feeling of being responsible for another person . . . but both of us felt some guilt. It might have been better had intercourse not occurred."

Two or three noted some negative effects. In the following history M is speaking of a casual liaison (and his only sex experience prior to marriage).

> M regrets the fact that he had sexual intercourse prior to marriage. It happened only once when he picked up an older woman in Germany while in the service. "Having been raised as I was I wasn't very pleased with myself. I had heard a lot about it from the fellows but it wasn't anything, and I was quite ashamed of myself for doing it. I didn't talk to her before or after; I just wanted to get rid of her." M confessed this experience to his priest although he has not told his wife about it. Neither did they talk about sex standards prior to marriage. M never made any sexual advances while he was dating his wife-to-be.

Another subject thinks that "it probably would have been better if we had not had intercourse." This subject had intercourse only with his fiancée, and then "just a few times."

The regretful subjects, it will be noted, were relatively inexperienced. Their expression of feeling offers an interesting opportunity for contrast with the self-evaluation of twelve individuals who were more promiscuous.

> 1. M had extensive experience with many prostitutes while he was in the service. Most were "one-night stands" and he can only estimate that there were around one hundred fifty such liaisons. There were also several non-affectional sexual associations which extended for periods of several months.
>
> His fiancée was determined to avoid premarital intercourse and so they did. They have now been married three years and have one child. M rates his marriage as being a "very satisfying one." He sees no effect on his marital adjustments of his extensive premarital experience, except that it made "it a little one-sided" for his wife. He had all the experience and she had none, so she has had much to learn.

2. M had eleven sexual partners including his wife prior to marriage. Most were with acquaintances. M has been married over a year and rates his marriage as "very satisfactory." He and his wife are very free in their sexual relationship and enjoy a very good sexual adjustment.

3. M had intercourse with eight persons prior to marriage. This included his wife with whom he had relations "a few times just before getting married." They have now been married about twenty-two months and have one child. M rates his marriage as "better-than-average."

4. M had intercourse with twelve partners other than his wife before they were married. He had intercourse with her about a year before they were married. M thinks they have "an average-to-good" marriage. They have been married nineteen months and have one child. M cannot see that his premarital experience had any effect on their marriage one way or another.

5. M, now twenty, has been married eleven months. He had intercourse with five or six persons—including his wife before marriage. He "wishes" they had not had intercourse before marriage, though he can't actually see that it made much difference. In some ways he thinks intercourse strengthened their relationship. M rates their marriage as "perfect."

6. M is twenty-three, and has been married about twenty-one months. He had intercourse with twelve persons while in the service. All were at the casual level. There was no intercourse with his wife. The general marriage adjustment is apparently poor. M rates it as "average," but at the same time expresses considerable dissatisfaction, and talks of conflicts which are apparently deep and unsettled. There is no evidence though, that premarital intercourse has had anything to do with this. In fact, M rates the sexual side of his marriage as "O.K."

7. M, now twenty-eight, had fourteen partners in premarital intercourse. He has been happily married for over six years. His wife refused to engage in sexual relations prior to marriage. M has had no extramarital sexual experience. He regards their sexual adjustment in marriage as "good."

8. M, age twenty-two, has been married eight months. He had nine partners. Six of these were prostitutes and three casual acquaintances. There was no intercourse with his fiancée. The marriage is "quite satisfactory." There was some difficulty in early sexual adjustment due to inexperience and hesitancy on the part of M's wife, but that has not been overcome.

9. M, now twenty-two, has been married and divorced, and after getting his fiancée pregnant is married again. He has been married about five months. He is "very satisfied" with his present marital and sexual adjustment. He feels, however, that his first marriage, contracted when he was nineteen, was based on sex.

10. M, age twenty-two, has been married five months. He had ten sexual partners before marrying his wife, with whom he had no sexual relations prior to marriage. M reports a poor sexual adjustment in marriage. His wife complains that M treats her like she was "a girl in the back seat of a car," and M agrees. The marital adjustment in general is apparently bad. M reports the existence of a number of problems, and in general seems rather unhappy with the marriage.

11. M, who is now twenty-three, has been married about eighteen months. He had intercourse with nineteen different persons including his wife prior to marriage. At the time of marriage, "no one thought the marriage would stand up" but in spite of some stresses M thinks they are "over the hump" and have a good marriage. Sexual adjustment is excellent. If anything, M thinks premarital intercourse helped the marriage.

12. M, age twenty-six, has been married about two and a half years. M estimates that he had twenty-five or thirty partners in intercourse prior to marriage. M is involved in an unsatisfying and unhappy marriage. He and his wife seem both temperamentally and sexually maladjusted. In fact, there is real doubt as to whether this marriage will stand up.

The data which have been surveyed suggest several possible hypotheses relative to the effect of premarital intercourse on general marital and marital sexual adjustments.

First, individuals who have had very limited premarital sexual experience seem more likely to relate evidence of personal disturbance, than positive effects on marital adjustments. They are often bothered by feelings of regret. They are guilty over having violated propriety, or feel they have been unfair to their partner. References to ways in which these experiences have had a direct effect in producing marital difficulties are infrequent.

Second, the promiscuous individual seems much less likely to express feelings of guilt or remorse. The probability is that most promiscuous individuals attach little or no moralistic meaning to extramarital intercourse and so can engage in intercourse without experiencing emotional disturbance. Had emotional upset been a likely outcome the individual would have been less likely to have behaved promiscuously in the first place.

These comments are not all-inclusive, however, particularly if we are concerned with the consequences of premarital intercourse for marital interpersonal relationships. In the case of the promiscuous individual, whether he has any feelings of regret or not, his sexual behavior may have very important consequences for interpersonal relations in marriage. Two possibilities suggest themselves, and each will be illustrated by a case history:

1. The promiscuous person may involve himself and others in consequences which can be severely damaging because there is no adequate way of caring for them even within marriage. A premarital pregnancy, or a premarital pregnancy with an abortion, illustrate happenings which may have a markedly disrupting effect even though marriage occurs.
2. Promiscuous sexual experience may generate attitudes toward sex and/or toward persons which are quite damaging to marriage relationships. Thus the wife of a man who had had extensive experience with prostitutes commented in regard to her husband, "About twice a week he takes me and uses me." In this study one of the subjects quotes his wife as saying that, "I treat her like a girl in the back seat of a car."

The first history shows the marital havoc which an unsupervised and seemingly irresponsible adolescent, intent upon securing sexual intercourse, and unmindful of the rights of others, can create. This picture emerges as the numerous details and ramifications of the total relationship are understood.

At the time M gave this case history he was just past his twentieth birthday, had fathered a child, and was divorced. The interview was obtained after three dates had been broken and three different excuses offered—"I forgot I was to come in"—"I slept in"—"I was just ready to leave when I got to talking with another fellow and I didn't get over."

> M had had intercourse with four girls before dating F. At this time M was eighteen and F seventeen. He began dating her because he liked her and she was physically attractive. From the beginning M made efforts to persuade F to have intercourse. She resisted but began to weaken because, M thinks, she was concerned with getting married. She came from a "pretty strict home" and was "not too happy" there.
>
> At the end of two months they became engaged, which fact M promptly used as an argument for beginning intercourse. F was concerned with possible pregnancy, and so M agreed that if pregnancy did occur they would get married.
>
> M used condoms the first three or four times since "I always carried them with me." Before long, however, M ceased taking any precautions, since "I didn't care much if she did get pregnant, and I think she didn't care if this happened either."
>
> M thinks that having intercourse strengthened their relationship. They had intercourse "practically every time we went out," and sometimes a couple of times in an evening. F responded by talking and planning for marriage more and more. In spite of M's statement that intercourse "strengthened" their relationship he mentioned incidents in which he teased or tormented F. "If we were around other girls I'd make passes at them, or pat them on the butt." This was more than F could take and she would become very angry, whereupon "I would tell her I was going to give her ring back." This always ended the argument. In the meantime so far as M was concerned the relationship came to rest more and more on sex.
>
> About four or five months after intercourse began F became pregnant, and about two or three months after she conceived they "went ahead and got married," with the knowledge and consent (but disappointment and disapproval) of their parents. By this time they were already getting along poorly, and M was both pleased and displeased with the idea of marrying F. They

lived together for a few months and had a most unsatisfactory experience. M began to drink some, and once came home "really crocked." He also gave F "a rough time." He "teased her and made fun of her big belly" until, a month or so before the baby was due, she returned to her parents. The parents sent her away for the birth of the baby, and M has never seen the child, though he has seen F. "We are just like total strangers." M gives the impression of feeling resentful and mistreated, and of feeling his own conduct to be not particularly out of line.

F instigated divorce proceedings and the decree has been granted, though it is not final. M has started going with another girl and from her actions he thinks she will likely be a willing sexual partner. "I'll have intercourse again if the right girl comes along. I'll always be ready for intercourse.*

How accurate was M's judgment as to the unifying consequences of premarital intercourse on his and F's relationship? Is his evaluation accurate in that the novelty of beginning intercourse with F, and practically unlimited access to intercourse made this a very attractive relationship for a time? Was F so eager for marriage that she was willing to marry almost anyone and do whatever was needed to make her aspirations come true? For her intercourse (and possibly pregnancy) may have been an indication that marriage was to be the outcome. Naturally she, too, if she thought this, clung closely, perhaps even desperately, to the relationship. Yet basically, despite positive assertion about a strong relationship, readiness to assume responsibility and willingness to protect, there was probably never a relationship between these two. Disastrous consequences clearly resulted from this association.

The next case history indicates how sexual experiences may generate attitudes that create difficulties in sexual and marital adjustment. A definite cause-effect relationship can not be established, but the circumstances warrant a strong assumption that it does exist. M himself feels that this is the case.

M is now twenty-six. He has been married for about two and a half years to a girl with whom he did not have intercourse prior to marriage. He had premarital intercourse with between twenty-

---

* M, in this history, probably would express "no regrets" over his past experience. This indicates how unrevealing an expression of "no regrets" can be of the impact of an experience of interpersonal relationships.

five and thirty persons. M's mother died when he was in middle childhood, and he was reared by his father.

M's first sexual intercourse occurred when he was about twelve with a girl who was twenty-two. "It was a rather peculiar happening. At the time my dad and I were building a house for my sister. There were four sisters in a family in our neighborhood. All of them at one time or another had been in some kind of a home. My dad had run around with each of them.

"We had the outside part of the house up and were working on the inside, when one of the girls came in to talk. After a short time my dad asked me to watch the door. I knew that he was going to have intercourse with her. In a few minutes, however, he called me into the room. The girl was sitting on my dad's coat. My dad said to me, 'Do you want a little?' So I said, 'Sure.'

"I went over to the girl. She helped me get ready and complete intercourse. After it was over she asked me if it was my first time. I said it was. This may be hard to believe, but she told me I was quite good at it, and that she would take me any time. I was quite surprised because it was my first orgasm and it was quite pleasurable. I had intercourse with her several more times later. My dad didn't have intercourse with her since she wouldn't take both of us, and he wanted me to have it."

M had no further intercourse until he was about fourteen or fifteen years of age. He had three different girls then. He got involved in petting with them, and they just worked into intercourse. These were schoolmates. M had chances to have intercourse with other girls during this period, but turned these chances down.

When he was seventeen or eighteen years of age he was engaged to a girl, but there was no intercourse. He liked this girl very much and wanted to marry her, but when he was overseas she began going with somebody else and finally married. He still thinks of this girl, and it bothers him somewhat that they didn't get married.

M left high school at age eighteen, and went into the military service. He was sent to Japan and Korea where over the period of several months he had some twenty-five partners in casual intercourse. M looks at his premarital relationships as being on the positive side of the ledger. He enjoyed them and he feels that all of his partners got pleasure from them also.

M met his wife when he was twenty-two after leaving the service. They were married about a year and a half later, when M was twenty-three and his wife was twenty-one.

The relationship at the time of the interview seemed a poor one. "My wife says she was a virgin, and I believe her. When we were first married, and the first few times we had intercourse, she was completely passive. I could never tell if she had reached a climax, as she showed no emotion. When I tried to explain to her about the movements, she thought it was nasty. I was quite disappointed in her. I think that in respect to intercourse her attitudes have hurt me. I had no trouble with premature ejaculations in my premarital intercourse, but with my wife I am not able to hold off. I did not have this trouble with the others."

M has tried talking with his wife hoping to persuade her to try different positions and mouth-genital relations, but she refuses. "This is making our marriage less satisfactory."

M says his wife does not want to talk about their troubles, particularly the sexual troubles. He has several theories about their difficulty. He thinks his wife does not like men because of a strict, dominating kind of father. She has put him in the place of her father and displays disinterest toward him as a way of getting back at her father.

M regards the marriage as an extremely poor one, and places most of the blame on sexual maladjustments. The fact that he had so many exciting and interesting premarital sexual relationships has ruined him, since he now has something with which to compare his marital sex relationship. If he had not had these experiences, he thinks his marital intercourse might have been just as poor, but he wouldn't have known how poor it was for lack of a comparison.

M's difficulties in sexual adjustment may be associated, as he suggests, with the extent and character of his premarital experience. There are other possibilities, also. One wonders what effects resulted from the kind of introduction M had to sex. Are both M and his wife trying to work out their personal difficulties through sex? There are still other possibilities, but one seems justified in feeling that for M and his wife premarital intercourse has had some negative effects upon marital sexual adjustment.

One married man, reporting sexual maladjustment, attributed it to premarital intercourse on the part of his wife. Before the two had met, his wife had been engaged to another man by whom she became premaritally pregnant. Apparently, the emotional shock of this event caused her to break with her fiancé. She bore the child and gave it out for adoption. After she became engaged to

M she told him what had occurred in the past. M accepted this, or thought he had, yet now he found himself pressing sexual demands upon his wife which she could not (or would not) meet. As M looks at the situation his analysis is that "perhaps I do this because I resent what happened in the past. I can't help having strong feelings about her relationships with the fellow to whom she was first engaged."

In trying to understand the relationship between premarital intercourse and marital sexual adjustment this important fact should be noted. Basic personality difficulties, i.e., emotional disturbances, neurotic characteristics, often underlie both personal adjustment problems and difficulties in sexual or marital relations with a spouse. The same personal characteristics or experiences may underlie both premarital sexual promiscuity, and sexual and general marital maladjustments in marriage. The individual may be using sex both in the premarital and postmarital period as a vehicle for working out his difficulties. The following case history will illustrate this possibility.

> M, age twenty-three, has been married for two years. At the time of the interview he said that he and his wife were in serious difficulty. In fact, the week before her parents had visited them and at this time their marital dissatisfaction had broken into the open. M's wife had told him that unless conditions improved she would divorce him. She was holding back at this point for the sake of their six-month-old infant. M cited both sexual and general marital difficulties.
>
> M gave a history of premarital experience which involved sexual relations with "something like eighteen to twenty pick-ups and prostitutes" while he was in the military service. Most of them had been overseas. M seemed bothered enough in the interview so that the interviewer spent considerable time with him exploring the background of the difficulty, and followed this with several more periods devoted to counseling.
>
> M came from a home in which he got along very poorly with his mother. She was very strict in her religious beliefs. She made almost any adolescent conduct outside of religious participation sinful. Any kind of sex activity in particular was forbidden. M engaged in masturbation, felt extremely guilty about it, fought it unremittingly and wholly unsuccessfully. He was very curious about intercourse, yet his desires in that direction only intensified his guilt and made him more disturbed.

He tried on many occasions to defy or break away from his mother, but was always defeated. The weapons his mother used were tears, prayers for M's salvation, and splitting headaches which put her in bed any time she was crossed or thwarted. When M got into the military service he reacted by engaging in all the activities his mother had forbidden. He was still unable to escape her, however, for his activities burdened him down even more with guilt.

After M left the military service he was approached by the minister of the church of the same denomination as his mother's. After a discussion, during which the pastor became aware of M's difficulties, M "confessed" his sins and entered the church. At this time he felt a tremendous release from his disturbed feelings.

The decision was aided somewhat by his having met within the church the girl who later became his fiancée and then his wife. She, too, came from an unhappy home, but was very religiously inclined. She and M probably found enough in common in their similar circumstances to persuade them that they should marry. Marriage, however, did not solve their problems. It went quite smoothly for a few months, but trouble gradually crept into the relationship. M became quite suspicious of his wife's conduct with other men. He felt she was indiscreet and invited sexual advances though he did not know positively that any misconduct had occurred. He also suspected that she had had premarital intercourse though she denied any such experience. He did not tell her of his own sexual experience.

At the time of the interview their sexual relations were, on the whole, unenjoyable. M's wife was almost completely passive, and he felt strong desires, yet he had a strong sense of guilt over them. This made intercourse unsatisfactory to both of them. The result was a decline in frequency of intercourse to once or twice a month.

M also felt that his wife was a dominating type of person and that he was becoming a henpecked husband. This led to a good many heated quarrels. This, in fact, had caused the quarrel referred to in the first paragraph. Differences had also arisen over religious matters—what was permissible in the conduct of each, and how devout they should be in their religious observances. M has found himself rebelling more and more against the religious attitudes and patterns of the church, and his wife.

M, when asked how his wife interpreted their difficulties, said that she charged him with being jealous and suspicious. She feels she can't be friendly with anyone without being charged with misconduct. She also says he builds every little happening up to something it doesn't mean at all—he makes "mountains out of molehills."

All in all, the picture indicates quite an unhappy and unsatisfactory marriage.

Discussions with M leave the feeling that his experience in premarital intercourse and his sexual and general marital difficulties are all of a piece. M is full of resentment and rebellion over the treatment he has received in his own home. He has tried to throw off the controls of his mother by excesses in the service, but got only an even heavier burden of guilt for his pains. He tried to solve the difficulty by retreating to religion, but this proved to be a futile effort.

Now in marriage he projects his own sense of shame and his guilt on his wife by trying to make her out as unfaithful, and as harboring immoral desires. In fact, since she has a strong religious background it is very likely that he is still fighting his mother through his wife. His sexual and marital difficulties are a reflection of his inability to throw off the yoke of his mother's domination, and come to terms with his own feelings of guilt and of disloyalty to his mother and his religion.

The apparent association between personal adjustment problems and sexual maladjustments has been noted by others. For example, Albert Ellis (29), a well-known psychotherapist, reported on the sexual problems of one hundred couples with whom he had counseled concerning marital difficulties. Of this number ninety-four had "distinct sex problems."

Concerning the relationship between sexual and marital difficulties Ellis wrote that

. . . the process [of becoming maladjusted] went something like this: (a) For a variety of reasons, one or both partners to the marriage were distinctly neurotic or psychotic prior to the wedding. (b) The difficulties of achieving a sound interpersonal relationship in marriage added to the original emotional disturbance. (c) Because of the original disturbance, as well as because of simple ignorance of sexual processes, considerable sexual disturbances existed in one or both of the mates prior to marriage. . . .

GENERAL OBSERVATIONS

The effect of premarital intercourse upon marital adjustments is very difficult to trace. A full and accurate understanding certainly cannot be gained from analyses confined to the experiences of both sexes if each is approached as a separate group. Attention must be given to the interaction of the two sexes in marriage, both as members of their respective sexes and as individual male and female. The unique qualities and experiences of a particular man and a particular woman, as they are associated in the marital relationship, are what create the marital and sexual adjustments of a couple.

The influences of cultural attitudes and practices upon the relationship between premarital intercourse and marital adjustment must also be assessed. This analysis is complicated by the existence of sub-cultures in which attitudes and practices at variance with one another are found. Thus, the usual adolescent, peer-group, sub-culture of a boy stresses very different sexual values, and accepts quite different practices than does the sub-culture of the girl, or of their parents and teachers.

Even after these individual and cultural factors are taken into account much of what is decided is necessarily in the nature of interpretation. The following concluding points, however, seem justified.

1. The effects of premarital intercourse upon marital adjustments are varied, and dependent upon the particular circumstances which surround the couple in question. These effects, from the couple's viewpoint, may range from positive, strengthening consequences for the relationship to very damaging and disrupting ones.

2. Persons who have been very strictly and severely taught are probably more likely to experience guilt and shame reactions growing out of premarital intercourse than those who have been more liberally taught. Those who have grown up with more freedom and fewer inhibitions are much less likely to experience personal disturbance in their marital adjustments from the experience.

3. In situations where sexual adjustment or maladjustment is attributed directly to premarital intercourse it is necessary to ana-

lyze the situation before one can decide if it is probably so, and if it is, why and to what extent.

4. The negative effects on marital adjustments attributed to premarital intercourse *per se* have probably been greatly exaggerated in our culture. The effects have been thought to result too largely simply from the fact of participation. The contribution of unique personality characteristics and of underlying cultural factors have been greatly underestimated, or ignored.

10

INTEGRATION OF SEX INTO

INTERPERSONAL RELATIONSHIPS

In the preceding chapters data relating to the affect of premarital intercourse on the interpersonal relationships of the participants have been presented. These data have, at least by implication, suggested that important and deep-seated social and cultural forces, not immediately observable in individual case histories, have much to do with the way premarital intercourse affects interpersonal relationships. This can be said another way. Any two persons participating in premarital intercourse live in a socio-cultural situation. The outcome of their experience will be determined not alone by what they are or do as individuals; it is also determined by the strength of the various influences which bear upon them both before and after they become sexual partners, and the way in which they deal with them.

The existence of these influences is recognized when people say "if we only had different social attitudes, premarital sexual freedom would be no problem." This argument has a certain theoretical validity, but few people comprehend the deep-seated and persistent nature of the social and cultural forces which so markedly condition what can and can not be done with sex.

The very nature of these forces prevents a quantitative determination of their strength and scope. Data concerning them were not collected in this study, though to a certain degree their impact could be documented. Yet their presence is recognized by practically every informed person once they have been pointed out.

This study would, therefore, portray only a part of the picture if it failed to note the existence of these factors and indicate how they may be related to the efforts to integrate sex and sexual expression satisfyingly into premarital interpersonal relationships. In this concluding chapter this will be done.

The discussion will go beyond the data that have been collected and move into the realm of theoretical analysis and speculation.

IMPEDING FORCES

Some very powerful forces appear to operate in such a way as to make it very difficult, if not impossible, to expect relationships of strength and integrity to result particularly from the more casual use of premarital intercourse. Eight of these forces will be noted.

1. *Sexual Exploitation.* There exists a long and extensive history of exploitation in the use of sex. This has an important consequence, for any impulse or force which has been so much used in an advantage-taking way will be surrounded by fears and misconceptions. In the case of sex this background makes its extremely difficult for the sexual impulse to be accepted as representing altruism and unselfishness; the fact that sex has often been used exploitively is not easily dispelled.

Sex is sometimes sold as a commodity. Under such circumstances the sexual association is devoid of relationship meaning. Intercourse is an episode, rather than a relationship. The individual who buys a sexual relationship ordinarily looks upon his partner as an object, not as a personality. The association is intentionally depersonalized by both parties.

Beyond this level premarital intercourse has been often used to satisfy individual desires and for personal satisfaction, with little regard for the needs or welfare of others. Thus, an individual may seek intercourse for physical pleasure, or use it as a bribe to attract or hold another person. Evidence that premarital intercourse is frequently used in this manner has been offered in the preceding chapters.

Selfish objectives are linked to sex in such a way as to make advantage-taking inevitable, and to distort the meaning of sex. Sex, it may be said, is being used as an aspect of love while it is actually being used for individual satisfaction. Genuine interest in and concern for the other person may be professed, but motives which are essentially self-centered and thus threaten relationships then begin to emerge. Instead of affection, disdain and disrespect may be the real feeling. Sensual pleasure may be the central objective, and the professions of affection prove to be a deception. In such cases the sexual relationship has been used to possess and to manipulate, rather than for sharing and mutual satisfaction.

An illustration was given in Chapter III in which a boy used an athletic sweater with an unusual emblem to open a friendly conversation with strange girls. If this effort was successful it was followed by a sexual approach. This approach certainly casts an aura of suspicion around both friendliness and sexual advances. As a result, friendly advances may become a signal for the erection of defensive barriers and distrustful attitudes. This has happened many times, not only with sex, but with other phases of living as well.

If the boy and the sweater, and his potential partner, could recognize openly that participation in intercourse is the central issue, they would at least be involved in honest communication. They would know what to expect from one another, and contribute a little to honesty in an area where it is badly needed.

Some advantage-taking is conscious and deliberately fostered; some of it is unconscious, but its consequences are still painful and disturbing. Regardless of the way in which the advantage-taking originates, the net effect would seem to be the same—sex is surrounded with feelings of suspicion and distrust.

The extensive use of sex and the common emphasis on sex appeal in the entertainment field, literature and in advertising, is another illustration of the exploitive use of sex. Sex, in all these sources, is commonly played upon in the interest of sales and promotion. It is commercialized, sensationalized, used to draw customers, and made the butt of levity and jokes.[1] Sexual seductiveness is suggested as a lure for attracting and holding a

---

[1] The extent and manner in which sex is used in mass media, the movies and on the stage have been well documented by Ellis (28).

partner of the other sex. The suggestion is made, if not outright, at least by implication, that the astute use of sexual attractiveness may gain one advancement and prestige in other phases of life, as indeed it may. As a result, it becomes increasingly difficult to believe that sex can or will be used honestly, and in the service of improved interpersonal relations. Sex is not unique in this matter. The problems that grow out of the exploitive use of sex are likewise the problems of other aspects of life which are abused. Because money and power have been so often misused the motives of a person seeking them, or in a position to use them, are probably regarded with as much skepticism as the motives of a person seeking nonmarital sex.

Feelings of suspicion and distrust remain even after the actual circumstances have changed, and continue to color thinking and reactions over a long period of time. For example, abuses in the financial and business community brought financiers and business men into disrepute, particularly in the 1930's. These feelings have not yet been entirely dissipated. Can anyone doubt that it will be a long time before the leaders of the United States and Russia can work together free from suspicion and distrust?

Distrustful attitudes arising from exploitation may seem to have disappeared. Yet frequently they have simply been pushed aside, and await only unusual stresses and strains for expression. A good example is the attitudes that have embroiled Negroes and whites in the current segregation-integration struggle. Many of the troublesome attitudes can be traced to the exploitive relationships that have existed between the two races for years. The hostilities and antagonisms which were generated and intensified during the period of slavery and the Civil War seemed for years to be subsiding, but under the impact of the current effort to attain equal rights for the Negro they have reappeared.

A long period during which people may experience honesty and sincerity in the use of sex in interpersonal relationship is needed. Until then they will find it difficult to think of sex, premaritally or extramaritally, without suspecting that self-centered, exploitive motives are probably involved.

2. *Difficulties in Communication.* A marked incapacity to communicate objectively and freely about sex is an outstanding characteristic of our society. Few persons realize how difficult frank, direct and full communication about sex actually is. The com-

plexity of the communication problem is illustrated in many ways. For years everyone has been taught in families and schools, and through social experiences, to regard sex as a taboo subject. An objective, serious discussion of sex is very unlikely ever to arise at a middle- or upper-class social gathering, for example. People have to become very well acquainted with one another before they feel free to enter into a free, broad-ranging objective discussion of sex with one another.

Children and youths can raise questions and discuss sexual matters much more freely than adults. Reticence and inhibitions in children and youths are more often observed when they are around adults than when they are around each other. The interest of small children in their bodies and reproductive matters is free and unabashed, though usually they soon learn not to let their elders become aware of their curiosity.

Teen-agers ordinarily speak quite freely with each other, for in other teen-agers they recognize kindred spirits struggling with the riddle of sex. Many of them feel strong sexual desires, which they, as unmarried individuals, are unable to express in acceptable ways. Youths, therefore, almost always make a ready, objective audience for discussions of sex. Given adequate leadership, and an accepting, permissive atmosphere, they are ready to recognize the presence and the motivating force of their sexual feelings quite openly and directly.

Adults, however, have ordinarily lowered an iron curtain which prevents any objective, extended, personalized discussions of sex. They will make sly, off-color comments, tell sex jokes, and engage in innuendoes; they may refer boastingly to their sexual experiences and conquests. They may discuss and judge the sexual conduct of others, but reference to their own sexual feelings and problems becomes very threatening. In any serious discussion of sex many adults are profoundly ill-at-ease.

An evidence of this incapacity for communication about any aspect of sex was found by Tebor (91) in his study of virgin college men. Here was a group which had followed the conventional patterns, and with whom it should have been easy to discuss their exemplary sexual behavior. Most of the subjects said, however, that their own sexual conduct had never been discussed with any adult. In fact, in very few instances did any adults know for sure of their sexual pattern, least of all those adults who are presumably most concerned, and who should therefore give them support—their parents, teachers, and religious leaders. Sex is simply not discussed in our culture in any context!

Youths and adults usually find it difficult to converse freely and objectively about sex with each other. About the best adults can do is to give youths physiological, depersonalized facts about reproduction. If the discussion relates to youthful conduct, adults can seldom be accepting or permissive. Their past experience compels them to be judgmental and forbidding.

On several occasions the writer has worked in high schools in which a premarital pregnancy has just come to light. The situation ordinarily produces much comment. The pupils discuss it among themselves, and so does the faculty. Both groups are careful to conceal their comments from the other. Seldom is the situation ever utilized as an opportunity for young people and adults to communicate directly with each other about the nature, uses, and misuses of sex.

Even professionally trained adults are unable to communicate their honest feelings about sex until they have had enough time to develop a close rapport with the person to whom they are speaking. Conventional attitudes are usually voiced, and unconventional ones are kept to oneself until they appear to have a good chance of acceptance. People who seem quite interested in sex are likely to be regarded with skepticism, and are often suspected of a morbid interest. People who are sincerely interested in seeing a change in sexual standards or in the general atmosphere surrounding sex speak hesitantly for fear of adverse public opinion.

Professional persons whose work requires them to deal with matters of sex, experience the same difficulties as nonprofessionals. They may be able to discuss the sexual needs and problems of other segments of the population objectively and at length, but any indication that they, too, have sexual feelings and problems is carefully avoided.

This fact was noted quite pointedly by a youth at a sex education conference. He had sat through two days of discussions by people with professional backgrounds. When asked for his appraisal of the conference, his comment was about as follows: "You professional people have engaged in discussion for two days. You have talked long and learnedly about the problems of youth. But as I have listened there hasn't been a single remark that would indicate that any of you personally ever had or now have any sexual feelings or problems."

An atmosphere in which frank, objective, and honest communication about sex, personal feelings and desires could take place, not just once but a number of times, would seem an absolute prerequisite to the non-exploitive use of premarital sex. That atmosphere does not exist at the present time.

3. *Negative Attitudes and Values.* Attitudes and values which interfere with objectivity and rational considerations concerning the use of sex are deeply imbedded in the culture. Certain specific attitudes have been mentioned in the perceding paragraphs, but others need to be considered. One is the common association of sexual experience with important non-sexual values. For some persons, particularly males, participation in sexual intercourse may be the symbol of success in the masculine sex role. Sex may be used to prove one's attractiveness to members of the other sex, or to demonstrate one's power. These associations are bolstered by some of the typical social attitudes, particularly those expressed through entertainment and mass media. These values lead to an irrational attitude toward, and a distorted use of, sex.

An irrational fear of sex[2] makes objectivity and effective communication very difficult. Parents who find their children experimenting with sex are likely to display much more shock and upset than if they had found them playing with a dangerous firecracker, or even a loaded gun. The children would doubtlessly be stopped in their experimentation in each instance. In the case of the firecracker or the gun the parents would probably give their children an objective and thoughtful explanation for their disapproval. Such an explanation is unlikely in the case of sexual experimentation.

The attitude toward youthful couples involved in premarital intercourse is likely to be one of marked upset and shock. Ordinarily, this is regarded as a serious immorality, meriting the sternest disapproval. But is this attitude based upon what is really involved in interpersonal relationships? And is it consistent with our attitude toward other matters?

---

[2] The writer feels that the aggressive impulse rather than the sexual impulse is to be most feared. The aggressive impulse, given free rein, brings destruction and death. This is the impulse most seriously in need of control.

Let us draw a parallel. Fast, irresponsible automobile driving endangers the well-being of the driver, his passengers, and others who are on the road as well. Yet the attitude toward those who engage in reckless driving is ordinarily much less severe and much more objective, than toward those who engage in premarital intercourse. Yet irresponsible driving is certainly a threat to the welfare of other persons, and an accident can damage many relationships or even wipe them out entirely.

Extremes of sanctimony and lasciviousness confuse people and make objectivity impossible and inconsistency certain. Most people are subjected to these extremes repeatedly. Educational and religious leaders are frequently so condemnatory and sanctimonious that their views are heavily discounted. On the other hand, movies, newspapers, magazines, the stage and other media, often make sex appear highly alluring and enticing; a morsel to be enjoyed if a person can obtain it without being caught. These extremes are sometimes found within a single individual. They interfere with the development of a balanced point of view.

This shifting and vacillation in attitudes toward sex is very unsettling and disturbing to everyone, particularly youth. It produces uncertainty, and chaos is its consequence. Until we can agree upon and accept a framework for moral judgment which embraces the whole of our lives there is little hope for consistency and rationality in our behavior. The important thing is that we cease treating sex as something shameful, and an aspect of life apart from all the rest. We need to make decisions about sex and evaluate them within the same framework which we use to judge the worth of our other capacities, be they our intelligence, intuitions, physical stamina or prowess, or other special talents. My contention is that judgment with regard to the use of all these capacities should be made within the framework of interpersonal relationships, as developed in Chapter 1.

Tremendous social pressures interfere with an objective and mature approach to the understanding and use of sex. These pressures bear heavily upon girls. They feel a definite social pressure to find a boy friend, to get a dating relationship established, to get engaged, to marry—in short, "to get a man."

The girls' problem is accentuated by the fact that the optimum period of mate selection for girls, already shorter than for boys, is being shortened by the growing tendency toward early marriage. The average age of first marriage for both men and women has been declining steadily. The average age of first marriage for girls is now between twenty and twenty and one-half years, and still falling. As it declines, the optimum period for mate selection for the girl is correspondingly shortened. Her optimum period is now roughly between eighteen and twenty-two years of age. This gives the girl a relatively short time in which to find a mate. At least half of the girls are either married or have prospects by the time they have reached their twentieth birthday. The girl who wishes to marry, and who reaches twenty-one with no marital prospects, is ordinarily uneasy if not disturbed about her situation. This sometimes produces injudicious behavior as it relates to setting up relationships, particularly with reference to sexual conduct.

The pressures involved are felt by girls while still in high school. Even though the pressure to marry may not be so marked at that time, the pressure to get a boy friend and to date is. At this time, as at later ages, sex may be used to entice or lure. The movies and those interests which profit from the commercialization of sex, dating, the wedding and honeymoon, have added their pressure. The romantic ideal is still another factor. Many girls react to these pressures with strenuous efforts to accomplish, at almost any cost, what is obviously expected of them—namely, the development of a male-female relationship.

Adolescent boys experience some pressures also. They are faced with the problem of establishing themselves as men. The culture is now quite removed from those social arrangements which formerly enabled a young man to become a farmer, a hunter, or a salaried worker by the time he was eighteen. The chances of the modern lad of eighteen gaining community recognition for his masculine achievements through economic and vocational activities are severely limited. Many young men have no chance to associate with adults in a way that would give them a meaningful and satisfying status in the adult world toward which they are moving. A few gain recognition by participation in competitive athletics (an activity valued highly by many adults), or by success in some kind of work venture.

Most boys, as they enter and pass puberty, find themselves excluded from activities which might provide them recognition as significant males in the adult world. They turn, therefore, to making a society of their own. In this world they gain recognition by methods of their own devising. "Souped-up" cars, reckless driving, dare-devil exploits, boisterous and bizarre behavior, drinking prowess, depreciation and defiance of adult values and standards, all figure in adolescent boys' efforts to be accounted men.

Aggressiveness, in the sense of "getting ahead," of being a "go-getter," of getting to the top, is extolled as a major virtue in our culture, particularly for males. This is usually considered as applying to sports, or the occupational and vocational efforts of men. Some of the statue-conferring values of aggressiveness have attached themselves to sexual striving.

The aggressive exercise of sexual powers is definitely a masculine characteristic. The female may receive and accept, but it is the male who has the physical strength to overpower, and who penetrates the female. This is a simple fact of biology which can never be altered, though its manifestations may be culturally modified. In our culture the male is generally the overt sexual aggressor. Certainly the youth sub-culture[3] places a high value on sexual prowess as an evidence of masculine achievement. As a result the line between aggressiveness and exploitation becomes very thin, indeed.

Sexual prowess through actual or demonstrated achievement is, therefore, a need of many adolescent boys. They feel this as a pressure, and they bring this pressure to bear on each other. Excerpts from liaison histories at various levels of involvement have been offered to show how these pressures affect masculine sexual behavior.

When these pressures combine in the persons of a boy and a girl in an unsupervised dating relationship, the outcome can be predicted. The situation, to put it bluntly, is that the girl wants a boy, and the boy wants sex. So in order to get the boy the girl provides (or offers) him sex hoping that this will entice him into a permanent association, or he seeks it aggressively to prove, to himself at least, that he is a man.

So long as these confusions and pressures exist sex is certain to

---

[3] Ehrmann (27) in his research on dating behavior has considerable data on the male and female sub-cultures in our society. Many of his findings coincide with our own, and the student of premarital dating behavior will want to study Ehrmann's research. Le Masters (67) has extensive expository material in his book on male and female sub-cultures.

be used more exploitively than would otherwise be the case. So long as false values are built about sex, marriage and mate selection, so long as youths are sexually over-stimulated, or encouraged to contract relationships for which they are unready, just so long will sex be used exploitively. Such circumstances make it difficult, if not impossible, to use sex as a constructive force in creating good interpersonal relationships.

4. *Sex Antagonisms and Hostilities.* A long-existing and deep-seated antagonism and hostility between the sexes is still another problem. Just as certain courtship pressures have probably always existed, so have rivalries and antagonisms between the sexes. These feelings easily give rise to the exploitive use of sex. Currently, there are several circumstances which have created much hostile feeling between the sexes.

One is the changing relationship between the sexes. Women have been moving steadily from a subordinate status to one of equality, and in some aspects of life to one of dominance. This changing relationship provides many opportunities for strong feelings to develop. Some women feel that their individual qualities, talents, and rights have been insufficiently recognized. Some men feel that women are invading the masculine world, which leads to complaints that "women are getting out of their place" and should be "kept in the home where they belong."

A second circumstance which touches more and more families merits consideration. With increasing urbanization and suburbanization, more and more children are being reared in a setting which is primarily matriarchal. This seems a problem, particularly so far as boys are concerned. Some boys are scarcely aware of any authority or influence in their rearing other than that exercised by women. At present a substantial body of opinion exists supporting the idea that a rearing experience which is largely matriarchal results in boys who are insecure in their masculine role, antagonistic toward women, and otherwise immature and poorly adjusted.

In a mother-dominated home the boy grows tired of being supervised, directed, and (as he feels) "bossed" by women. These hostilities are "taken out" by the boy on the girls he dates, the woman he marries, or the daughter he begets. Excerpts from some of the case histories can be interpreted as supporting this view. Careful studies need to be made in order to determine the significance of this kind of family authority pattern on the feelings and behavior of the children.

Another source of rivalry and hostility between the sexes is found in the numerous double standards which exist. The term "double standard" ordinarily relates to masculine freedom-feminine denial in sexual conduct. Actually a double standard exists in many phases of male-female relations. In the occupational world sex membership affects the rate of pay, the quality of available and accessible positions, and the top limits in achievement to which the individual can aspire. The double standard in the political field kept woman from voting for years, and it still exists as a strong barrier to women holding high political office.

These double standards operate in very complex and confusing ways. Sometimes they become double-double standards as when some women who regard themselves as pure and virtuous enforce a standard of conduct toward certain members of their own sex which sets the latter group off as "cheap" and non-virtuous. Women may support a double standard of sexual conduct even when it apparently works against their long-run good. Nor are all double standards favorable to men, as for example the standard which permits women relative freedom in the expression of their tenderer emotional feelings while denying it to men.

The double standard in sexual conduct makes the exploitive use of sex especially easy. Thus, the responsibility for determining "how far" a couple shall go is frequently left entirely to the girl, who accepts it as her rightful responsibility. In many dating relationships the girl is the one who has to set the limits. Unless she halts progress into petting and toward intercourse it does not stop. Simply stopping the move toward intercourse often does not settle the matter. In addition the girl may have to resist the arguments, the persistence, and sometimes even the physical efforts of the boy to carry his advances into intercourse, as is shown by the studies of Kirkpatrick and Kanin (64), and Kanin (54). If the girl has had intercourse previously, and especially if she is a divorcée, many men regard her as fair game. The object is to outwit her and outguess her. Her legitimate needs and the realities of her situation are not considered.

The wily girl may also take advantage of this situation to ensnare the male. She is coy and conventional enough to establish the concept of virtue which is important to her, but alluring enough to give the male the urgency with which he overthrows her virtue. And so under the double standard each exploits the other.

Sex is frequently used to vent hostilities and to satisfy other strong feelings men and women may bear for each other. It is used in the service of the non-democratic but age-old philosophy of masculine dominance and feminine subordination. The outcome is its frequent use for exploitation and advantage-taking objectives.

5. *Biological and Social Sex Differences*. Differences in the biological and the social status of the two sexes make it very difficult to arrive at decisions relative to premarital sex practices which are acceptable to and make comparable demands upon members of both sexes. Research studies, with predictable regularity, show that males are more willing and more ready to urge the casual use of sex than are females. Sex can hardly be the casual, readily-accepted experience in the life of a woman that it can be in the life of a man. This circumstance produces the well-established difference in viewpoints between the two sexes, a difference which is not the result of chance. It rests quite solidly upon two factors. One is the unchangeable biological differences between men and women. The other is the deep-seated social attitudes and conventions toward what is involved in participation by men and by women in the various forms of sexual behavior.

Biologically, women can and do become the victims of irresponsible sexual behavior far more easily than men. The masculine role in the reproductive process is simply to penetrate the female and deposit the sperm. At this point, from the standpoint of physiological processes he has contributed all he can. Beyond the possible contraction of a disease there seems no way in which he can be physically victimized by casual sex experience.

On the other hand, the female's whole pattern of living is changed as she becomes pregnant, moves toward, and enters parenthood. Whether this experience is one she bears easily, and accepts as a desirable experience, depends a great deal upon the willingness of the man who impregnated her to share the reproductive responsibilities and give her support. If he is unwilling to do this, the demands of the reproductive process are likely to be disproportionately heavy for her. In other words, she has become the biological victim of sex.

Throughout life awareness of sex and its consequences bears more heavily upon women than men. Physiological processes which begin for both sexes at puberty, i.e., menstruation, seminal emissions, condition behavior and influence daily practices much more for the female than for the male. The same holds true for intercourse, reproduction, child-care, and the middle-age change-of-life. Potentially and actually the woman's pattern of life is always much more altered by these experiences than the man's. In order to protect themselves and their position women must be more guarded and circumspect in their sexual behavior than men. This, in turn, introduces an element of considerable complexity into the development and maintenance of satisfying interpersonal relations.

6. *Deficiencies in Personal Adjustments.* The fragmentation, purposelessness,[4] immaturities, and psychological maladjustments that characterize the lives of many people interfere with their capacity to create satisfying interpersonal relations. A long and extended discussion to prove the prevalence of these conditions is unnecessary. The evidence that they exist is all about us. The important question is what effect this kind of circumstance has upon the use of sex.

In the first place these conditions render people much less capable of handling sex in a mature, non-exploitive way than they could otherwise handle it. People who lack purpose and meaning in their personal lives may seek the fulfillment which they are unable to attain otherwise through sex. Since sex in itself can not sustain a lasting relationship their efforts to attain satisfaction in this manner are ordinarily as fruitless as their efforts in other directions.

Neurotic immaturities are often reflected in sexual behavior. Psychiatric analysis of individuals and psychiatrically-oriented research have established this fact quite clearly.

A study (Wittkower, 95) was conducted during World War II by two psychiatrists in the British Army. They took a random

---

[4] For an excellent discussion of the fragmentation and purposelessness in our society see Wheelis (94).

sample of two hundred venereal-disease patients who were classified as promiscuous, and a control group of eighty-seven patients
who were hospitalized for impetigo. These patients were then
interviewed and classified as to the maturity of their personalities.
The results were as follows:

	Venereal Disease Patients	Control Patients
Immature personality types	59%	19%
Borderline	30%	19%
Mature personality types	11%	62%

These psychiatrists wrote, "There is not the slightest evidence
for the view which attractively links up health, virility, and promiscuity." On the contrary, "True promiscuity has an acute or
chronic neurotic motivation," and cannot be accounted for on the
basis of physiological necessity.

Similar evidence has also been revealed in a study (Lion, 69)
of two hundred eighty-seven promiscuous and seventy-eight potentially promiscuous girls made in the San Francisco Psychiatric
Clinic during 1943 and 1944. These girls represented typical pick-
ups and prostitutes. The study was made for the purpose of determining the kinds of families, the type of personalities, and other
pertinent factors common to this group of girls.

The following passages are taken from the report:

> Family disorganization was characteristic in the case histories.
> . . . Among 60 per cent of the patients, parents were either sepa-
> rated, divorced, or deceased. In many of these broken homes the
> parents had remarried one or more times. In a few instances the
> patients had no knowledge of their fathers, and illegitimacy of
> the patients was known or suspected. To this story of broken
> homes there was the sequel of placement in boarding schools,
> foster homes, or in the homes of relatives for varying periods
> of time.
>
> The effect of broken homes was evident in a majority of cases.
> . . . Inconsistencies in training and discipline were frequently
> the result of constant shifting from the care of one parent to
> that of another. . . . Emotional ties to one parent and rejection
> of the other were frequently seen. In some instances there was an
> absence of loyalty to the family group and of affectional ties to
> any member of the family. . . . Many . . . identified themselves
> with men and rejected their own feminine role. . . .

Approximately three-fourths of the promiscuous patients and nearly two-thirds of those potentially promiscuous had had voluntary premarital intercourse. . . . The first experience was usually with a boy friend or fiancé. . . . To be considered "one of the crowd" often prompted patients to experiment initially with sexual intercourse. . . .

Some personality characteristics were common to the patients as a group. Noteworthy among these was the uneven development in the areas of physical, intellectual, emotional, and social maturity for individual patients . . . ability to accept organized group experiences was lacking or limited. Usually their associates were men and women who, like themselves, had not reached maturity although they attempted to fulfill the adult role. . . . Immaturity in characterological development was prevalent and was expressed especially in the patients' inability and unwillingness to assume responsibility for their behavior. Allocation of blame upon parents, husbands, and others to account for their own shortcomings was common. . . .

Contrary to popular belief, no evidence was revealed to indicate that this problem is produced by above average sex drive. In fact, *the majority of habitually promiscuous patients were promiscuous in an attempt to meet other problems rather than in an attempt to secure sexual satisfaction.* . . . (Italics in the original)

A later investigation made by the Psychiatric Service of the San Francisco City Clinic was devoted to an analysis of male promiscuity. A total of two hundred fifty-five men were included in this study.

In discussing the motivation for habitual promiscuity in men, the investigators (Safier, 88) say:

Promiscuity . . . was revealed to be a problem in interpersonal relationships. The degree of (sexual) satisfaction experienced by the promiscuous men was greater than that experienced by the promiscuous women; however, it appeared that in many cases, as with the women, promiscuity was engaged in as an attempt to solve other problems. In nearly all cases this behavior appeared to be the result of conflicts, inadequacies, or disorganization within the personality. Incapacity for sustained love relationships or impairment of that capacity was revealed by almost every patient. Active hostility toward women was present in varying degrees among some of the men. . . .

> . . . no evidence could be secured that promiscuity was the
> result of greater than average sex drive. With the exception of
> two patients the men did not themselves offer this explanation,
> and in those two cases it appeared that this explanation was a
> rationalization offered to cover up difficulties in relationship to
> women and sexual conflicts. Neither clinical data nor Rorschach
> studies revealed greater than average sensuality.

These quotations show how closely promiscuity is related to
personality adjustments and social conditions, and how home deficiencies and personal inadequacies are really factors that afford
openings through which these individuals take advantage, or are
taken advantage of and exploited.

Some interesting reinforcing evidence is offered by Maslow (72)
in the data developed from a study of "self-actualizing," i.e., out-
standingly mature people. Maslow, in interpreting his findings, is
emphatic in pointing out several things.

1. Self-actualizing people are able and willing to take the welfare of others into account in their sexual expressions.
2. Self-actualizing people "enjoy" sexual experience much more
   intensely than the average person, though at the same time
   they consider it "much less important in the total frame of
   reference."
3. Self-actualizing people tend to join sex and love in a very complete merger. While they may be able to enjoy sexual pleasure
   without love they are much less likely than other people to
   care for it that way.

So evidence from both ends of the adjustment continuum indicates that fragmentation, purposelessness, and psychological maladjustments contribute to the extensive misuse of sex. Neurotic
immaturities are related to promiscuity and casual, irresponsible
sexual exploration; emotionally healthy persons can enjoy sex, but
still put it in a perspective where it will effectively support satisfying interpersonal relationships.

7. *An Irrational Moral Code.* The moral code of society today is
primarily focused upon acts. So long as we focus on the absence
or occurrence of specific acts as our basis for making moral decisions and judgments, we will be defeated in trying to think constructively about motivation, meaning, and the consequences of
behavior for interpersonal relationships. In premarital sexual be-

havior we ordinarily consider participation in a sexual act as an evidence of immorality. If we accept the improvement of interpersonal relationships as a criterion for moral judgments then we find that some very immoral experiences may occur in the realm of sex without any overt sexual action having occurred.

A movement toward using the criterion of interpersonal relationships as the basis for making moral judgments is hampered by our concentration on certain other goals as major social values. The attainment of these goals is inconsistent with an emphasis on the importance of interpersonal relationships. As this is not the place to engage in a prolonged discussion of values, it seems sufficient to say that so long as power or high position, almost regardless of how gained, or material wealth, is used as a measure of success a light value will be placed on interpersonal relationships as a goal. When the improvement of interpersonal relations is accepted as a paramount value it will force the reconsideration of many of our other social values.

8. *Inadequate Societal Arrangements.* The successful integration of sex into a social pattern is dependent upon the development of certain supporting features within the society. These features are evolved to afford a needed measure of protection to its members. Thus, the family is commonly said to have as one of its functions the provision of sexual satisfaction for husband and wife and nurturance and support for the offspring.

In a society in which premarital intercourse is acceptable, and which is at the same time concerned with the improvement of interpersonal relationships some important social features seem necessary. One would be that responsibility be automatically assumed with participation in a sexual relationship. This responsibility should involve both male and female and should extend to all the possible ramifications of the sexual relationship. The most obvious responsibility relates to possible pregnancy. Responsible concern for possible emotional outcomes and developments in other relationships should be included also.

A second supporting feature which is necessary would be satisfactory social arrangements and attitudes to help unmarried mothers and children born out of wedlock. Undoubtedly, as premarital intercourse becomes more widely practiced, the number of premarital conceptions will increase, and more premarital pregnancies will be carried to birth. Dealing with this as a social problem is an approach with which our culture has had less experience than some others. Such things as the adoption of children into good families, the assumption by the father of a reasonable and definite share of responsibility for the conception and rearing of the child, and the removal of the stigma on unmarried mothers and illegitimate children, are possible arrangements.

How social arrangements that are expected to achieve certain outcomes will actually work out is hard to predict. Thus, early marriage is a social development which has been suggested as a solution to the sex problems of youth. Some have assumed that early marriage would reduce the number of couples entering premarital intercourse. Whether early marriages have had any effect on the amount of premarital intercourse no one knows, but there is reason for questioning the validity of this assumption.[5] In fact, the reverse may be true.

As already noted, the trend toward early marriage is having the important effect of shortening the optimum period of mate selection for women. Whether this tempts them more and more to use whatever methods they can to move toward marriage is an open question. Data in this study would indicate that one consequence may be the use of intercourse as a lure to engagement and marriage.

Evidence also exists to indicate that a sizable number of early marriages are the result of premarital pregnancies. This is not surprising, since some young men and women are active participants in sexual relationships which may produce progeny six, eight, or even ten years before they can support themselves economically.

Another possibility is that the trend toward early marriage may result in more non-marital intercourse. Kinsey's study of males (57) indicates that men who marry as virgins are more likely to have extramarital intercourse than men who marry with experience in premarital relationships. The marriage of more and more men at an early age, before they have had premarital sexual experience, may be reflected in a future rise in the amount of extramarital experiences.

The experience of other cultures might be of value at this point.

---

[5] See reference 14 for a comprehensive summary of the research on early marriage.

The Scandinavian countries are often cited as having been more successful in dealing with the premarital sex problem than our own. Any comparative analysis of sexual customs needs, however, to take all the various cultural features into account. Americans interested in sexual freedom are prone to cite sexual freedom as characteristic of the Scandinavian countries, but overlook the concepts of individual and state responsibility which accompany it. They also fail to recognize the various interlocking and supporting features which have developed in these cultures to undergird the accepted patterns of sexual behavior. Illustrations are subsidies for unmarried mothers and for families, a firm assessment of masculine responsibility, an acceptance of full equality between the sexes, the removal of the stigma on children born out of wedlock, and state assistance in the care of all children.[6]

As experience broadens, still other social features which have implications for the use of sex in the premarital period will doubtlessly emerge.

FACILITATING FORCES

Certain forces or conditions, outlined below, are modifying our attitudes and sexual practices in the direction of greater liberality and more freedom. These forces would seem to reduce some of the hazards which premarital intercourse poses to interpersonal relationships.

1. *A Growing Objectivity Toward Sex.* The difficulties involved in discussing sexual problems objectively were noted earlier in this chapter. It is a satisfaction to recognize that progress is being made toward objectivity. Definite advances in frank, straightforward discussion have resulted from scientific publications and research findings in this area. The writings of Freud and Havelock Ellis broke through the barriers. Later the studies of Dickinson and Beam (25) and Hamilton (48) and the more recent studies by Kinsey, swept away many more of the remaining obstacles. The problem now is to increase the capacity for objective discussion and to use this capacity for the improvement of interpersonal relationships.

---

[6] For an interesting discussion of the social arrangements in the Scandinavian countries see reference 32.

2. *Growing Insights Into Nature and Needs.* Psychological insights concerning human nature, the character of sex, and the needs of men and women in their interpersonal associations have been increasing. This is all to the good.

The writer holds with those authorities who regard the essential nature of man as co-operative, loving, and accepting of others. These authorities also accept sex as a positive force—a part of the same capacity which makes the normal individual responsive to others, and appreciative of warm, embracing relationships. Thus regarded the sexual impulse is not to be feared but utilized in helping build the kind of relationships which make possible genuine freedom, enriching associations, and satisfying fulfillment of individual potentialities.

The growing strength of these views on the nature of man and sex is reflected in the writings of a number of religious leaders. As they consider the place of sex in the modern social setting, the rigid, unyielding standards, based on the omission or commission of acts, are being abandoned. In the writings of outstanding leaders, more and more expression is being given to a concern of the improvement of interpersonal relations. The reader concerned with the views of modern religious leaders should consult the publications of such men as Buber (13), Hiltner (50), Cole (19, 20).

It seems reasonable to hope for the eventual development of social arrangements that will harmonize with our psychological knowledge. Regard for what we learn and adherence to basic human relationship principles will keep freedom from becoming irresponsibility, liberty from becoming license, and place sex in perspective with other human needs.

This is one of the most hopeful of the various trends. It is a far more fruitful approach to the development of satisfying interpersonal relationships than an attempt to set up rigid patterns of behavior and conduct.

3. *An Increasing Tolerance for Sexual Expression.* Over the years there has been an increasing readiness to accept a freer expression of sex in the premarital period. In the main this development has applied to sexual expressions other than premarital intercourse.[7] Masturbation, for example, is no longer considered a

---

[7] Goldsen (43) feels, and the writer would agree, that among college stu-

heinous crime or even a psychologically dangerous experience by students of sexual behavior. In fact, many people are now willing to accept masturbation as a normal, even desirable, premarital sex adjustment. Such disapproval as still exists is based primarily on religious teachings.

Physical expression between dating partners which results in sexual arousal, i.e., petting, seems to be increasingly accepted, particularly in middle-class groups. The number of engaged couples who experience intercourse before marriage would indicate a growing tolerance for sexual expression at this level.

Various sexual aberrations, e.g., homosexuality, are now being recognized as an evidence of disturbances in relationships rather than as expressions of willful misconduct. As this point of view becomes more widely and firmly held, prejudices and hampering misconceptions will disappear. Objective and honest communication becomes possible, and attention can be given to the meaning and consequence of various kinds of sexual expression.

4. *Increased Control over Consequences*. Scientific advances have made it more possible to regulate the possible consequences of sexual intercourse both within and outside of marriage. Contraceptive devices and prophylactic advances have much reduced the dangers of unwanted conception and venereal disease. More effective devices are even now being developed. The real problem is probably less the adequacy of the devices than human failure—the irresponsibility, the unwillingness, or the inability of the participants to use those devices.

5. *Availability of Advisory Service*. The past few years have seen an increase in the number of counselors who can help individuals deal with sexual and relationship problems. An enumeration of sources of available advisory help would be impossible. The sources range, however, from individual doctors and private

---

dents there is now a very permissive attitude toward premarital intercourse. She writes, "Few students say they insist strictly on chastity in their potential mates . . . few students say they consider 'no previous sex experience' as an important criterion for choosing a mate. Less than one college man in a hundred—and not one college woman (sic)—selected this as *the* most important criterion. Fewer than one out of five men, and one out of seven women, said it was important at all." But, Goldsen cautions, this "does not mean that college students are unconcerned about the premarital chastity of their mates," it simply means they do not consider it decisive.

counselors to well-organized and established groups like the Planned Parenthood Federation of America, or the American Association of Marriage Counselors. Counselors in some public schools may help youth while marriage counseling services serve husbands and wives. Family service agencies deal with whole families, and there are special services to work with unwed mothers, adoptions, or fertility problems.

The presence of such services in the community serves to increase insight and understanding, and to make possible a more intelligent and humane approach to problems of sex.

6. *Decline of the Double Standard.*[8] This development is included with some reservation. The decline of the double standard would appear to be a gain, for it erases an artificial distinction between the sexes and moves toward the judgment of individuals on the basis of merit. Punishing competitiveness between the sexes may be diminishing. Even so, there is considerable doubt that the single standard as it is evolving has reduced exploitation.

We are still far from having placed the concern for developing non-exploitive interpersonal relationships, whether sexual or otherwise, first in our hierarchy of values. We lack both the necessary understanding and the attitudes. Until one of our major values becomes the development of good interpersonal relationships, a change in the extent to which we adhere to the double standard may make little difference. The result may be simply a single standard with exploitation appearing in a different guise, but as hurtful as ever.

7. *An Increasing Amount of Sexual Research.* Research in human sex behavior is a comparatively recent social innovation. The pioneer studies in the United States took place early in this century. G. V. Hamilton (48), Katherine Davis (22), Robert L. Dickinson and Lura Beam (25) opened the way for the most extensive and ambitious of all studies, the one conducted by Alfred C. Kinsey (57, 58) and his associates. Researchers up to this time have been much concerned with the *incidence* of sexual behavior. Much time and effort has gone into counting and into comparisons

---

[8] Reiss (85) presents an excellent analysis in which he distinguishes four premarital sex standards of which one is the double standard. Reiss feels the strength of the double standard is declining, and that we are moving toward a standard of permissiveness with affection.

of the behavior of specific groups. We are now seeing a growing concern with *understanding* sexual behavior. This is being reflected in research. References to the studies made at the Psychiatric Clinic of the City of San Francisco examining the cause of promiscuous sexual behavior were made earlier in this chapter.

Loeb (71) is at present engaged in studies attempting to distinguish the basic personality characteristics that differentiate between those who do and those who do not participate in premarital intercourse. He advances three tentative conclusions:

> First, teen-agers who trust themselves and their ability to contribute to others and who have learned to rely on others socially and emotionally are least likely to be involved in irresponsible sexual activity.

> Second, teen-agers who have learned to be comfortable in their appropriate sex roles (boys who like being boys and wish to be men, and girls who like being girls and wish to be women) are least likely to be involved in activities leading to indiscriminate sexuality.

> Third, both boys and girls have a need to discuss serious problems with adults who they feel can be helpful—that is to say, trusted.

Loeb's conclusions, though tentative, provide an appropriate note upon which to close this chapter. They suggest again that responsible sexual behavior and satisfying interpersonal relations are closely linked: as one finds satisfaction in his interpersonal associations and in his sex role his sexual behavior patterns are influenced. This is, of course, in keeping with the underlying assumption of this study, and with other cited examples of research.

Perhaps this brings us nearer, too, to a definition of the kind of love that needs to undergird our sexual practices. The statement is frequently made that sex should be exercised within a context of "love." "Love" is usually taken to mean a romantic love, a surging emotional attachment between male and female. The writer regards this as a restrictive and limiting definition of love. The concern for interpersonal relationships, the central concern of this study, greatly enlarges the scope and meaning of love. Sex standards, genuinely set within the framework of this broader concept of love, will not go far wrong.

CONCLUSION

The evidence marshaled in this study, and its interpretation, suggest certain features which may be helpful in an effort to use our sexual endowments in the service of satisfying interpersonal relationships. These features have already been indicated, and so need only to be brought together here in summary. They are:

1. Adherence to a value system which makes a concern for the improvement of interpersonal relations a paramount value.

2. Acceptance of the fact that the sexual impulse is essentially positive and life-giving in nature. Rather than fearing it, our task is learning how to direct and utilize it.

3. Much discussion and objective consideration of the nature of sex, and its place in relationships. These discussions need to cut across age and sex lines, and to be approached in the same manner as we approach discussions on other subjects.

4. Scrupulous care to avoid exploitive, self-centered use of sex.

5. Much attention to ways in which satisfying and complementing sex roles can be developed.

6. The release of pressures and the elimination of commercial uses which attach extraneous values to sex.

7. A continuation of research which will increase insights into all aspects of human adjustment, including sex.

These suggestions are offered in the belief that as they are realized our culture may move toward a more responsible, satisfying, and a more fulfilling use of sex, not only in the premarital period but throughout life.

STATISTICAL FINDINGS

The data contained in this Appendix provide an overview of certain aspects of the study. They permit inter-level comparisons and indicate trends which are not so clearly visible in a level-by-level examination. They also permit a different type of analysis than is possible through the descriptive data used in Chapters II-VII.

General Data

Table 10* indicates the level-designation of the six hundred sixty-eight liaisons reported by the two hundred subjects participating in this study. The level assigned was the one which existed at the time intercourse was initiated. The liaisons are also arrayed according to the ages of the subjects. The large number of liaisons (123) which were reported without the ages of the subject being recorded represent a failure in data collection. Over half of the liaisons for which an age was not recorded were in Levels I and II (prostitutes and pick-ups). The failure to record the age re-

---

* Seven tables with background data, with data relating to specific levels, or to liaison movement are found in Chapters I-VIII.

sulted from the fact that a number of prostitute relationships were reported as occurring when "I was in the service" or "When I was in high school." Since the investigation was concentrated strongly on the relationship aspects of these experiences, rather than upon the age at which intercourse first occurred, I often let such a statement stand without raising the question of exact age.

Table 10

LIAISON LEVELS ARRAYED BY AGE OF SUBJECT AT

TIME OF INTERCOURSE

AGE	Level of Liaison						TOTAL
	I	II	III	IV	V	VI	
Not Recorded	33	32	28	18	12	0	123
9	0	0	1	0	0	0	1
10	0	0	1	0	0	0	1
12	0	0	0	1	0	0	1
13	1	1	3	1	1	0	7
14	1	4	7	5	3	0	20
15	3	7	20	3	1	0	34
16	7	6	23	10	16	0	62
17	5	19	24	15	20	4	87
18	15	23	41	25	20	7	131
19	9	9	33	13	9	8	81
20	9	5	22	14	8	2	60
21	2	2	10	4	3	4	25
22	4	6	6	3	0	0	19
23	3	4	2	1	0	0	10
24	0	0	1	0	1	0	2
26	0	0	0	1	1	0	2
27	0	0	0	2	0	0	2
TOTAL	92	118	222	116	95	25	668
Per Cent	13.8	17.6	33.2	17.4	14.2	3.8	100.0
Average Age	18.46	17.60	17.78	17.19	17.71	18.80	

Only six liaisons are recorded for men from twenty-four to twenty-seven years of age, and only ten subjects are in the twenty-three years-of-age group. Certain important selective factors are operating here. First, the proportion of all men in their mid- or late twenties who are in college is small. Second, if they are in college they are more likely to be married than are the younger men, and so were less likely to be reached by this investigation.

The data in Table 10 shows that the boys under sixteen years of age in our sample were unlikely to have had their sexual experience with prostitutes. Their liaisons are more likely to be with a neighborhood girl who takes the lead, or with a girl who is herself interested in experimenting.

Another striking feature of the data set forth in Table 10 is the small number of liaisons reported at Level VI. Only twenty-five,* or less than four per cent of the total, are Level VI liaisons. Level V liaisons comprise 14 per cent of the total. In other words, only 16 per cent of all liaisons are reported at the two upper levels.

Several points may have a bearing upon this distribution. The manner in which the subjects were obtained may have by-passed men who were involved in Level V and VI liaisons. Since these are liaisons in which the partners are mutually affectionate, some subjects may have chosen not to report liaisons at these levels. The investigator occasionally had evidence of greater hesitancy on the part of interviewees to report current Level V and VI liaisons then to report liaisons at lower levels. This is probably because Level VI men felt the need for protecting their partners from possible criticism, or from the revelation of an existing relationship. Without doubt, Level VI subjects have a sense of loyalty for their partners which they do not feel toward persons with whom they are associated at levels of lesser emotional involvement.

The largest portion of the liaisons, 33 per cent, occurred at the casual dating level (Level III), while Levels II and IV each account for about 18 per cent of the total. Level I accounts for about 14 per cent of all liaisons reported. This means that 82 per

---

* It was later found that twenty-eight (4.2 per cent) liaisons fell in this category. Three had been erroneously included in Level V; but since all the IBM data have been processed and calculations made, the decision was to let the data stand. This at the same time reduced the Level V liaisons to ninety-two.

cent of the recorded intercourse relationships occurred at levels which by definition represent minimal emotional attachments or no attachment whatsoever. As has been demonstrated in the preceding chapters, the impact of premarital intercourse on interpersonal relationships differs greatly with the degree of emotional involvement felt by the couple. Obviously the preponderant impact of premarital intercourse within this group is that which is common to the minimal levels of emotional involvement.

This raises another important question, but at present an unanswered one. What liaison distribution according to levels would be found if all premarital intercourse relationships were reported? Would the liaisons be equally distributed among the levels, or is the distribution found in this study fairly accurate? The data collected in this study provide no answer to these questions.

Table 11

SUBJECTS EXPERIENCING INTERCOURSE AND HAVING
INITIAL INTERCOURSE BY LIAISON LEVELS

Level	COLUMN A Subject Experiencing Intercourse	COLUMN B Subjects Having Initial Experience	Per Cent Column A Is of Column B
I	38	18	47.5%
II	60	27	45.0%
III	98	53	54.0%
IV	87	43	49.5%
V	77	41	53.2%
VI	28	18	64.3%
Total	388	200	

Table 11 shows the number of men participating in intercourse at each level, and the proportion at these levels who were having their initial experience. The smallest proportion of virgins among those participating at any of the levels was found at Level II. Here 45 per cent of the participants had their initial experience. The largest proportion was found at Level VI. Here 64 per cent of the participants had intercourse for the first time. From these data one might anticipate, with a larger population, an increase as one moved from levels of minimal to maximal emotional involvements in the proportion of the participants who experienced their first intercourse at that level. On the other hand, when the total participating population (200 subjects) is studied it is found that more men had their initial experience at Level III than at any other level. The next highest levels in terms of initial experience were Levels IV and V.

Obviously the whole matter of distribution needs further study. In a large population what proportions of all the liaisons experienced would be found at the various levels? What proportion of all the men with premarital experience begin intercourse at the various levels; and how do they combine these levels when they have intercourse with more than one partner? These are unanswered questions.

Table 12 and Figure A indicate that the length of time during which the overall relationship had existed before intercourse occurred is related to the liaison level into which the sexual relationship fell. The reason for all of the Level I liaisons (prostitutes) falling in the "less than a week's acquaintance" category is obvious. The fact that only nineteen of the relationships in which intercourse occurred in less than two months' time were classified as Level IV, and only two as Level V liaisons, is of especial interest. None were classified as Level VI.

On the other hand, of the hundred and sixteen liaisons in which intercourse did not occur until after a year or more of acquaintances, 100, or 86.1 per cent, were classified as Level IV, V or VI liaisons. At levels V and VI there was, by definition, some affectional attachment. In fact, exactly half (58) of the hundred sixteen were classified as Level V liaisons. Of the twenty-five Level VI (strong emotional attachments) liaisons, intercourse occurred in only one instance under six months of acquaintance, in four instances in less than a year, and in twenty instances after an acquaintance of more than a year.

Further evidence that the investment of time in the overall relationship results in closer ties between the partners is found in Tables 13 and 14, and Figures B and C. These tables indicate the kind of verbal communication which occurred before and after intercourse, and relate it to the length of time the overall relationship had existed before intercourse occurred. In many of the liaison histories no evidence of communication between the partners

Table 12

LEVEL OF SEXUAL LIAISON AND LENGTH OF TIME THE RELATIONSHIP HAD EXISTED PRIOR TO INTERCOURSE

Liaison Level	Less Than One Week (N : % down)	One Week to Two Months (N : % down)	Two to Six Months (N : % down)	Six Months to One Year (N : % down)	Over One Year (N : % down)	Length of Time Unknown (N : % down)	TOTAL (N : % down)
I	91 : 32.5	0 :	0 :	0 :	0 :	1 : 8.3	92 : 13.7
% across	98.9 :	:	:	:	:	1.1 :	100.0 :
II	112 : 40.0	3 : 2.5	1 : 1.1	0 :	0 :	2 : 16.6	118 : 17.7
% across	94.9 :	2.5 :	0.8 :	:	:	1.7 :	100.0 :
III	69 : 24.6	95 : 79.8	32 : 34.0	7 : 14.9	16 : 13.9	3 : 25.0	222 : 33.2
% across	31.1 :	42.8 :	14.4 :	3.2 :	7.2 :	1.4 :	100.0 :
IV	8 : 2.8	19 : 16.0	42 : 44.6	21 : 44.7	22 : 18.9	4 : 33.3	116 : 17.4
% across	6.9 :	16.4 :	36.2 :	18.1 :	19.0 :	3.4 :	100.0 :
V	0 :	2 : 1.7	18 : 19.1	15 : 31.9	58 : 50.0	2 : 16.6	95 : 14.2
% across	:	2.1 :	18.9 :	15.8 :	61.1 :	2.1 :	100.0 :
VI	0 :	0 :	1 : 1.1	4 : 8.5	20 : 17.2	0 :	25 : 3.7
% across	:	:	4.0 :	16.0 :	80.0 :	:	100.0 :
TOTAL	280 : 100.0	119 : 100.0	94 : 100.0	47 : 100.0	116 : 100.0	12 : 100.0	668 : 100.0
% across	41.9 :	17.8 :	14.1 :	7.0 :	17.3 :	1.8 :	100.0 :

Span of Relationship Prior to Intercourse

Figure A

LENGTH OF TIME RELATIONSHIP EXISTING PRIOR TO INTERCOURSE
BY PERCENT AND LIAISON LEVEL (TABLE 12).

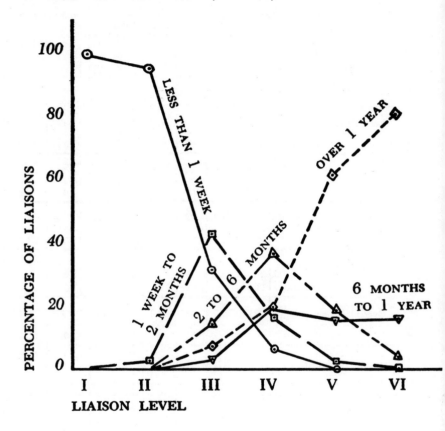

Table 13

LENGTH OF OVERALL RELATIONSHIP PRIOR TO INTERCOURSE AND TYPE OF COMMUNICATION CONCERNING POSSIBLE INTERCOURSE

Span of Time Before Intercourse	Type of Communication			TOTAL	
	Argumentative Persuasive	Understanding	No Communication or Unclassified		
	N : % : down	N : % : down	N : % : down	N : % : down	
Less Than One Week	17 : 20.0	9 : 8.6	254 : 53.0	280 : 42.0	
% across	6.1 :	3.2 :	90.7 :	100.0 :	
One—Two Weeks	18 : 22.0	13 : 12.4	88 : 18.0	119 : 17.8	
% across	15.1 :	10.9 :	73.9 :	100.0 :	
Two Weeks—Six Months	15 : 18.0	22 : 21.0	57 : 12.0	94 : 14.0	
% across	16.0 :	23.4 :	60.6 :	100.0 :	
Six Months—One Year	11 : 13.3	17 : 16.2	19 : 4.0	47 : 7.0	
% across	23.4 :	36.2 :	40.4 :	100.0 :	
Over One Year	21 : 25.0	43 : 41.0	52 : 11.0	116 : 17.4	
% across	18.1 :	37.1 :	44.8 :	100.0 :	
Length of Time Not Known	2 : 1.5	1 : 0.8	9 : 2.0	12 : 1.8	
% across	16.7 :	8.3 :	75.0 :	100.0 :	
TOTAL	84 : 100.0	105 : 100.0	479 : 100.0	668 : 100.0	
% across	12.6 :	15.7 :	71.7 :	100.0 :	

Figure B

LENGTH OF OVERALL RELATIONSHIPS PRIOR TO INTERCOURSE AND TYPE
OF COMMUNICATION CONCERNING POSSIBLE INTERCOURSE (TABLE 13).

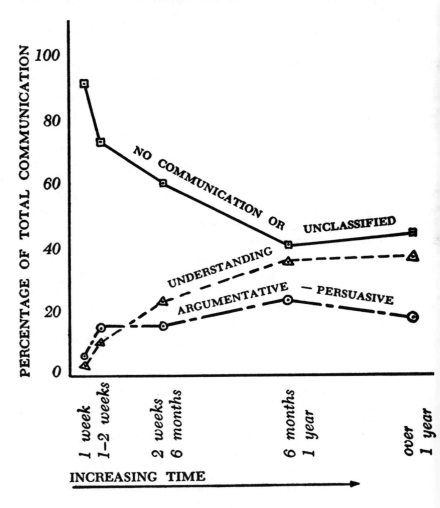

was found, while in a few of the histories the evidence was too scanty to permit classification. In these liaisons only a remark or two may ever have passed between the partners relative to sexual involvement.

In the rest of the liaisons the evidence permitted one or two classifications. First, the communication could be classified as "argumentative-persuasive." In this case it was usually a tug-and-pull contest over whether intercourse should occur or not. An attempt was being made by one partner to persuade the other to a course of action. Ordinarily, the boy was urging the girl to have intercourse. Second, the communication could be classified as "understanding" communication. This type of communication was engaged in for the purpose of understanding each other's feelings, attitudes, and desires.

Prior to intercourse a much larger proportion of the classifiable communication was argumentative-persuasive than was the case after intercourse (12.6 per cent as compared to 2.8 per cent). This may mean that in many associations after intercourse occurred the reason for argumentative-persuasive discussion had disappeared. In still other liaisons the feeling resulting from intercourse produced a tension and created a barrier which made communication of any sort impossible. This may explain in part the increase of seventy-five liaisons (from 479 to 554) in the "non communication or not classifiable" column in the pre- and post-intercourse tables (Tables 13-14). In some instances the relationship broke very shortly after the initial experience in intercourse, with no further communication having occurred.

The proportion of "understanding" communication in relationships which had existed for over a year before intercourse occurred is worth noting. In the hundred and five liaisons in which "understanding" communication occurred before intercourse forty-three (41 per cent) were in relationships which had existed for over a year. In the ninety-five liaisons in which "understanding" communication occurred after intercourse forty-seven (49 per cent) were in relationships which had existed for more than a year before intercourse took place. This carries the hint that for a few couples who have been associated for that length of time before intercourse occurs, experience in intercourse may move them toward "understanding" communication. Consideration of this point will be found in Chapter VII.

Some further data relating to verbal communication are pertinent at this point. Each interviewee was asked to indicate the amount (much, some, little, none) of discussion, regardless of kind, between himself and his sexual partner, both before and after intercourse had occurred. The data on amount as related to liaison levels are found in Tables 15 and 16, and Figures D and E.

Several items of interest are found in these tables. One is the increase in the number of liaisons in which, following intercourse, "no communication" occurred, compared to the number with "no communication" prior to intercourse (308 to 451). This increase is accompanied by a decrease in the number of liaisons in the "much" (from 57 to 36) and the "some" (from 120 to 68) communication categories. These figures harmonize with the impression gained through analysis about the amount of communication which occurred in the liaisons. Communication about sex is very difficult. There are many couples who engage in the petting preliminary to intercourse, in intercourse itself, and who ultimately separate, even as friends, without ever recognizing to each other verbally that they have been so involved. Generally speaking, it seems much easier to engage in actual intercourse than it is to refer openly to it. This point was reinforced by illustrations in the chapters discussing the various levels.

Table 15 on "communication before intercourse" indicates that in no Level I or II liaison was "much" communication reported. "Much" communication was reported, however, in thirteen Level III liaisons. Level V and VI liaisons accounted for 64.9 per cent of the "much" communication while Levels IV, V, and VI liaisons accounted for 60.8 per cent of the "some" communication. The "little" or "no" communication liaisons are heavily concentrated in Levels I, II, and III, with 72.6 per cent of the "little" and 77.8 per cent of the "no" communication there. Conversely, only 27.4 per cent of the "little" and 22.1 per cent of the "no" communication liaisons are found at Levels IV, V, and VI. Evidently a period of extended association is necessary before couples find it possible to speak openly about their own sexual relationships.

An examination of Table 16, "communication after intercourse," indicates that the distribution of liaisons arranged by levels into the various communication categories is not greatly changed over the "before intercourse" distribution. The most obvious point, as has been noted before, is the large increase in the number of liai-

Table 14

LENGTH OF OVERALL RELATIONSHIP PRIOR TO INTERCOURSE AND TYPE OF COMMUNICATION OCCURRING AFTERWARD

Span of Time Before Intercourse	Type of Communication			TOTAL	
	Argumentative Persuasive	Understanding	No Communication or Unclassified		
	N : % : down	N : % : down	N : % : down	N : % : down	
Less Than One Week	2 : 10.0	1 : 1.0	277 : 50.0	280 : 42.0
% across	0.7 :	0.4 :	98.9 :	100.0 :
One—Two Weeks	5 : 26.0	14 : 15.5	100 : 18.0	119 : 17.8
% across	4.2 :	11.8 :	84.0 :	100.0 :
Two Weeks—Six Months	4 : 22.0	17 : 18.0	73 : 13.0	94 : 14.0
% across	4.3 :	18.1 :	77.7 :	100.0 :
Six Months—One Year	5 : 26.0	13 : 14.0	29 : 29.0	47 : 7.0
% across	10.6 :	27.7 :	61.7 :	100.0 :
Over One Year	3 : 16.0	47 : 49.0	66 : 12.0	116 : 17.4
% across	2.6 :	40.5 :	56.9 :	100.0 :
Length of Time Not Known	0 :	3 : 2.5	9 : 2.0	12 : 1.8
% across	:	25.0 :	75.0 :	100.0 :
TOTAL	19 : 100.0	95 : 100.0	554 : 100.0	668 : 100.0
% across	2.8 :	14.2 :	82.9 :	100.0 :

Figure C

LENGTH OF TIME IN OVERALL RELATIONSHIPS PRIOR TO INTERCOURSE
AND TYPE OF COMMUNICATION OCCURRING AFTERWARD (TABLE 14).

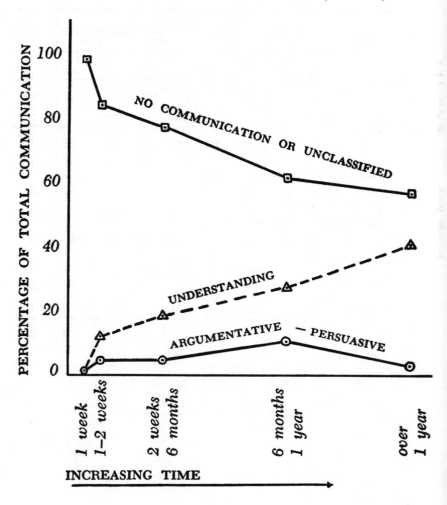

Table 15

AMOUNT OF COMMUNICATION PRIOR TO INTERCOURSE BY NUMBER AND PERCENTAGE OF LIAISONS AT VARIOUS LEVELS

| Liaison Level | Amount of Communication | | | | | | | | TOTAL | |
| | Much | | Some | | Little | | None | | | |
	N	% down	N	% down	N	% down	N	% down	N	% down
I	0		0		21	11.5	71	23.1	92	13.7
% across					22.8		77.2		100.0	
II	0		11	9.2	40	21.8	67	21.8	118	17.7
% across			9.3		33.9		56.8		100.0	
III	13	22.8	36	30.0	72	39.3	101	32.9	222	33.2
% across	5.9		16.2		32.4		45.5		100.0	
IV	7	12.3	35	29.2	32	17.6	42	13.7	116	17.4
% across	6.0		30.2		27.6		36.2		100.0	
V	26	45.6	31	25.8	17	9.3	21	6.8	95	14.2
% across	27.4		32.6		17.9		22.1		100.0	
VI	11	19.3	7	5.8	1	0.5	6	1.6	25	3.7
% across	44.0		28.0		4.0		24.0		100.0	
TOTAL	57	100.0	120	100.0	183	100.0	308	100.0	668	100.0
% across	8.5		18.0		27.4		46.1		100.0	

Figure D

AMOUNT OF COMMUNICATION PRIOR TO INTERCOURSE BY LIAISON
LEVEL (TABLE 15).

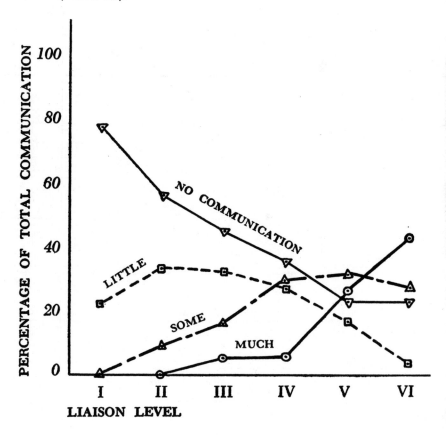

Table 16

AMOUNT OF COMMUNICATION FOLLOWING INTERCOURSE BY NUMBER
AND PERCENTAGE OF LIAISONS AT VARIOUS LEVELS

| Liaison Level | Amount of Communication | | | | | | | | TOTAL | |
| | Much | | Some | | Little | | None | | | |
	N	% down	N	% down	N	% down	N	% down	N	% down
I	0		2	2.9	19	16.8	71	15.7	92	13.7
% across			2.2		20.7		77.2		100.0	
II	1	2.8	. 2	2.9	37	32.7	78	17.3	118	17.7
% across	0.8		1.7		31.4		66.1		100.0	
III	5	13.9	16	23.5	42	37.2	159	35.2	222	33.2
% across	2.3		7.2		18.9		71.6		100.0	
IV	4	11.1	31	45.6	11	9.7	70	15.5	116	17.4
% across	3.4		26.7		9.5		60.3		100.0	
V	18	50.0	15	22.1	3	2.6	59	13.1	95	14.2
% across	18.9		15.8		3.2		62.1		100.0	
VI	8	22.2	2	2.9	1	0.9	14	3.1	25	3.7
% across	32.0		8.0		4.0		56.0		100.0	
TOTAL	36	100.0	68	100.0	113	100.0	451	100.0	668	100.0
% across	5.4		10.2		16.9		67.5		100.0	

Figure E

AMOUNT OF COMMUNICATION FOLLOWING INTERCOURSE BY LIAISON
LEVEL (TABLE 16).

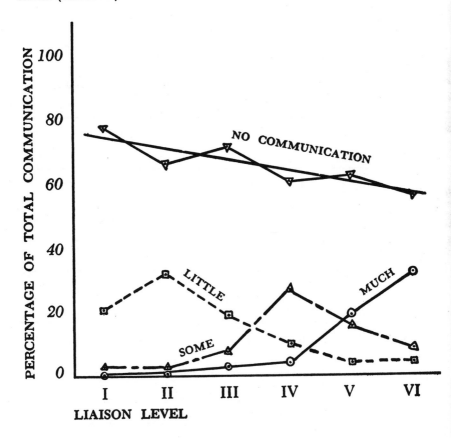

Table 17

NATURE OF COMMUNICATION PRIOR TO INTERCOURSE BY NUMBER
AND PERCENTAGE OF LIAISONS AT VARIOUS LEVELS

Liaison Level	Nature of Communication						TOTAL	
	Argumentative-Persuasive		Understanding		No Communication or Unclassified			
	N	% down	N	% down	N	% down	N	% down
I	0		0		92	19.2	92	13.7
% across					100.0		100.0	
II	11	13.1	2	1.9	105	21.9	118	17.7
% across	9.3		1.7		89.0		100.0	
III	35	41.6	18	17.1	169	35.2	222	33.2
% across	15.8		8.1		76.1		100.0	
IV	15	17.9	32	30.5	69	14.4	116	17.4
% across	12.9		27.6		59.5		100.0	
V	20	23.8	38	36.2	37	7.7	95	14.2
% across	21.0		40.0		38.9		100.0	
VI	3	3.6	15	14.3	7	1.1	25	3.7
% across	12.0		60.0		28.0		100.0	
TOTAL	85	100.0	105	100.0	479	100.0	668	100.0
% across	12.6		15.7		71.7		100.0	

Figure F

NATURE OF COMMUNICATION PRIOR TO INTERCOURSE BY LIAISON LEVEL (TABLE 17).

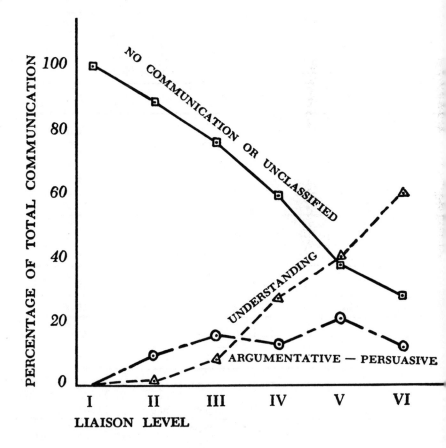

Table 18

NATURE OF COMMUNICATION FOLLOWING INTERCOURSE BY
NUMBER AND PERCENTAGE OF LIAISONS AT VARIOUS LEVELS

| Liaison Level | Nature of Communication | | | TOTAL |
| | Argumentative Persuasive | Understanding | No Communication or Unclassified | |
	N : % down	N : % down	N : % down	N : % down
I	0 :	0 :	92 : 16.8	92 : 13.7
% across	:	:	100.0 :	100.0 :
II	2 : 10.5	0 :	116 : 20.8	118 : 17.7
% across	1.7 :	:	98.3 :	100.0 :
III	8 : 42.8	18 : 18.9	196 : 35.4	222 : 33.2
% across	3.6 :	8.1 :	88.3 :	100.0 :
IV	2 : 15.8	26 : 27.4	87 : 15.7	116 : 17.4
% across	2.6 :	22.4 :	75.0 :	100.0 :
V	5 : 26.3	41 : 43.1	49 : 8.9	95 : 14.2
% across	5.3 :	43.2 :	51.6 :	100.0 :
VI	1 : 5.3	10 : 10.5	14 : 2.6	25 : 3.7
% across	4.0 :	40.0 :	56.0 :	100.0 :
TOTAL	19 : 100.0	95 : 100.0	554 :100.0	668 : 100.0
% across	2.8 :	14.2 :	82.9 :	100.0 :

Figure G

NATURE OF COMMUNICATION FOLLOWING INTERCOURSE BY LIAISON
LEVEL (TABLE 18).

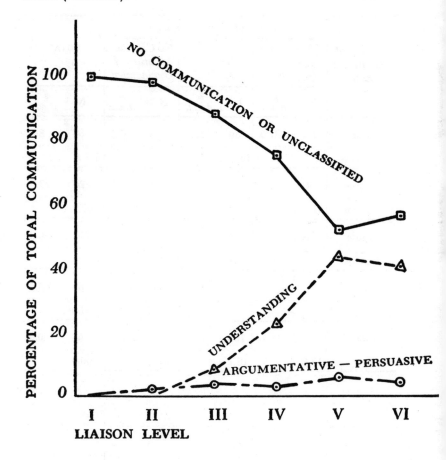

Table 19

AMOUNT AND NATURE OF COMMUNICATION PRIOR TO
INTERCOURSE BY NUMBER OF LIAISONS

Amount of Communication	Nature of Communication						TOTAL	
	Argumentative Persuasive		Understanding		No Communication or Unclassified			
	N	% down	N	% down	N	% down	N	% down
Much	26	31.0	30	28.6	1	0.2	57	8.5
% across	45.6		52.6		1.8		100.0	
Some	50	59.5	64	61.0	6	1.2	120	17.9
% across	41.7		53.3		5.0		100.0	
Little	8	9.5	11	10.4	183	38.1	202	30.3
% across	4.0		5.4		90.6		100.0	
None	0		0		289	60.5	289	43.3
% across					100.0		100.0	
TOTAL	84	100.0	105	100.0	479	100.0	668	100.0
% across	12.6		15.7		71.7		100.0	

Figure H

AMOUNT AND NATURE OF COMMUNICATION PRIOR TO INTERCOURSE
DATE (TABLE 19).

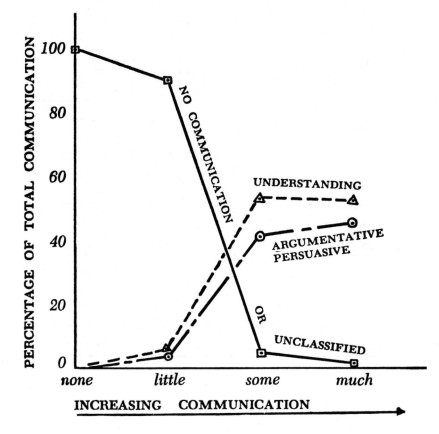

Table 20

AMOUNT AND NATURE OF COMMUNICATION FOLLOWING
INTERCOURSE BY NUMBER OF LIAISONS

Amount of Communication	Nature of Communication			TOTAL	
	Argumentative Persuasive		Understanding		No Communication or Unclassified		TOTAL	
	N : % down	N : % down	N : % down	N : % down
Much	9 : 47.4	25 : 26.4	2 : 0.4	36 : 8.4
% across	25.0 :	69.4 :	5.6 :	100.0 :
Some	5 : 26.3	41 : 43.1	22 : 4.0	68 : 10.2
% across	7.4 :	60.3 :	32.4 :	100.0 :
Little	5 : 26.3	29 : 30.5	113 : 20.4	147 : 22.0
% across	3.4 :	19.7 :	76.9 :	100.0 :
None	0 :	0 :	417 : 75.2	417 : 62.4
% across	:	:	100.0 :	100.0 :
TOTAL	19 : 100.0	95 : 100.0	554 : 100.0	668 : 100.0
% across	2.8 :	14.2 :	82.9 :	100.0 :

Figure I

AMOUNT AND NATURE OF COMMUNICATION FOLLOWING INTERCOURSE
(TABLE 20).

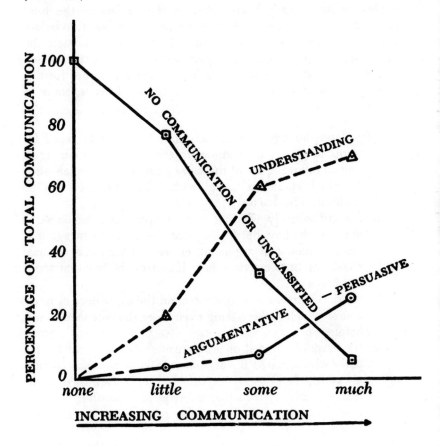

sons showing "no" communication following intercourse at Levels II and above.

Tables 17 and 18 and Figures F and G provide data on the nature of the communication which occurred before and after intercourse. The most obvious and interesting feature of these tables, as has already been noted, is the decline in the total amount of communication after intercourse as compared to before intercourse. This decline is accounted for largely through the lesser amount of argumentative-persuasive communication which occurred after intercourse. There may be several reasons for this decline, some of which are found in certain liaisons, some in others.

1. After intercourse is secured there may be no further need for attempts to persuade or argue. Intercourse may occur again and again following about the same pattern as was established in the initial experience, though with no verbal reference to the fact. This may be due to:

   a. the girl actually wanting to participate in intercourse as much as the boy, but feeling that she needs to engage in a certain amount of argument, either to satisfy conventional standards, or to convince herself and/or the boy that she is a virtuous girl.

   b. the development of tensions around the experience of intercourse which make talking even more difficult than it was before.

   c. the diminished need once intercourse has occurred for the party who initiated the arguments and persuasions (almost always the boy) to say anything more. In fact, there is the fear, particularly if further intercourse is possible, that further discussion will disturb the relationship he has been seeking.

2. The relationship may break very shortly after the beginning of intercourse. In such circumstances there is little or no opportunity for further discussion of any kind.

There are some instances in which experience in intercourse seems to result in more communication. Thus, the couple may have entered intercourse with no communication at all, but once it has occurred arguments and persuasion will be engaged in to maintain the relationship. In some instances "understanding" communication may be easier after intercourse. The experience breaks the barriers to understanding communication, and the couple engages in "understanding" communication in a way which was impossible before.

An interesting feature in Tables 19 and 20 and figures H and I is the slight decrease following intercourse (from 15.7 per cent to 14.2 per cent) in the proportion of liaisons in which there was "understanding" communication. There is a definite increase, however (from 10.4 per cent to 30.5 per cent), in the proportion of liaisons showing a little "understanding" communication. The reasons for these differences are not apparent, but the writer believes that some couples, once they have entered intercourse, are then inclined to leave the situation as it is. "Say nothing" and avoid disturbing the situation, is their reaction. They therefore avoid any discussion of what is occurring.

Tables 21 and 22 indicate the frequency with which the subject of marriage was raised before and after intercourse, the liaison levels at which the subject was raised, and whether it was raised by male, female, or by both jointly. Several interesting trends are immediately obvious. One is that the men, according to their reports, seldom raise the subject of marriage either before or after intercourse. Neither do the women raise it frequently before intercourse, nor very frequently after intercourse, though the chances are much higher that if the subject is raised by the woman, it will be after intercourse. Only four women were reported as raising the subject before intercourse, and thirty-two (or eight times as many) brought up the subject after intercourse.

The above facts raise some interesting questions. Why do neither the men nor the women bring up the subject of marriage prior to intercourse? Are the reasons for remaining silent different? Do the women use intercourse as a means of either rationalizing their wish to marry, or of forcing the issue? Do they become frightened after intercourse and seek security through marriage? Is this particularly the case for girls who are involved in Level III and IV liaisons? Is the desire to marry one of the motivations which prompt some girls to accept intercourse? In how many of the situations in which marriage was discussed "jointly" was the subject really raised by the girls?

There is more likelihood of a joint approach at Levels IV, V,

Table 21

MARRIAGE AS SUBJECT OF DISCUSSION PRIOR TO INTERCOURSE
BY LEVELS AND PERSON RAISING THE SUBJECT

| Liaison Level | Person Raising the Subject | | | | | | | | TOTAL | |
| | Male | | Female | | Jointly | | No Evidence | | | |
	N	% down	N	% down	N	% down	N	% down	N	% down
I	0		0		0		92	14.4	92	13.7
% across							100.0		100.0	
II	0		0		0		118	18.5	118	17.7
% across							100.0		100.0	
III	0		2	50.0	0		220	34.6	222	33.2
% across			0.9				99.1		100.0	
IV	0		2	50.0	6	22.2	108	16.9	116	17.4
% across			1.7		5.2		93.1		100.0	
V	0		0		11	40.7	84	13.2	95	14.2
% across					11.6		88.4		100.0	
VI	1	100.0	0		10	37.0	14	2.2	25	3.7
% across	4.0				40.0		56.0		100.0	
TOTAL	1	100.0	4	100.0	27	100.0	636	100.0	668	100.0
% across	0.1		0.6		4.0		95.2		100.0	

Table 22

MARRIAGE AS SUBJECT OF DISCUSSION FOLLOWING INTERCOURSE
BY LEVELS AND PERSON RAISING THE SUBJECT

Liaison Level	Person Raising the Subject								TOTAL	
	Male		Female		Jointly		No Evidence			
	N	% down	N	% down	N	% down	N	% down	N	% down
I	0		0		0		92	16.1	92	13.7
% across							100.0		100.0	
II	0		0		1	1.6	117	20.4	118	17.7
% across					0.8		99.2		100.0	
III	0		15	46.9	5	8.3	202	35.2	222	33.2
% across			6.8		2.3		91.0		100.0	
IV	2	100.0	14	43.8	11	18.0	89	15.6	116	17.4
% across	1.7		12.1		9.5		76.7		100.0	
V	0		3	9.4	34	55.7	58	10.1	95	14.2
% across			3.2		35.8		61.1		100.0	
VI	0		0		10	16.4	15	2.6	25	3.7
% across					40.0		60.0		100.0	
TOTAL	2	100.0	32	100.0	61	100.0	53	100.0	668	100.0
% across	0.3		4.8		9.1		85.8		100.0	

Table 23

POSSIBLE PREGNANCY AS SUBJECT OF DISCUSSION PRIOR TO INTERCOURSE BY LEVELS AND PERSON RAISING THE SUBJECT

Liaison Level	Person Raising the Subject								TOTAL	
	Male		Female		Jointly		No Evidence			
	N	% down	N	% down	N	% down	N	% down	N	% down
I	0 :		0 :		0 :		92 :	14.2	92 :	13.7
% across	:		:		:		100.0 :		100.0 :	
II	0 :		0 :		0 :		118 :	16.2	118 :	17.7
% across	:		:		:		100.0 :		100.0 :	
III	0 :		2 :	100.0	2 :	11.7	218 :	33.7	222 :	33.2
% across	:		0.9 :		0.9 :		98.2 :		100.0 :	
IV	1 :	33.3	0 :		6 :	35.4	109 :	16.9	116 :	17.4
% across	0.9 :		:		5.2 :		94.0 :		100.0 :	
V	1 :	33.3	0 :		5 :	29.4	89 :	13.7	95 :	14.2
% across	1.1 :		:		5.3 :		93.7 :		100.0 :	
VI	1 :	33.3	0 :		4 :	23.5	20 :	3.1	25 :	3.7
% across	4.0 :		:		16.0 :		80.0 :		100.0 :	
TOTAL	3 :	100.0	2 :	100.0	17 :	100.0	646 :	100.0	668 :	100.0
% across	0.4 :		0.3 :		2.5 :		96.7 :		100.0 :	

Table 24

POSSIBLE PREGNANCY AS SUBJECT OF DISCUSSION FOLLOWING INTERCOURSE
BY LEVELS AND PERSON RAISING THE SUBJECT

| Liaison Level | Person Raising the Subject | | | | | | | | TOTAL | |
| | Male | | Female | | Jointly | | No Evidence | | | |
	N	% down	N	% down	N	% down	N	% down	N	% down
I	0		0		0		92	15.9	92	13.7
% across							100.0		100.0	
II	0		1	12.5	1	1.2	116	20.0	118	17.7
% across			0.8		0.8		98.6		100.0	
III	0		4	50.0	9	11.3	209	36.1	222	33.2
% across			1.8		4.1		94.1		100.0	
IV	1	100.0	3	37.5	22	27.3	90	15.5	116	17.4
% across	0.9		2.6		19.0		77.6		100.0	
V	0		0		34	43.8	61	10.5	95	14.2
% across					35.8		64.2		100.0	
VI	0		0		14	17.4	11	1.9	25	3.7
% across					56.0		44.0		100.0	
TOTAL	1	100.0	8	100.0	80	100.0	579	100.0	.668	100.0
% across	0.1		1.2		12.0		86.7		100.0	

and VI, than at earlier levels. All of the joint discussions of marriage prior to intercourse occurred at these levels, as did 90.1 per cent of all the post-intercourse discussions.

Data with reference to discussions about possible pregnancy are reported in Tables 23 and 24. Possible pregnancy is seldom mentioned by either men or women prior to intercourse, but it was more often mentioned following intercourse. The increase occurred predominantly at Levels IV, V, and VI. Some 90.3 per cent of the jointly-initiated discussions of possible pregnancy prior to intercourse were at these levels, and 88.5 per cent of the jointly-initiated post-intercourse discussions.

Table 25

INSTANCES OF ACTUAL OR FEARED PREGNANCY RELATED TO THE
USE OR NON-USE OF CONTRACEPTIVES

| Use of Contra-ceptive | Pregnancy | | | | | | TOTAL | |
| | Actual | | Feared | | No Pregnancy | | | |
	N	% down	N	% down	N	% down	N	% down
YES	6	100.0	45	91.8	337	55.0	388	58.1
% across	1.5		11.6		86.9		100.0	
NO	0		3	6.1	108	17.6	111	16.6
% across			2.7		97.3		100.0	
NO EVIDENCE	0		1	2.0	168	27.4	169	25.3
% across			0.6		99.4		100.0	
TOTAL	6	100.0	49	100.0	613	100.0	668	100.0
% across	0.9		7.3		91.8		100.0	

Table 25 indicates the extent to which contraceptives were used, the actual number of pregnancies reported, and the number of times pregnancy was feared. Actual pregnancies were reported in only six, or 0.9 per cent, of the liaisons on which data were collected.[1] There could easily have been more pregnancies than these, however. Many of the intercourse relationships occurred under such casual conditions that the male could never have known if a pregnancy had occurred. This likelihood is certainly increased by the lack of attention some of the subjects paid to the use of contraceptives in their casual sexual relationships.

Table 26 indicates that the use of contraceptives is closely associated with the liaison level of the overall relationship. An examination of the data indicates that contraceptive measures are more likely to be taken in relationships where there is a definite degree of attachment than in relationships where there is little or no attachment. This indication becomes even stronger when data in the "no evidence" column are examined. The largest proportion (91.7 per cent) of these liaisons are found at Levels I, II, and III. Considering the casual nature of the sexual relationship at these levels, undoubtedly many of these liaisons took place without the use of contraceptives.

In some liaisons with a number of intercourse experiences it is certain that some of them occurred without the benefit of contraceptives. A number of subjects indicated that while they used contraceptives most of the time, there were occasions when they were forgotten or ignored.

The subjects were also asked if there was any specific planning or discussion, either before or after intercourse, as to what should be done in case of pregnancy. The data on this point, found in Table 27, indicate that of the six hundred sixty-eight liaisons there was such planning in seventy (10.5 per cent) liaisons, none in two hundred thirty-eight (35.6 per cent) and no evidence of such planning in three hundred sixty (53.9 per cent). When such planning did take place it was more likely to occur at Levels IV, V, and VI.

The development of unequal affectional attachments is another feature which causes difficulty in relationships where premarital intercourse has occurred. The interviewees were asked to report

---

[1] Kinsey (57, p. 327) found that about 18 per cent of all females who engaged in premarital intercourse became pregnant and that conception apparently occurred about once in every thousand experiences in intercourse. Gebhard (40, pp. 45-47) indicated that college-educated girls had a significantly lower rate of pregnancy, due in large part to the greater use of contraceptives.

Table 26

USE OR NON-USE OF CONTRACEPTIVE MEASURES
BY LIAISON LEVELS

| Liaison Level | Contraceptive Used | | | | | | TOTAL | |
| | Yes | | No | | No Evidence | | | |
	N	% down	N	% down	N	% down	N	% down
I	0 :		8 :	7.2	84 :	49.8	92 :	13.7
% across	:		8.7 :		91.3 :		100.0 :	
II	42 :	10.8	31 :	27.9	45 :	26.6	118 :	17.7
% across	35:6 :		26.3 :		38.1 :		100.0 :	
III	149 :	38.4	47 :	42.5	26 :	15.3	222 :	33.2
% across	67.1 :		21.2 :		11.7 :		100.0 :	
IV	92 :	27.7	19 :	17.1	5 :	2.9	116 :	17.4
% across	79.3 :		16.4 :		4.3 :		100.0 :	
V	82 :	21.1	6 :	5.4	7 :	4.2	95 :	14.2
% across	86.3 :		6.3 :		7.4 :		100.0 :	
VI	23 :	5.9	0 :		2 :	1.2	25 :	3.7
% across	92.0 :		:		8.0 :		100.0 :	
TOTAL	388 :	100.0	111 :	100.0	169 :	100.0	668 :	100.0
% across	58.1 :		16.6 :		25.3 :		100.0 :	

Table 27

PLANS FOR COPING WITH POSSIBLE PREGNANCY
BY LIAISON LEVEL

Liaison Level	Amount of Planning						TOTAL	
	Planning		No Planning		No Evidence			
	N	% down	N	% down	N	% down	N	% down
I	0 :		11 :	4.6	8 :	22.3	92 :	13.7
% across	:		12.0 :		88.0 :		100.0 :	
II	1 :	1.4	46 :	19.3	71 :	20.0	118 :	17.7
% across	0.9 :		39.0 :		60.1 :		100.0 :	
III	7 :	10.0	80 :	33.6	135 :	37.4	222 :	33.2
% across	3.2 :		36.0 :		60.8 :		100.0 :	
IV	15 :	21.4	59 :	24.8	42 :	11.7	116 :	17.4
% across	12.9 :		50.9 :		36.2 :		100.0 :	
V	37 :	52.8	33 :	13.8	25 :	6.7	95 :	14.2
% across	40.0 :		34.7 :		25.3 :		100.0 :	
VI	10 :	14.3	9 :	3.7	6 :	1.6	25 :	3.7
% across	40.0 :		36.0 :		24.0 :		100.0 :	
TOTAL	70 :	100.0	238 :	100.0	360 :	100.0	668 :	100.0
% across	10.5		35.6 :		53.9 :		100.0 :	

Table 28

DEGREE OF ATTACHMENT FELT BY PARTNERS BY LIAISON LEVEL

Liaison Level	Degree of Attachment								TOTAL	
	Male Stronger		Equal		Female Stronger		No Evidence			
	N	% down	N	% down	N	% down	N	% down	N	% down
I	0		19	9.7	0		73	21.1	92	13.7
% across			20.7				79.3		100.0	
II	1	1.1	24	12.2	2	1.7	91	26.4	118	17.7
% across	0.9		20.3		1.7		77.1		100.0	
III	0		38	19.4	57	48.3	127	36.8	222	33.2
% across			17.1		25.7		57.2		100.0	
IV	2	22.2	34	17.3	40	33.9	40	11.6	116	17.4
% across	1.7		29.3		34.5		34.5		100.0	
V	5	55.5	63	32.1	16	13.5	11	3.2	95	14.2
% across	5.3		66.3		16.8		11.6		100.0	
VI	1	11.1	18	9.2	3	2.5	3	0.8	25	3.7
% across	4.0		72.0		12.0		12.0		100.0	
TOTAL	9	100.0	196	100.0	118	100.0	345	100.0	668	
% across	1.3		29.3		17.7		51.6		100.0	

for each liaison whether the feelings of the male and the female for each other were equal, or whether one felt a stronger attachment than the other. Table 28 offers data on this point.

The data show that judging from masculine responses females displayed the more intense attachments much more frequently than males. The evidence is, in fact, quite impressive—the men in nine liaisons stating that they were more attached than the girls with whom they were associated, as against one hundred eighteen liaisons in which the men indicated they felt the girls were more attached than they were. The data also indicate that sex differences in affectional attachments are most likely to be found at Levels III, IV, and V. In fact, nearly half of all the liaisons in which the women appeared to be the more attached were found at Level III. Yet Level III liaisons were defined (from the masculine point of view) as those in which the dating relationship was casual, and the association was initiated to obtain intercourse.

These data also raise some interesting questions. If the women had been reporting, would they have given a similar report? Does this situation (assuming the data are reasonably accurate) reflect the greater need for women, as compared with men, to set up an attachment with members of the other sex? Is it the result of an undue social pressure placed upon a woman to get a boy friend, to get engaged, to get married? Were the women pretending, as the men sometimes were, an affectional relationship?

Experience in working with young people, as well as the experience in interviewing, leaves the impression that these data reflect an actual situation. Many of the girls were undoubtedly hoping that the relationship in which they found themselves would develop into something permanent. Girls, much more than men, feel under pressure to get engaged and to marry. Consequently, they are disposed to hope for each particular relationship to develop into something strong and permanent. They are psychologically ready to "fall in love," and so they imagine themselves in love. They talk and act the language of love, whether or not they have had time to grow into love. The reader will recall that the data in Tables 21 and 22 indicated that girls were much more likely than boys to bring up the subject of marriage following intercourse. That evidence provides support for the belief that many girls accept intercourse because they hope this will please the boy, and consequently place the relationship on a firm, enduring base. They may, in fact, think (a view which the male sometimes encourages) that the introduction of intercourse will strengthen the relationship, and so they may initiate intercourse themselves. This variation on the old saying that the way to a man's heart is through his stomach, turns out to be tragically untrue for many girls.

An accurate analysis of the motives which existed in the various liaisons is obviously impossible. One procedure was utilized, however, in the hope that it might throw some light on the question of motivation. In the process of organizing the data for tabulation on the IBM machines, the two research assistants analyzed the case histories to classify features in them according to the category analysis system which had been devised. They were asked, after they had analyzed each liaison, to rate it according to whether the male and the female about whom the male was reporting were predominatly partner-centered, or predominantly self-centered in their motivations. If the ratings as given by the raters did not agree, or evidence was insufficient, the liaison was placed in the "inconclusive evidence" column.

This kind of rating procedure is admittedly highly subjective. The reliability of the ratings is open to question, even though the ratings of the two analysts had to coincide. Moreover, the rating for the female involved in premarital intercourse was based upon the male's report of his interpretation of her reactions. Add to this the fact that people can never be sure of their feelings, and it is clear that these data can only suggest direction and raise questions for further research. The interpretation should extend no further than this. The reader should keep this in mind as he examines the data in Tables 29, 30 and 31.

In Table 29, a much larger proportion of female participants (474) than male subjects (145) fell in the "inconclusive evidence" category. Almost 75 per cent of the "inconclusive evidence" ratings for the females were from liaisons at the most casual level of involvement where self-centeredness would undoubtedly be high. Another part of the problem is surely the inability of the males to report clearly on the motivations of their female partners. Another interesting feature of the data in Table 29 is the extent to which males were judged to be more self-centered than females. The male was judged to be self-centered in four hundred ninety-six liaisons, whereas the female was judged so in one hundred

Table 29

PARTNER-CENTERED/SELF-CENTERED MOTIVATION BY SEX AS JUDGED BY RATERS

		Female						TOTAL	
		Partner		Self		Inconclusive Evidence			
		N	% down	N	% down	N	% down	N	% down
Male	Partner	21	48.8	1	0.7	5	1.1	27	4.0
	% across	77.8		3.7		18.5		100.0	
	Self	18	41.9	146	96.7	332	70.0	496	74.2
	% across	3.6		29.3		67.0		100.0	
	Inconclusive Evidence	4	9.3	4	2.6	137	28.9	145	21.8
	% across	2.8		2.8		96.5		100.0	
	TOTAL	43	100.0	151	100.0	474	100.0	668	100.0
	% across	6.4		22.6		71.0		100.0	

Read Table 29 as follows: In the first horizontal line both raters judged that in 21 liaisons both male and female were partner-centered; in one liaison the female was judged to be self-centered and the male partner-centered, etc. In the left-hand vertical column in 18 liaisons the males were judged to be self-centered, and the female partner-centered, etc.

fifty-one liaisons. The male was rated as partner-centered in twenty-seven liaisons, while the female was thought to be partner-centered in forty-three liaisons. Allowing for some errors in both rater judgment and in the subjects' reporting, these ratings still seem to indicate a real sex difference.

Does the difference result simply from the fact that the man, having reported most fully on the person he knows best—himself —is more exposed to adverse rater judgments than his partners? If the four hundred seventy-four liaisons in which there was too little evidence for judging females could actually be rated for partner-centeredness or self-centeredness, what kind of distribution would be obtained? Are the females equally self-centered, but possessed with the ability to conceal this successfully from their male partners? Does the judgment of male self-centeredness result from the fact that the man, as a result of cultural expectations and probably by virtue of biology, is the sexual aggressor, and is therefore judged to be more self-centered than the woman, simply because he assumes the aggressive role? Does the woman's passivity (which in itself may invite aggression) mask her self-centeredness? Is the woman's partner-centeredness, which may arise from her greater desire for a relationship, really more self-centered than is generally realized? Or are women genuinely less self-centered than men? If these questions were to be answered one way with reference to sexual conduct, would the answers be in the same direction when other aspects of male-female relationships are considered? These are challenging questions, and the answers are important in the understanding of sexual behavior. Unfortunately, they can not be answered from the data in this research.

Tables 30 and 31 display the data resulting from the raters' judgments on self-centered partner-centered motivations by liaison level. That there is some consistency to the raters' judgments, and hence some merit in the speculations above, is indicated by the fact that the liaisons rated as showing partner-centered motivations are more heavily concentrated in Levels IV, V, and VI (more intense emotional involvements), and those rated as showing self-centered motivations are more heavily concentrated in Levels I, II, and III (minimal emotional involvements).

Table 30

PARTNER-CENTERED/SELF-CENTERED MOTIVATION OF MALES
BY LIAISON LEVEL AS JUDGED BY RATERS

Level	Partner Centered		Self Centered		Inconclusive Evidence		TOTAL	
	N	% down	N	% down	N	% down	N	% down
I	0		92	18.5	0		92	13.8
% across			100.0				100.0	
II	0		113	22.8	5	3.4	118	17.6
% across			95.8		4.2		100.0	
III	1	3.7	200	40.3	21	14.5	222	33.2
% across	0.5		90.1		9.5		100.0	
IV	4	14.8	60	12.1	52	35.9	116	17.4
% across	3.4		51.7		44.8		100.0	
V	13	48.1	25	5.0	57	39.3	95	14.2
% across	13.7		26.3		60.0		100.0	
VI	9	33.3	6	1.2	10	6.9	25	3.8
% across	36.0		24.0		40.0		100.0	
TOTAL	27	100.0	496	100.0	145	100.0	668	100.0
% across	4.0		74.3		21.7		100.0	

Table 31

PARTNER-CENTERED/SELF-CENTERED MOTIVATION OF FEMALES
BY LIAISON LEVEL AS JUDGED BY RATERS

Level	Partner Centered		Self Centered		Inconclusive Evidence		TOTAL	
	N	% down	N	% down	N	% down	N	% down
I	0 :		37 :	24.5	55 :	11.6	92 :	13.8
% across	:		40.2 :		59.8 :		100.0 :	
II	0 :		22 :	14.6	96 :	20.3	118 :	17.6
% across	:		18.6 :		81.4 :		100.0 :	
III	3 :	7.0	62 :	41.1	157 :	33.1	222 :	33.2
% across	1.4 :		27.9 :		70.7 :		100.0 :	
IV	12 :	27.9	24 :	15.9	80 :	16.9	116 :	17.4
% across	10.3 :		20.7 :		69.0 :		100.0 :	
V	20 :	46.5	5 :	3.3	70 :	14.8	95 :	14.2
% across	21.1 :		5.3 :		73.7 :		100.0 :	
VI	8 :	18.6	1 :	0.7	16 :	3.4	25 :	3.8
% across	32.0 :		4.0 :		64.0 :		100.0 :	
TOTAL	43 :	100.0	151 :	100.0	474 :	100.0	668 :	100.0
% across	6.4 :		22.6 :		71.0 :		100.0 :	

CONCLUSIONS

The following conclusions are suggested by the statistical data. These conclusions should not be extended beyond the population which was involved in the study.

1. The longer the time the couple had known each other prior to intercourse, the greater the likelihood that the sexual liaison would be classified at a level denoting strong or intense emotional involvements.

2. The capacity of couples to communicate concerning their sexual relationship, whether before or after intercourse occurred, grew with the intensity of the emotional attachment in the total relationship.

3. The amount of argumentative-persuasive communication decreased sharply once intercourse had occurred.

4. Experience in intercourse did not facilitate communication, for the number of subjects who reported "no communication" following the beginning of intercourse was greater than the number who reported "no communication" prior to intercourse.

5. Neither possible marriage nor potential pregnancy is a subject for much discussion by couples prior to intercourse.

6. Possible pregnancy raised jointly by sexual partners as a subject of conversation increased sharply after intercourse had occurred.

7. Girls much more frequently than boys became more attached to their sexual partner than their partner was to them.

8. The use of contraceptive practices and plans for coping with possible pregnancy were found more frequently at levels of marked emotional involvement as contrasted to levels of minimal emotional involvement.[2]

---

[2] Bell and Blumberg (8) in a study of the intimacy attitudes of two hundred fifty college females and one hundred sixty college males at certain stages of courtship arrived at a similar conclusion. They say "Our male respondents tended to perceive the dating relationship in a much greater hedonistic manner than the females. Progressively, as the other person was perceived more as a potential marriage partner, a greater feeling of 'responsibility' by the male entered the evaluation of the intimacy behavior." Green (44) and Vincent (97) also have some pertinent observations relative to masculine ego involvement in relationships involving premarital intercourse.

9. The data indicate that the men who were the subjects of this study were considerably more self-centered than partner-centered in their attitudes toward the persons with whom they were involved.

BIBLIOGRAPHY

1. Abraham, K. *Selected Papers on Psychoanalysis*. New York: Basic Books, 1953.
2. Allee, W. C. *Cooperation Among Animals*. New York: Henry Schuman, 1951.
3. —— "Where Angels Fear to Tread: A Contribution From General Sociology to Human Ethics." *Science* 97:517-25; June 11, 1943.
4. American Psychiatric Association. "Psychiatric Implications of Surveys on Sexual Behavior." *Psychoanalytic Review* 43:471-500; October, 1956.
5. Ansbacher, Heinz L. and Rowena R. Ansbacher. *The Individual Psychology of Alfred Adler*. New York: Basic Books, 1956.
6. Arieti, Silvano. *American Handbook of Psychiatry*. New York: Basic Books, 1959, Volume II.
7. Beach, Frank. "Characteristics of Masculine 'Sex Drive.'" In Nebraska Symposium on Motivation, *Current Theory and Research in Motivation*, edited by Marshall R. Jones. Lincoln: University of Nebraska Press, 1956, Volume IV.
8. Bell, Robert R. and Leonard Blumberg. "Courtship Stages and Intimacy Attitudes." *Family Life Coordinator* 8:61-63; March, 1960.
9. Bloch, Herbert and Arthur Niederhoffer. *The Gang*. New York: Philosophical Library, 1958.

10. Blood, Robert O. "Romance and Premarital Intercourse—Incompatibles?" *Marriage and Family Living* 14:105-8; May, 1952.

11. Bowlby, J. *Maternal Care and Mental Health.* Geneva: World Health Organization, 1951.

12. Bowman, H. A. *Marriage For Moderns.* New York: McGraw-Hill, 1954.

13. Buber, Martin. *I and Thou.* New York: Charles Scribner's Sons, 1955 (eighth edition).

14. Burchinal, Lee G. "Research on Young Marriage: Implications for Family Life Education." *Family Life Coordinator* 9:6-24; September-December, 1960.

15. Burgess, Ernest W. and Paul Wallin. *Engagement and Marriage.* Philadelphia: J. B. Lippincott, 1953.

16. Chesser, Eustace. *Live and Let Live.* New York: Philosophical Library, 1958.

17. Chisholm, G. B. *The Psychiatry of Enduring Peace and Social Progress.* The William Alanson White Psychiatric Foundation, 1947.

18. Christensen, Harold T. "Cultural Relativism and Premarital Sex Norms." *American Sociological Review* 25:31-39; February, 1960.

19. Cole, William G. *Sex in Christianity and Psychoanalysis.* New York: Oxford University Press, 1955.

20. —— *Sex and Love in the Bible.* New York: Association Press, 1959.

21. Comfort, Alex. *Sexual Behavior in Society.* New York: Viking Press, 1950.

22. Davis, Katherine B. *Factors in the Sex Life of Twenty-two Hundred Women.* New York: Harper's, 1929.

23. Davis, Kingsley. "The Sociology of Prostitution." *American Sociological Review* 2:744-55; October, 1937.

24. Deutsch, Helene. *The Psychology of Women.* New York: Grune and Stratton, 1945.

25. Dickinson, R. L. and Lura Beam. *A Thousand Marriages, A Medical Study of Sex Adjustment.* Baltimore: Williams and Wilkins Co., 1951.

26. Duvall, E. M., and Reuben Hill. *When You Marry.* New York: Association Press, 1953.

27. Ehrmann, Winston. *Premarital Dating Behavior.* New York: Henry Holt, 1959.

28. Ellis, Albert. *The Folklore of Sex.* New York: Boni, 1951.

29. —— "Sex Problems of Couples Seen for Marriage Counseling." *The Journal of Family Welfare* 3:81-4; March, 1957.

30. Ellis, Havelock. "Sex in Relation to Society." *Studies in the Psy-*

chology of Sex. New York: Random House, 1936, Vol. II, Part III.

31. Emerson, A. E. "The Biological Basis of Social Cooperation." *Illinois Academy of Science Transactions,* Vol. 39, 1946.

32. Encyclopedia of Sexual Behavior, "Scandinavian Countries, Sex Life of," Edited by Albert Ellis and Albert Abarbanel. New York: Hawthorne Books, 1961, Volume II, pages 910-25.

33. Erikson, E. H. *Childhood and Society.* New York: Norton, 1950.

34. Friend, Jeanette G. and Ernest A. Haggard. "Work Adjustments in Relation to Family Background." *Applied Psychology Monographs* No. 16, 1948.

35. Fromm, E. *The Art of Loving.* New York: Harper's, 1956.

36. —— *Escape from Freedom.* New York: Rinehart, 1941.

37. —— *Man for Himself.* New York: Rinehart, 1947.

38. —— *The Sane Society.* New York: Rinehart, 1955.

39. Gardner, George E. "Sex Behavior of Adolescents in Wartime." *The Annals of the American Academy of Political and Social Science,* pp. 236-65, November, 1944.

40. Gebhard, Paul H., *et al. Pregnancy, Birth and Abortion.* New York: Harper's, 1958.

41. Glover, E. "The Abnormality of Prostitution." *Women,* edited by A. N. Krich. New York: Dell Publishing Co., 1953.

42. Goldfarb, William. "Psychological Privation in Infancy and Subsequent Adjustment." *American Journal of Orthopsychiatry* 15:247-55; April, 1945.

43. Goldsen, Rose K., *et al. What College Students Think.* Princeton, New Jersey: Van Nostrand Co., 1960.

44. Green, Arnold. "The 'Cult of Personality' and Sexual Relations." *Psychiatry* 4:344-8; August, 1941.

45. Greenwald, Harold. *The Call Girl.* New York: Ballantine Books, 1958.

46. Hall, Calvin S. and Gardner Lindzey. *Theories of Personality.* New York: John Wiley, 1957.

47. Hamblin, Robert L. and Robert O. Blood, Jr. "Pre-marital Experience and the Wife's Sexual Adjustment." *Social Problems* 4:122-30; October, 1956.

48. Hamilton, G. V. *A Research in Marriage.* New York: Lear, 1924.

49. Heider, Fritz. *The Psychology of Interpersonal Relations.* New York: John Wiley, 1958.

50. Hiltner, Seward. *Sex Ethics and the Kinsey Reports.* New York: Association Press, 1953.

51. Hohman, Leslie B. and B. Schaffner. "The Sex Lives of Unmarried Men." *The American Journal of Sociology* 52:501-7; May, 1947.

52. Horney, Karen. *Our Inner Conflicts.* New York: Norton, 1945.
53. —— *Neurosis and Human Growth.* New York: Norton, 1950.
54. Kanin, Eugene J. "Male Aggression in Dating-Courtship Relations." *American Journal of Sociology* 63:197-204; September, 1957.
55. —— "Premarital Sex Adjustments, Social Class, and Associated Behaviors." *Marriage and Family Living* 22:258-63, August, 1960.
56. —— and David H. Howard. "Postmarital Consequences of Premarital Sex Adjustments." *American Sociological Review*, October, 1958.
57. Kinsey, Alfred C., *et al. Sexual Behavior in the Human Female.* Philadelphia: W. B. Saunders Co., 1953.
58. —— *Sexual Behavior in the Human Male.* Philadelphia: W. B. Saunders Co., 1948.
59. Kirkendall, Lester A. "Premarital Sex Standards: The Problem and Its Implications." *Pastoral Psychology* 7:43-46; April, 1956.
60. —— *Sex Education as Human Relations.* Sweet Springs, Missouri: Inor Publishing Co., 1950.
61. —— "A Suggested Approach to the Teaching of Sexual Morality." *Journal of Family Welfare*, Bombay, India, 5:26-30; June, 1959.
62. —— "Toward a Clarification of the Concept of Male Sex Drive." *Marriage and Family Living* 20:367-72; November, 1958.
63. —— and Curtis E. Avery. "Ethics and Interpersonal Relationships." *The Humanist* 16:261-67; November-December, 1956.
64. Kirkpatrick, Clifford and E. Kanin. "Male Sex Aggression on a University Campus." *American Sociological Review* 22:52-58; February, 1957.
65. Kronhausen, Phyllis and Eberhard Kronhausen. *Sex Histories of American College Men.* New York: Ballantine Books, 1960.
66. Leary, T. *Interpersonal Diagnosis of Personality.* New York: The Ronald Press, 1957.
67. LeMasters, E. E. *Modern Courtship and Marriage.* New York: Macmillan, 1957.
68. Lindesmith, Alfred R. and Anselm Strauss. *Social Psychology.* New York: Holt-Dryden, 1956.
69. Lion, Ernest G. *et al. An Experiment in the Psychiatric Treatment of Promiscuous Girls.* San Francisco, California: City and County of San Francisco, Department of Public Health, 1945.
70. Locke, Harvey J. *Predicting Adjustment in Marriage: A Comparison of a Divorced and a Happily Married Group.* New York: Henry Holt, 1951.
71. Loeb, Martin B. "Social Role and Sexual Identity in Adolescent

Males." In *Casework Papers, 1959.* New York: National Association of Social Workers, 1959.

72. Maslow, A. H. *Motivation and Personality.* New York: Harper's, 1954.
73. May, R. "A Psychologist Looks at Mental Health in Today's World. *Mental Hygiene* 38:1-11; January, 1954.
74. Montagu, Ashley. *The Direction of Human Development.* New York: Harper's, 1955.
75. —— *On Being Human.* New York: Henry Schuman, 1951.
76. Mowrer, O. H. "Biological vs. Moral Frustration in Personality Disturbances." *Progressive Education* 26:65-9; January, 1949.
77. —— *The Crisis in Psychiatry and Religion.* Princeton, N.J.: D. Van Nostrand Co., 1960.
78. Mullahy, Patrick. *A Study of Interpersonal Relations.* New York: Hermitage Press, 1949.
79. Murphy, Gardner. *Personality: A Biosocial Approach to Origins and Structures.* New York: Harper's 1947.
80. Murtagh, John and Sara Harris. *Cast the First Stone.* New York: McGraw-Hill, 1957.
81. Olive, John F. *Sexual Hygiene and Pathology.* Philadelphia: J. B. Lippincott, 1955.
82. Peck, Robert F. and Robert J. Havighurst. *The Psychology of Character Development.* New York: Wiley and Sons, 1960.
83. Reevy, William R. "Premarital Petting Behavior and Marital Happiness Prediction." *Marriage and Family Living* 21:349-55; November, 1959.
84. Reich, Wilhelm. *The Sexual Revolution.* New York: Orgone Institute Press, 1945.
85. Reiss, Ira L. *Premarital Sex Standards in America.* Glencoe, Ill.: Free Press, 1960.
86. —— "The Treatment of Premarital Coitus in Marriage and the Family Texts." *Social Problems* 4:334-38; April, 1957.
87. Ribble, Margaret. *The Rights of Infants.* New York: Columbia University Press, 1943.
88. Safier, Benno, M.D. *A Psychiatric Approach to the Treatment of Promiscuity.* New York: American Social Hygiene Association, 1949.
89. Sullivan, H. S. *The Psychiatric Interview.* New York: Norton, 1954.
90. —— *The Interpersonal Theory of Psychiatry.* New York: Norton, 1953.
91. Tebor, Irving. *Selected Attributes, Interpersonal Relationships and Aspects of Psychosexual Behavior of One Hundred College*

Freshmen, Virgin Men. Unpublished Ph.D. Thesis, Oregon State College, 1957.

92. Terman, Lewis M. *Psychological Factors in Marital Happiness.* New York: McGraw-Hill, 1936.

93. Weinberg, S. Kirson. *Social Problems in Our Time.* Engelwood Cliffs, New Jersey: Prentice-Hall, 1960.

94. Wheelis, Allen. *The Quest for Identity.* New York: Norton, 1958.

95. Wittkower, E. B. and J. Cowan. "Some Psychological Aspects of Sexual Promiscuity." *Psychomatic Medicine* 6:287-94; October, 1944.

96. Wolfenden, Sir John, Chm. *Report of the Committee on Homosexual Offences and Prostitution.* London: Her Majesty's Stationery Office, 1957.

97. Vincent, Clark E. "Ego Involment in Sexual Relations." *American Journal of Sociology* 65:287-95; November, 1959.

ABOUT THE AUTHOR

Lester A. Kirkendall, Professor of Family Life, Oregon State University, has been actively engaged in marriage and family life education for many years. He has served as director of the Association of Family Living, Chicago, Illinois, on the boards of the National Council of Family Relations and the Sex Information and Education Council of the United States, and has taught and lectured at many colleges and universities throughout the nation. He is acknowledged to be one of the leading authorities on sex education and has contributed extensively to the literature on this subject.